Virginia's Private War

VIRGINIA'S PRIVATE WAR

*Feeding Body and Soul
in the Confederacy,
1861–1865*

William Blair

New York • Oxford
Oxford University Press
1998

Oxford University Press

Oxford   New York
Athens   Auckland   Bangkok   Bogota   Bombay
Buenos Aires   Calcutta   Cape Town   Dar es Salaam
Delhi   Florence   Hong Kong   Istanbul   Karachi
Kuala Lampur   Madras   Madrid   Melbourne
Mexico City   Nairobi   Paris   Singapore
Taipei   Tokyo   Toronto   Warsaw

and associated companies in
Berlin   Ibadan

Copyright © 1998 by Oxford University Press, Inc.

Published by Oxford University Press, Inc.
198 Madison Avenue, New York, New York 10016

Oxford is a registered trademark of Oxford University Press

Library of Congress Cataloging-in-Publication Data
Blair, William Alan.
Virginia's private war : feeding body and soul
in the Confederacy, 1861–1865 / William Alan Blair.
p. cm.
Includes bibliographical references and index.
ISBN 0-19-511864-2
1. Virginia—History—Civil War, 1861–1865—Public opinion.
2. Virginia—History—Civil War, 1861–1865—Social aspects.
3. United States—History—Civil War, 1861–1865—Public opinion.
4. United States—History—Civil War, 1861–1865—Social aspects.
I. Title.
E581.B57 1998
973.7′13′09755—dc21   97-51657

1   3   5   7   9   8   6   4   2
Printed in the United States of America
on acid-free paper

For Mary Ann
For always being there

Acknowledgments

Every scholarly venture comes to fruition with help from others. I especially acknowledge that of Frances Pollard and the wonderful staff at the Virginia Historical Society, as well as Minor Weisiger, John Kneebone, and Brent Tartar at the Library of Virginia. The people at both locations performed their jobs with a professionalism and helpfulness that eased the strain of researching far from home on a limited budget. The materials at these locations, along with the rich collections at the Alderman Library at the University of Virginia in Charlottesville, also provided invaluable windows into the past. I also must thank the archivists at the Wilson Library of the University of North Carolina at Chapel Hill, especially John White, and the Perkins Library at Duke University for extending warm hospitality. Robert K. Krick of Fredericksburg-Spotsylvania National Military Park deserves special thanks for opening his own research files and allowing me to stay within commuting distance of Richmond. Finally, I must acknowledge the wonderful cooperation of Mildred Allen and her fine staff in the microforms section of Pattee Library at the Pennsylvania State University. Without their services, this book never would have been born.

At Penn State a resurgent intellectual community also helped me. The History Department advanced this project through a Sparks Fellowship that funded a great deal of the archival work. Among my peers I particularly must thank Susan E. Shirk for challenging my ideas during Friday afternoon coffee sessions, which provided more stimulus than the caffeine, and for becoming a valuable colleague. Joe Fischer patiently critiqued ideas on our many runs. Peter S. Carmichael sharpened my focus and taught me a few things about the worldview of young Virginians. With the kind consent and superb hospitality of Tara, he also provided a place from which to launch research forays into Richmond. Charles Holden helped me find my way back to the Civil War, as well as my sanity, and Steve Knox stretched and clarified thinking about class struggle, although I doubt that I followed his advice fully. As to faculty, Nan Elizabeth Woodruff inspired me to find new ways to view history, especially the obligation to understand people on their own terms and the richness of exploring the South. Gary W. Gallagher also has encumbered me with enormous debts for his consistent support over the years. With him lies the blame for nurturing an infection with the Civil War through his own enthusiasm. The doctor in this case helped the disease thrive, for which the patient is eternally grateful. He and Eileen Ann also offered personal encouragement and support that will always be remembered.

Beyond Penn State I have benefited from the wisdom of a number of scholars. George C. Rable offered important insights and critique while this work formed as a dissertation. Elizabeth Fox-Genovese and Howard Lamar read the work as jurors for the Nevins Prize for dissertations and encouraged me to continue with the project. I am also grateful for the close reading of the manuscript by the reviewers for Oxford University Press, including Orville Vernon Burton for providing a substantial and solid overview that improved the book. At the University of North Carolina at Greensboro, my colleagues have been tremendously supportive. UNCG also provided support through various faculty grants that allowed me to concentrate on finishing this project.

Most of all, this work is a testament to the support of one special person. Few spouses would allow the other at the age of 34 to exchange a successful position for another career with less promise of material reward. Neither would they so easily forgive the considerable time that these pursuits consume, nor so wonderfully add to the richness of life through wit, warmth, and common sense. Above all, this work is dedicated to Mary Ann, with my thanks and love.

Contents

Virginia's Private War

Introduction

The 1970s proved troublesome for the Confederacy as worldwide events stimulated a reevaluation of the southern cause. Vietnam shook the American psyche in many ways, but it also taught a hard lesson about what an outnumbered people could accomplish against a foe with superior resources and firepower. New efforts to write the histories of people previously outside of the mainstream—combined with the experience of Vietnam and disenchantment with the overt nationalism of the Cold War—affected the way Americans understood their own Civil War. A generation that treated nationalism more skeptically, if not cynically, found Confederate patriotism wanting. Scholars rediscovered discontent on the Confederate home front: the bread riots that broke out in at least seven southern cities in 1863, the desertion that plagued the Confederate armies, and the public anger over legislation that put the poor into the army while the rich stayed at home. By the 1990s, the scholarly consensus held that southerners did not have what it took to win spiritually—that the reason for Confederate defeat lay not on the battlefield but in a failure of national heart, especially when compared to the efforts of the North Vietnamese or the various nationalist groups that resumed hostilities after the Soviet Union collapsed.[1]

As a person who came of age during the Vietnam era, I brought many of these assumptions to a project in 1992 to learn how the common folk could be persuaded to follow their leaders. I was interested in how people identify with a nation, especially how interests and self-image merge in a way that allows one group to feel so intensely about their "imagined community" that they would kill other people and die for it themselves.[2] I selected Virginia for this study largely because its home front had been neglected in the literature and because it was the most important Confederate state in terms of population, industrial resources, and proximity to the national capital. I intended to carry the study through 1885, expecting that the wartime portion would reaffirm the interpretation that class anger and hostility weakened the Confederacy. At the time, the war seemed the smaller portion of a broader project emphasizing the postwar world. I was more interested in how postbellum white southerners, despite a wartime experience to the contrary, constructed an identity of united sacrifice against the North during the conflict.

Despite my intention to focus on the postbellum years, the evidence kept leading me back toward the war and toward a story I had not expected and still find difficult to express. To my surprise, I arrived at an interpretation that Virginians did not lose because of failed nationalism or internal conflicts. Yet that statement does not capture the complex relationship of Virginia's civilians to the nation. I fear that my argument will be misinterpreted as resurrecting the romantic notion of a unified South nobly defending its way of life in a Lost Cause when I, too, found discontent among the public. I had not counted on the complicated way in which dissent functioned as a catalyst for change or how Confederates could still identify with a cause even when they lost faith in a particular government.[3] Virginians demonstrated that although they had qualms about certain aspects of their nascent nation, their sense of purpose remained strong enough to win until the winter of 1864–1865, when the pressure of the Union army and the lack of resources finally took their toll on the spirits of all but the heartiest souls.

As I probed for discontent in letters from citizens to their state or Confederate leaders, contradictions with current interpretations led me to these conclusions. The correspondence indicated resentment of favoritism that allowed planters to stay home when poorer folks had to serve in the military. Hunger also eroded the spirit, as did taxes that became too burdensome. The letters and petitions, however, seemed to ask for a fair enforcement of policies rather than abolishing the system. When I examined the evidence that many cite as proof of a collapse of will, I found a more complicated story.

Desertion in Virginia was at its highest in 1862 and had come under control by 1864. By the end of the war more than 80 percent of adult males between 17 and 50 years of age had served in the army or were involved in war-related industries. Riots faded from the scene after the spring of 1863, although discontent over food shortages never disappeared. Although southern morale had its ups and downs, I wondered what Ulysses S. Grant would have said if someone had approached him in 1864 and asked if he noticed a lack of national spirit in the enemy that inflicted 65,000 casualties in the Army of the Potomac between early May and mid-June.

Perhaps the biggest surprise came when examining the centralizing tendencies of government that many point to as conflicting with the states' rights principles of the South. First, it became clear that the expansion of government occurred in part because people in Virginia's communities asked for it, recognizing that the measures were temporary because of the wartime emergency. Even the exemptions in conscription legislation took shape in response to the needs of the public, as expressed in petitions that flooded the War Department from the Virginia home front. The public was not always happy with the policy that resulted, or its enforcement, but that is another story. More to the point, the letters to officials—and the changes in policy that followed—showed that planters had not checked their political savvy at the door when they entered the war. They responded to their constituents and crafted legislation to answer the concerns of civilians while considering their own concerns as well. The beneficiaries of that policy—whether the poor, the skilled workers, or the planters—changed over time to fit the circumstances. The measures did not always resolve problems effectively or employ means that seem logical to us today. Yet I had to wonder if the effort helped morale particularly because it came during a war—when an enemy and not just an inept government could reasonably be blamed for the hardships.

As the war progressed, dissent helped force the government to crack down on planters while easing the burden on the poor and the families of soldiers. Legislation in the beginning of the conflict retained a class bias by allowing the rich to purchase substitutes or gain exemptions under the twenty-Negro law. Bread riots and particularly desertion served as a wake-up call to local, state, and Confederate authorities. Something had to be done to handle the problems posed both by an enemy army and by the public's discontent. The turning point came in late 1863 when the elections indicated a turn in public support from secessionists toward prewar leaders, many of them former Whigs and Unionists. Rather than demonstrating a lack of support for the cause, this signaled a change to leaders who because of their more national outlook prosecuted the war more fully and exacted greater sacrifices from other planters. Beginning in January 1864 the war became more of a rich man's fight as the Confederate government ended substitution, forced men who had purchased substitutes into the army, and instituted procedures that allowed the needy and soldiers' families to purchase food at government-controlled prices. Coupled with impressive efforts at the state and local levels, these policies sent the Confederacy toward the brink of becoming a welfare state.[4]

In the end, even welfare fell short largely because the odds were so strongly stacked against success. Local impressment officers contended with national authorities for the same food needed to feed civilians and soldiers. There simply was not enough to go around for the home front and the armies. The Union army also prevented Virginians from maintaining any equilibrium for long. The constant pressure by "Yankees" took its toll on the crops and psyches of Virginians as the Union army employed increasingly tougher measures against civilian property and continued to kill Confederate soldiers' family members. When the Confederate army suffered defeats in 1865, the war spirit declined precipitously, although, remarkably, it still burned in a number of hearts—especially among upper-class women.

To tell this story required a specific kind of inquiry and presentation. The dynamic of dissent and response dictated a chronological narrative. The first chapters of this book establish the grounds for Virginia unity and then show how discontent built to a crescendo in 1863. Chapter 4 marks the turning point toward a rich man's fight and chapter 5 indicates how the Union army cut deeper into the state and disrupted the home front. These chapters highlight the material components that affected morale on the Virginia home front: the implications of raising troops, food, and other resources. The final chapter examines how Virginians forged an ideological bond with the Confederacy. Here I emphasize the role of the enemy in crafting a Virginia-Confederate identity by providing evidence of a barbaric Yankee who was out to plunder homes, victimize helpless women, and steal slaves. I also analyze how Virginia's geographic location promoted Confederate identity, allowing its people to fight for the nation by protecting their homes. Because of this last feature,

I cannot claim that Virginia's experience speaks for the Confederacy as a whole. The Old Dominion's position on the frontier and its attachment to the Confederate government through Richmond presented unique factors that reinforced identification with the national cause.[5] But this study adds another piece to the puzzle of the southern war effort. In this case, the irony is that one of the last states to join the Confederacy ended up being one of its strongest supporters.

This study, then, needed to focus on communities to gain an understanding of how national, state, and local policies intersected. Shortly into the work I saw that we did not have a solid enough idea of the way in which policies that historians believe broke the Confederacy apart also enjoyed public support. Impressment, for instance, became a blessing to the poor and to families of soldiers around February 1864 as it stabilized prices and enabled these groups to purchase provisions at government rates. It did not, however, benefit the more prosperous farmers who purchased equipment, seed, and other materials in a free market while selling portions of their crops in a regulated market. If anything, planters and owners of large farms had more complaints with the government than the "rebellious" common folk as 1864 progressed.

To understand this process better, I selected three counties in the state—places in the interior that remained part of the Confederate cause and thus retained some choice in continuing to support the effort. I did not select these communities through statistical analysis of wealth or other social data beyond very simple demographics. That kind of approach can be invaluable but was not the method for my madness. It was important for me to learn the pattern of public complaints and determine whether they varied from larger to smaller slaveholding regions or by economic interests. To do so, I needed to narrow my research to several communities to have any hope of completing a tour through archival material, including examination of more than 150 reels of microfilm containing the letters received by the Confederate secretary of war.

I chose Albemarle, Campbell, and Augusta counties because of the advantages they offered for such a study. They contained a range of plantation agriculture and grain farming. Campbell with its neighboring town of Lynchburg provided a glimpse into the tobacco belt of the southern Piedmont, an area that had remained faithful to plantation agriculture. Augusta County provided another side of the story because this area in the Shenandoah Valley had fewer slaveholders and more workers than farmers. In the northern Piedmont,

Albemarle lay squarely in between, with a diverse mix of crops, no large town, and many owners of large numbers of slaves. It also had an ideological center in the University of Virginia, home to key proslavery ideologues of the antebellum South. Each community had newspapers and caches of private correspondence at various archives. Finally, Staunton, Charlottesville, and Lynchburg had similar experiences in becoming sites for hospitals and other Confederate installations. This meant that reports would be available from government officials about those sections of the state. Both Augusta and Albemarle also became targets for Union activity late in the war, providing the chance to see how these incursions affected morale, manpower, and provisions.

A random check of other regions—through diaries, correspondence, and newspapers—helped round out the picture. For these I followed the trail of the richest sources, such as conscription records that survived in Rockingham County, the published county minutes of Henrico, and the papers of William Sutherlin, a Confederate impressment commissioner. I simply looked for material that provided insight into the complex patterns of loyalty and disloyalty in a Confederate state. Consequently, this work represents not a community study per se but an attempt to use communities to tell a much broader story.

When deciding what to emphasize in this work I chose to concentrate on elements that added the freshest material to the studies of Confederate defeat. This involved an in-depth look at conscription, impressment, privation, and desertion—key components in the argument for loss of morale. I also saw the class unity of Virginians as less monolithic than suggested in earlier works. Here I followed the lead of George Rable, who has portrayed a ruling elite united in its commitment to a slaveholding society but sharply divided over whether government should be more central or more local in nature. I also benefited from Raimondo Luraghi's work suggesting that a *political class*—a term he borrowed from Antonio Gramsci—had formed in the Confederacy to serve as the conscience of its social group. These leaders operated either on a higher political plane or were shrewd enough to recognize that their own power depended on incorporating the interests of subordinate groups.[6] I do not view the Virginia politicians as constituting a separate class from planters, but I do think that rival groups of leaders existed, with different visions of nationalism and with followers composed of a cross section from subordinate groups. Last but not least, I hoped to restore the importance of military events to the question of Confederate defeat, not just as an influence on morale but as a factor that disrupted the lives of people caught in the path of the armies. Virginians fought no abstraction. Portions of the state were ravaged every bit as much as central Georgia, and over a much longer period of time.

It is important to clarify what this study does not do. Although including slaves and free blacks in the story, I did not feature them because their "support" for the Confederacy came mostly through coercion. Nor did I analyze religion or women in any but the most rudimentary fashion, not because either is unimportant but because others have focused on and developed these topics.[7] I add to their solid work in two ways: reaffirming that upper-class women remained committed to the cause even when Lee's army surrendered, and showing how men's roles as protectors—strengthened in response to incidents of Union soldiers entering the homes of defenseless women—formed an important component of Confederate identity. Apart from bread riots, I found on the part of Virginia's women no other protest that captured the attention of authorities, although officials worried about how to care for the wives of soldiers in order to keep their husbands in the army. County and state governments thus assumed the role of male protectors through charitable campaigns, although they were an admittedly imperfect substitute.

This brings me to a confession about a deficiency in my study. Try as I might, I could find only scattered testimony from either the poor or families of soldiers about their perception of the relief measures adopted by local, state, and Confederate authorities from mid-1863 to the end of the conflict. I came across indirect evidence that these efforts did ease the suffering, such as comments from a woman touring the poorer sections of Richmond in 1864 who indicated that starvation had declined and that people could get by if they chose to swallow their pride and accept relief. But this kind of evidence rarely shows itself: people are more likely to criticize the government than send a note of thanks. Few hesitated to chastize officials for failing to crack down on rich men who remained at home: one man wrote, "I think that iff you would do justice to the poor and to your country, you would have these men put in ranks and then they would no how the poor soldiers money comes."[8] Yet I do not know if this individual gloated when conscription officers forced those rich men into the army in 1864. I also do not know if a poor woman who requested government help ever nodded in thanks to the local justice of the peace when entering Sunday service. If this work does nothing else, I hope it leads someone to a fuller representation of this dynamic, even if it proves my suspicion wrong that Virginian-Confederates viewed the Yankees as a worse enemy than their own government.

Ultimately, this book focuses on the internal battles among the Confederate populace, or "Virginia's private war." The concerns within communities invariably involved how the recruiting of soldiers for the army stripped neighborhoods of people who were important for producing food and other goods. Because of the South's disadvantage in population, the question of manpower raised repercussions beyond the battlefield. Each person entering the ranks removed someone important from the local economy and thus changed that community. The burden fell particularly hard on regions with fewer slaves because the military consumed the men who would have produced goods for civilians. As communities suffered, soldiers sometimes risked execution by leaving the ranks to tend to emergencies at home. The struggles for manpower and provisions were thus related—involving a quest to feed not only the Confederate body but also its soul.

1

A Slave Society Goes to War

The problem is precisely to explain the impressive degree of class collaboration and social unity in the face of so many internal strains.
— Eugene D. Genovese, "Yeomen Farmers in a
Slaveholders' Democracy"

After learning the fate of Fort Sumter and Lincoln's call for 75,000 troops to quell the rebellion, a Shenandoah Valley farmer assembled his sons. "Boys," began the Augusta County Unionist, "this war is over the nigger. You can do what you want to fight or get substitutes." Joseph, the second oldest son, replied: "Well, I have the niggers—guess I'll fight."[1] Few phrased matters so crudely or linked the war so closely to slavery. Instead, most Confederate Virginians pointed to Lincoln's proclamation as "revolutionizing" the state by providing compelling evidence that "subjugation was the object, subjugation of all who would not subscribe to the creed of the conqueror." Although a Richmond editor proclaimed that slavery "begets and fosters the war spirit," people interpreted dissolution of the Union as necessary to preserve liberty against an increasingly tyrannical government that would use force against southerners—a statement easily proved by the army gathering across the Potomac River.[2]

Virginia offers a fairly typical example of the way Confederates understood their reasons for separating from the Union. Issues regarding slavery's expansion into the territories brought on the war, yet most white people quickly expressed their reasons for fighting in terms of guarding their liberties rather than protecting slave property. The significant number of Virginians who did own slaves rarely shied away from admitting that they left the Union to protect their chattel property from abolitionists. At the same time, they understood that they could mobilize the entire state only if the citizenry feared that a threat existed to more than "the peculiar institution"— that the actions of the Republicans continued a broad assault on individual freedom. One community leader from Augusta County put it bluntly: "The non slaveholder will fight for his section as soon as the slaveholder if you can convince him that *his* political rights are threatened, as a *citizen*. But he is not willing to leave his family & offer his life in a struggle which he believes is a mere contest between politicians for the spoils of office."[3]

It would be easy to misread such comments as indicating that southern society divided neatly into nonslaveholders and slaveholders; that only the latter would support a war over the peculiar institution. The concepts of slavery and liberty did not necessarily conflict. When southerners referred to protecting a way of life, or their liberties, slavery appeared high on the list of treasures worth guarding. The peculiar institution was one of the elements that defined Virginians as southerners. White people enjoyed the benefits of slaves even when not owning them—by hiring them, for instance, or by regarding all white men as superior racially to African Americans. Also, slavery's bonds among white Virginians had tightened by the time the Civil War began, contrary to accepted wisdom that the institution had lost salience in the state.[4] Commitment to the institution increased during the 1850s among a core of Virginians as the economy rebounded and more small-acreage farmers turned to tobacco production with the eventual goal of becoming masters themselves. Friction occurred between planters and farmers but usually over the kinds of disputes that surround the wealthy today—the rich trying to hold on to, if not extend, their advantages while the less prosperous protest the resulting inequities.

Yet it would be equally wrong to suppose that slavery formed the only tie that bound white Virginians to each other and to the southern cause. People lived in close, sometimes isolated communities in which they did not view each other solely as slaveholder or nonslaveholder. Most of the leaders owned slaves, but they were known by name and reputation rather than simply by occupation. Planter, farmer, and day laborer saw each other at church or at community barbecues. They may have drilled together in militia companies, raised barns, shucked corn, or ridden on slave patrols. They may indeed have been related.[5] None of this means that Virginians existed in an agricultural Eden where all the citizens got along nicely; obviously, they did not. But their political culture and the sectional crisis masked many of these differences by channeling discontent against a common enemy—something that will become clearer after first looking at the economic changes to life in the 1850s and then at the challenges that the North presented.

Events before the Civil War created fresh interest in an old money crop as the economy of the Old Dominion revitalized during the 1850s. Virginia's tobacco belt had languished beginning in the 1820s as prices fell internationally and the soil burned out. Thousands of sons and daughters had left the state to find a better living in the West. While the eastern section of Virginia suffered the most, other regions held their own and prospered through diversifying. Northern Virginia developed as a food manufacturer and distribution point for livestock. Along the coast, vegetable farming became profitable and planters everywhere started growing more wheat and corn, as well as selling off slaves to the Cotton South. The addition of more grain to Virginia's agricultural makeup came at the best possible time: international markets required more of the crop as the Crimean War disrupted trade with traditional sources. Demand for labor also had escalated with a resulting boon to slave traders and masters who benefited from increasing values for their property. All told, the economy was humming once again, although the depression had left some older farmers with a cautious outlook that would carry over into the secession crisis.[6]

Railroad and canal building helped fuel the recovery. The Virginia Central Railroad had worked its way into the Shenandoah Valley while the Virginia and Tennessee Road connected the southwest with new markets. The richest and poorest farmers turned to tobacco to profit from the new opportunities. While this resurgence concentrated east of the Blue Ridge, the crop became more prevalent in the Shenandoah Valley and established holds in both the southwest and the northwest. Putnam County in the Kanawha River Valley of the northwest produced a mere 37,122 pounds of tobacco in 1850, but the harvest had ballooned to 406,992 pounds by 1860. This was somewhat exceptional in that region, yet it is not clear how far tobacco would have spread—and slave owning would have entrenched—had the war not come. One thing is certain: slave owning in the late antebellum era was following the advance of transportation, especially the railroad.[7]

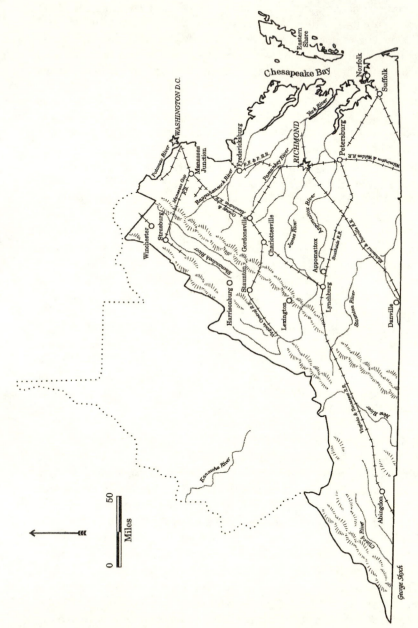

Figure 1.1 Key Features of Virginia, 1860

Given the choice between wheat and tobacco, marginal farmers grew the latter. Producing wheat for the market rather than the table was often beyond their means because the grain required more labor and three times as much land to yield a profit comparable to a small tobacco patch.[8] Albemarle County records indicate that the greatest gains in tobacco occurred among the richest and poorest families. Between 1850 and 1859, total hogsheads produced in the county more than tripled, from 1,214 to 4,525. Although landowning increased, the most significant shifts came among people with acreage valued at $1 to $499 and $10,000 and above. Staple production flourished at the expense of subsistence crops. Corn growing declined among all groups except for middling producers. Predictably, the tobacco fever contributed to a drop in home manufactures, making Virginians even more dependent upon finished goods from the North. An economic study of the county concluded: "Small farmers abandoned grains and vegetables and rushed to put their acreage into tobacco."[9]

The speculation fever extended beyond Albemarle County. The president of the Virginia and Tennessee Railroad reported in 1858 that 14,000 fewer hogs passed over his road than during the prior season. He warned farmers about the folly of producing tobacco at the expense of pork. "Two or three hundred dollars per annum, for bacon, is a much more serious tax, and bears much more heavily on the farmers than the taxes paid the sheriffs, and about which we hear so much grumbling." He concluded: "We say to the farmers, make more corn and less tobacco."[10]

For small-scale farmers who entered the tobacco market in the 1850s, slave ownership remained the next logical step toward economic stability and social respectability; however, an increase in the number of slaves did not occur. In fact, between 1850 and 1860 the number of slaves in the Old Dominion dropped from 33 percent to 30 percent of the population. At first, this seems to support the argument that slavery declined in the Old Dominion as a viable, thriving institution. The reasons behind the drop, however, are more complicated. For one thing, not all regions suffered. The Piedmont, Tidewater, and southwest posted gains in slaveholding during the decade.[11]

The sale of slaves, especially to the Deep South, and the migration of young planters to other states accounted for a large portion of the decline. Missouri in particular drew men from the southern Piedmont, such as Robert H. Early of Franklin County. In the

mid-1850s, Early left home for the Show Me State with fifteen or so
of his father's slaves. He did not own land but worked as a tenant
farmer growing hemp. Yet he was hardly poor. He generated $1,000
per year from hiring out his human chattel, eventually buying his
own farm through these means. The westward flow of masters and
slaves occurred within the state, although to a more limited extent.
Robert's father, Joab, moved to the Kanawha River Valley to take advantage of the fresh land for tobacco production.[12]

Another part of the decline in slave owning came from masters
capitalizing on the better prices for chattel. Sometimes they sold off
slaves to raise money for starting farms and planting tobacco. During
the 1850s, a significant number of persons became small, independent farmers in this manner. A study of the tobacco region concluded that in the 1850s landless slaveholders made up 11 percent of
the households. Ten years later, that percentage had dropped by half
while slave owning declined by about 6 percent. "What the figures
most plausibly suggest," the study concluded, "is that capital in-
vested in slaves was being diverted into land and that small masters
were therefore experiencing more of a change in form of wealth than
a change in actual status. It is plain, moreover, that they were mainly
responsible for the de-emphasis of slavery."[13] While these people
technically appear as nonslaveholders, they once had owned slaves
and would have been intensely interested in the peculiar institution's fate during the sectional crisis.

Farmers were not the only ones to use slave labor. Skilled workers or artisans often resorted to this form of help in the shop. *Mechanic* was a term that nineteenth-century Americans used to refer to
carpenters, brick layers, stone masons, skilled factory workers, and
others who bent nature to mechanical will. This category also included engineers, inventors, and manufacturers who turned to slaveholding as readily as large farmers did. In Lynchburg, 73 percent of
the craftsmen owned at least one slave, a greater percentage than
the professional occupations of doctor, lawyer, teacher, and minister.
Those who did not own slaves were drawn into the proslavery orbit
through a variety of means, including economic relationships, kin
ties, and service on slave patrols.[14]

Opposition to planters sometimes came from mechanics and
workingmen, although most of the labor-consciousness before the
war confined itself to opposite ends of Virginia. In the southwest,
railroad building created a critical mass of mechanics and laborers
along the Virginia and Tennessee Railroad at Abingdon. Anger over

domination by the wealthy and powerful ebbed, however, with changes to the constitution in 1851 that expanded suffrage and opened more public offices to elections. In the east, the iron industry in Richmond provided opportunities for a nascent working-class mentality. As early as 1847, white laborers at the Tredegar Iron Works had struck because they feared losing their jobs after teaching their craft to slaves. Owner Joseph R. Anderson dismissed the protesters and took them before the mayor's court on charges of forming an illegal combination. Although the charges were dropped, the action broke the strike.[15]

For the most part, these disputes neither assumed dangerous proportions nor struck at slavery's foundation. Virginia had few cities in which a working class could gestate; additionally, an improving economy with more job opportunities smoothed over worker discontent. Disputes also ran along racially determined class lines. Mechanics reacted strongly whenever manufacturers turned to slave laborers for skilled work, but the workers desired no overthrow of the slave system. The discontent of mechanics sometimes prompted reform in slave hiring, such as regulation of payments to slaves for boarding. The effect of these protests, one historian has concluded, "was thus not to weaken slavery but to entrench it more firmly in southern society."[16]

While the evidence reinforces the often-noted ties to the slave system among people living in or near the tobacco belt, can the same be said for residents west of the Blue Ridge? The Shenandoah Valley and trans-appalachian regions contained fewer slaveowners and the most rebellious elements within the Old Dominion. A substantial number of the farmers who settled in the Valley during the colonial period had migrated from Germany, setting up farms that focused first on subsistence and then on grains produced commercially. Even the location of markets reinforced the separate identities of easterners and westerners. Flour from the Shenandoah Valley traveled to Martinsburg and on to Baltimore instead of Richmond; the northwest floated its commerce down the Kanawha to the Ohio River and to points north such as Pittsburgh or Cincinnati. Because the Shenandoah Valley also contained significant communities of Mennonites, Dunkards, and Quakers who opposed slavery and secession, it might seem easier to explain why nonslaveholders there would quickly tire of the war for a slaveholders' republic.[17]

Demographics can cloud the growing importance of slavery in the Shenandoah Valley. Although certainly not as entrenched as in the tobacco belt, slave owning west of the Blue Ridge consistently increased before 1850 when the slave populations in the Valley counties averaged 18.8 percent and seven boasted of slave populations exceeding 25 percent. The 1850s snapped the trend of consistent growth, bringing a decline in the western sections—but not in key areas. Once again, modern transportation attracted the peculiar institution. Primarily because the Virginia Central Railroad cut across the Blue Ridge, slaveholding during the 1850s grew by roughly 10 percent in the counties of Augusta, Rockingham, Pendleton, and Highland.[18]

When considering the impact of slave owning by households, not individuals, the connection to slavery also increases. Although Augusta County contained only 811 slave owners—or 4 percent of the white population of 21,547—that number embraced 22 percent of all households. As much as one out of every five families potentially had a direct tie to slavery, although that estimate is likely the uppermost limit. The actual figure could be a few percentage points lower because of shortcomings in the census.[19] Slave hiring, however, would have enhanced these ties. Throughout Virginia, the practice had grown as slave owners weathered the depression partly by hiring out their laborers. By the 1850s, slaves worked in small shops; in iron and tobacco manufactories; in mining, canal, and railroad companies; and in public facilities such as institutes for the blind. Around Staunton in 1860, roughly 10 percent of all slaves were hired. The iron industry in particular used these arrangements. By 1847, Rockbridge, Alleghany, and Botetourt counties had 600 slaves working at iron furnaces.[20]

As the 1850s approached, Valley residents also crossed an ideological divide toward resembling eastern planters in their intolerance of abolition. In 1847 Henry Ruffner wrote a pamphlet that called for the gradual emancipation of slaves. A highly respected man as the president of Washington College, Ruffner had alleged that the institution impeded the material progress of the state. A number of people shared Ruffner's concerns about the impact of slavery on the economy, but few accepted his suggestion for gradual emancipation, even though he acknowledged that this solution would be impractical for eastern Virginia. Only sixteen years after the General Assembly had entertained a similar plan, hostility toward antislavery sentiments had advanced too far for anyone within the Old Dominion to suggest such a thing. Within a short time after the pamphlet appeared, Ruffner had to resign from office and move from the Valley.[21]

To say that slavery became an increasingly viable institution, even in some nonslaveholding regions does not mean that everyone had unquestioning faith in the peculiar institution or a love for the planters who led the state. Concern about the economic impact of the peculiar institution—especially in enabling the South to compete with an industrializing North—manifested itself even among planters.[22]

The northwest in particular contained the people with the least stake in the peculiar institution and perhaps the greatest resentment of the Tidewater. Ironically, the improving economy heightened the tensions between the northwest and the east. The trans-appalachian region remained the most unhappy with the constitutional resolution of 1851 that exempted slave property from full taxation. As slave prices rebounded, planters welcomed increases in the worth of their human property without a corresponding rise in taxes because of a $300 ceiling on the tax value of individual slaves. Nonslaveholders thus bore a greater portion of the tax burden that transportation improvements brought—an issue that remained a sore point well into the 1861 secession convention.[23] Additionally, the trans-appalachian region had a different nature because of trade and settlement patterns. Commerce occurred more often with northerners than southerners. A Clarksburg man captured the marked differences between the two regions in this manner: "We are not slaveholders, many of us are of Northern birth, we read almost exclusively Northern newspapers and books, and listen to Northern preachers."[24]

What emerged by the 1850s was a Virginia consisting of five major sections: the Tidewater, the Piedmont, the Shenandoah Valley, the southwest, and the northwest, or trans-appalachian region. Each contained its own characteristics, priorities, and subidentities, but as the war approached at least eastern Virginia (comprising the Tidewater and the Piedmont), the Valley, and the southwest operated together on a variety of questions that included slavery and southern rights. The most disconnected people lived beyond the Appalachian Mountains. When the time came for people to choose sides, it would come as little surprise which way the northwest would go. The section's rupture arose from long-standing grievances rooted in different economic and cultural patterns; however, the decision to remain with the Union was neither easy nor without controversy.[25]

Although key portions of the state had come into the proslavery orbit as the war neared, a host of factors contributed to creating the

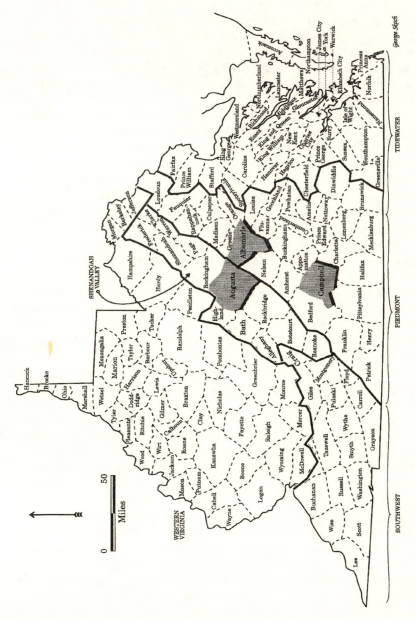

Figure 1.2 Regions and Counties of Virginia, 1860. *Source:* Shanks, *The Secession Movement in Virginia*

southern identity that would form the basis of a Confederate one. Race, for instance, provided an important social glue for white Virginians, as did religion and other cultural factors. But the political culture offers the focal point of this analysis because it shaped the way Virginians identified friend and foe during the sectional crisis. Also, the same relationships constructed within Virginia society over several of centuries would persist throughout the war, shaping even the nature of contact between officers and citizen-soldiers.

Virginia's political culture mirrored the South's: planters dominated yet they understood that their authority depended upon representing subordinate groups of cantankerous, independent-minded people. Community leaders had to earn the deference they received by fulfilling their responsibilities. Two things complicated this minuet of mutual obligations: followers often proved intransigent, and rivalries existed among the leaders. This created contentious politics heightened by the national debate over slavery. Yet antebellum dissent caused no serious fissures as disputes took on the form of rival groups led by opposing members of the elite.[26]

People in the Old Dominion backed local champions for a host of reasons, such as family tradition and church habits. In these alignments, the character of an individual leader more than party discipline might determine the loyalty of supporters, who voted as a group rather than as individuals.[27] Each section of Virginia had its own leaders associated with prominent families: the Garlands in Lynchburg, the Stuarts in Augusta County, the Randolphs in Albemarle, the Floyds in the southwest, and the Wises and Ruffins in the southeast. "We are all right clannish," a Campbell County woman admitted, "we think a great deal of our kin."[28]

As the antebellum period progressed, the economy, demographics, and constitutional changes combined to give yeoman farmers increasing influence in state affairs. With a majority of the white population finally living west of the Blue Ridge by 1850, the western portions of Virginia succeeded in a decades-long attempt to break the autocracy of eastern planters. The new constitution of 1851 opened more public offices to elections, including the governor, the lieutenant governor, judges, and commonwealth attorneys.[29] This change came reluctantly to Old-line Whigs who formed the heart of Unionist sentiment in the tobacco belt. Staunch Whigs resented extending power to the rabble, although this did not mean that political leaders could act with impunity. The same men who bemoaned expanded democracy retained their paternalistic ideal that considered care for the needy as a personal responsibility of the more fortunate citizens.[30]

Despite the vote being exercised by the poor, planters and other slaveholders retained their preeminent position in Virginia society and politics. They controlled not only state offices but local ones, with one means of dominance coming through the county governments that touched the lives of everyone within their jurisdiction. Planters and slave owners controlled an incredible range of public life through their service as justices of county courts. More than legal matters were resolved in these venues. County court in the Old Dominion combined executive, judicial, and legislative powers all in the same persons. As justices, planters served as both judges and county commissioners. They settled debts, established taxes, bound out the poor as apprentices, doled out local patronage by picking surveyors of roads or tax collectors, ruled on who could perform marriage services or be guardians for children, supervised the poor houses, qualified jurors, and established procedures for elections. Typically, they chose the candidates for office; subordinates trusted the leaders to make the correct selections. The tendency for slaveholders to hold these positions of power held true even in the west. By 1861, the southwest still sent three owners of large numbers of slaves to the state senate despite the fact that poorer people constituted more than 80 percent of the population in those districts. Even in the Shenandoah Valley, residents aligned themselves behind their favorite slave-owning champion, although it is unlikely that the masses identified them as such. They simply were rich and powerful men—people like Augusta County leaders Alexander H. H. Stuart, who served in James Buchanan's cabinet, and John B. Baldwin, a member of the U.S. Congress.[31]

Important community decisions occurred through an obligatory ritual of participatory democracy. Leaders and followers performed these rituals at public gatherings where individuals affirmed their public consent either through an open vote or, just as often, through signing a statement endorsing a particular course of action, such as secession. County meetings conducted at regular court days or during emergency sessions often served as the venue for forging such agreement, which newspapers invariably reported. If appropriate, minutes of these sessions were mailed to representatives or the governor to present the wishes of the electorate. Slaveholding leaders obviously could limit the boundaries of dissent by packing the room or establishing procedures that allowed the chair to control subjects for debate. The meetings, however, reinforced both the power of slaveholding leaders and their reliance on public consent. Similar sessions would be conducted at crucial times throughout the war— even in the army, as officers tried to build consensus for policies among enlisted men.[32]

Equally important, slave-owning leaders east and west of the Blue Ridge served as the conduit for subordinate classes attempting to influence government or gain favors. Petitions from meetings or from poorer citizens requesting clemency were often endorsed by a prominent person before being mailed to public officials. This was especially true with pardons for crimes. More than seventy people from Augusta County in 1860 asked the governor for mercy on behalf of James McMullen, sentenced to three years in the penitentiary for stealing bacon. John B. Baldwin, a member of the U.S. House of Representatives, sponsored the petition that asked for the release of McMullen who was "extremely poor & has a wife and two small children who were entirely dependent upon his daily labor for their support." Jailing the man, the document argued, forced the family to rely on the parish for support.[33] This patron-client system worked not only for law and order but also for issues such as taxation and attempting to secure public office. It would continue to function during the war as communities petitioned for military exemptions of local blacksmiths, tanners, and other people essential to the neighborhood economy.

Also helping to bind together white Virginians was a strong love of independence, coupled with an equally strong fear of enslavement. Northern freeholders shared this ideal of maintaining independence through self-sufficiency, but slavery provided a special context for southerners by defining dependence partly in racial terms. Workers feared a fall from independent producer to dependent proletarian, which in their eyes was not very far from slave status.[34] A code of honor reinforced this sensitivity over the independence of white people. They took seriously any encroachment on their liberties, whether from governments, politicians, or planters who treated them without the proper respect in social settings. When David Hunter Strother published a traveler's account of Virginia just before the war for *Harper's* magazine, he told of a teamster almost starting a fight with a gentleman who refused to share a drink. The innkeeper calmed tensions by reminding the teamster that his rules did not apply to all people, adding that the man had "no right to put your law in force on strangers in this here free country." Strother added: "This argument touched Tim's weak point, which was an inordinate love of liberty, both of speech and action." The gentleman helped matters by raising a glass of water, proving he would drink with a person cut from rougher cloth.[35]

The aversion to being told how to live extended to religious matters, especially when someone other than God judged their morality. Denominational disputes convinced congregations that northerners wanted to ignore southern wishes. When the Methodist Church split into northern and southern wings because of slavery during the 1840s, arguments continued in the northern portions of Virginia's Shenandoah Valley and Piedmont that remained under northern jurisdiction. As the war approached, Methodist congregations in this disputed territory increasingly wanted to cleanse the area of what they considered to be antislavery Methodism. At a regional session held in 1860 at Winchester, Virginia, Methodists from the Shenandoah Valley—including Staunton Station, Augusta Circuit, Rockingham Circuit, Churchville Circuit, Lexington Station, and Rockbridge Circuit—protested that the bishop had sided with northern Methodists in the General Conference by expressing sympathy for antislavery. Members from the Valley appealed to the Conference to "come out from the Northern abolition branch of the Methodist Episcopal Church, whose principles are in direct conflict with the ministers and members of the Methodist Church in Virginia" and declared that "on the action of the Conference [concerning slavery] depends the prospect of the Church in the Valley." Within these churches, slave owners and non–slave owners would argue on the same side.[36]

The acquisition of new lands from the Mexican War escalated the debate over slavery in the territories and pricked at sensibilities shared by planters and plain folk. Abolitionists stirred up concern for liberty when they fought officials over the return of fugitive slaves, killed men in Kansas who were in favor of slavery, called for obedience of a higher law rather than a Constitution that condoned slavery, spoke of an irrepressible conflict, and helped fund John Brown's failed expedition into Harpers Ferry. It appeared that abolitionists would resort to any measure to get their way. These events are well known and affected the Old Dominion as much as the rest of the South. In Virginia's case, however, state pride also pushed residents over to the southern cause even as it gave some leaders extra incentive to keep the Union together.

State pride encompassed as broad a concept as the "southern way of life." In the 1850s it included issues ranging from education to tobacco but stemmed from a desire to reaffirm Virginia's "place" as a leader of both the South and the Union. Virginians were aware that they had lost ground economically and politically through the 1830s and 1840s. During that time, the Cotton South experienced a boom impossible for the Upper South to duplicate. It also made men from the Deep South powerful and cocky. In Congress, South Carolina and Kentucky provided the more prominent spokesmen for the region. To Virginians of the 1850s, the state seemed poised to reclaim the prominence that it had suffered. But the way to accomplish this was not entirely clear. The Old Dominion could follow neither the cotton-producing states nor the northern example of free labor. It had to find its own way toward self-sufficiency while maintaining slave labor. This problem posed a number of questions. How could the state stimulate more manufactures to break the reliance on the North for finished goods? How much education should the masses have? Would learning increase agricultural efficiency or merely create a class of lazy men who fancied themselves as planters? Should tobacco, or something else, be the leading crop? How could young men be encouraged to stay in the state and overcome their apparent resistance to manufacturing work? Should northern manufacturers be invited in, or would their ideals about free labor cause more problems than they were worth? Differences existed over how to answer these questions, but many Virginians were optimistic that greater self-sufficiency could come if the citizenry could only recapture the spirit of the Revolutionary generation.

The agricultural reform movement provides a window through which to view these concerns and how they intersected with the sectional crisis. Within their clubs and through farm journals, planters debated how to boost the economy without suffering a loss of power to northerners or to southern merchants and manufacturers. New farming clubs and the state agricultural society attracted the more prominent members of Virginia society—men who would be instrumental in the secession debates of 1861. They were intensely aware that the northern economy had progressed beyond that of the South and that population statistics warned of continued domination by Yankees in economic and political affairs. Organizers hoped that renewed economic vigor would restore the state's position as a molder of public opinion.

Farmers' associations had existed since the early 1800s, but their revival took on new urgency as planters attempted to unite farmers across the state. Founded in Richmond in 1852, the Virginia State Agricultural Society was formed by owners of larger farms. Edmund Ruffin led the effort to avoid exhausting soil through greed, cheap land, and poor management. As a group, the men blamed the tobacco depression on "land skinners" who neglected to restore fertility to the soil. An address issued at the organization's formation warned: "As other States accumulate the means of material greatness, we slight the warnings of dull statistics, and drive lazily along the field of ancient customs, or stop the *plough* to speed the *politician.*" The writers believed that state pride could make matters worse if traditional methods caused farmers to repeat the wasteful practices of the past.[37]

While sensitive to the gap in production with the northern industrial regions, agricultural society members could not always agree on why they had fallen behind. At one point they debated whether disparities lay in the tobacco culture itself. A planter named John H. Cocke blamed the "noxious" crop for creating an addiction that led to indolence, delirium, and other character traits that sapped moral fiber. Most planters brushed aside these arguments as nonsense. No one was about to give up planting tobacco based on the proposals of one man. Nonetheless, all agreed that something had gone wrong with prior practices. Wasteful farming had exhausted the soil, and monocrop practices had left the state vulnerable when the depression in prices came. Scientific agricultural methods featuring crop diversification and fertilization suggested a possible cure; otherwise the South risked becoming even more dependent on the North when the economic boom ended.[38]

Editorialists also feared that the young generation contributed to the lack of industrial advances. In this they probably exaggerated, as most do about the sins of the younger generation. Yet the farm journals reflected a worry that young men had become spoiled. Soft life under a new economy, critics alleged, created youths who ignored the mechanical arts because of a stigma that associated menial handwork with the kind that slaves should do. "The truth is," a writer complained in the most popular farm journal in the Old Dominion, " . . . we must learn to appreciate and to honour intelligent usefulness, to co-operate with and sustain it, if we would be released from a degrading sense of dependence on those who despise us, for nearly every necessary article—from the brush of the toilet to the tacks in our boots."[39] The desire to stimulate interest in mechanical arts and manufacturing overlapped into the broader goal to foster a home market for goods. This meant attracting more manufacturing to increase the number of mechanics, who ought to buy more products than a farmer. Edmund Ruffin also hoped to bring the mechanic and manufacturer nearer the farmer to encourage greater diversity of crops and provide local markets for foodstuffs.[40] Along these lines, writers in farm journals encouraged the entire South in the late 1850s to start a homespun movement to hurt northern textile manufacturers and improve southern self-sufficiency.

The way in which education should be managed in order to contribute to the process created intense differences during the 1850s as planters walked a tightrope between favoring formal education for a deserving few and denying compulsory free schools for the masses. Some within the ranks of this elite had the temerity to advocate free public schools supported by taxes. Governor Henry Wise won his election—and the label of demagogue from rivals—partly on the promise to push for this change, but he could not overcome biases against education. Much of the public still equated schools with increased taxes and feared loss of local control that a centralized system might bring.[41] Nearly as many doubted whether free schools benefited a region of farmers who learned what they needed through practical experience. Persons of this persuasion proudly called themselves "clodhoppers" as opposed to the "swell-head farmers" who valued formal education for agricultural work. The clodhoppers often suspected the overeducated swell-heads of using their learning to sway voters.[42]

By 1856, membership in the organization had reached 10,000 people from regions of the state that would demonstrate the strongest Confederate support. Although the vicinity of Richmond contained the heaviest concentration of members with 1,569, Augusta County in the Shenandoah Valley had the next highest number with 505. Albemarle was right behind with 495. The Piedmont and Tidewater dominated the organization, while support declined farther to the southwest and northwest. Western Virginians especially took little or no interest in the organization, reflecting their long-held animosities toward eastern planters.[43]

Despite a strong core of influence, the organization accomplished little when it tried to flex its political muscle. There was too much contention within the organization to present a united front on many issues. In 1858, the group failed to stop a combination of merchants in Richmond from forming a tobacco exchange that consolidated pricing and sales from several warehouses under one roof. It also could not win enactment of a new fence law to cut down the open grazing land for the poor.[44] Tensions were apparent as Edmund Ruffin—who for a time led the effort for political lobbying—moved to restrict democracy within the organization. Letting everyone have a voice was not an efficient way to get things done. Mass meetings in which each member voted were too "tumultuous & disorderly." Ruffin preferred forming the Farmers Assembly; this was a smaller group, elected by the membership in their various counties, that could be kept in check through close association with the Executive Committee, which controlled who would be nominated.[45] Although this system was instituted, the approach failed because other members saw it for what it was—an attempt to have a small group of men rule the society. Although the first Farmers Assembly dutifully convened on October 28, 1856, the numbers subsequently declined and the body rarely mustered a quorum. One of Ruffin's closest friends and supporters openly admitted that the bulk of members understood that their voices mattered little.[46] Conflicting sentiments characterized Virginia's leaders—a situation that would not end with the war.

Although the farmer societies achieved mixed results legislatively, the members found common ground in two vital areas. They reiterated their faith in slavery and the importance of Revolutionary heritage for making the Old Dominion great. A fair number of the top proslavery ideologues in the South hailed from Virginia, beginning in the 1820s with Thomas Dew, whom many credit with the transition from treating slavery as a necessary evil to touting its good aspects. Virginians who took up this task in the late antebellum period included George Fitzhugh, Edmund Ruffin, A. T. Bledsoe, and James P. Holcombe. All were active in the Virginia State Agricultural Society and used the farming press of the South to promote their cause. Fitzhugh pushed matters further than most by advocating slavery for all workers, black or white, but he fell squarely with the majority of these ideologues who, in general, challenged the notions of equality for all men that Thomas Jefferson had espoused.[47] Through farm journals and personal addresses to agricultural clubs, county fairs, and state fairs that attracted a wide range of farmers and mechanics, these men spread the gospel of proslavery.

State pride became bound up in this process, especially the desire to capitalize on the special heritage of Virginians. Chance gave the state the ability to celebrate its contributions to the Union. In 1857, residents observed the 250th anniversary of the founding of

Jamestown. No better reminder existed of Virginia's importance in the nation's origins. Commemoration of George Washington also grew during this time, especially among women's groups. Upper-class women formed the Mount Vernon Association to raise funds to purchase and refurbish Washington's estate.[48] In a similar vein, the General Assembly of Virginia disinterred the body of James Monroe from New York to make him the centerpiece of a circle of notaries who were buried at the Hollywood Cemetery in Richmond. Revolutionary figures increased their hold on the public and provided an important foundation for the identity of Virginians. While this appeared most noticeably among the upper classes, this pride in heritage extended into the black community. In Staunton, a free black man named Tom Evans held a one-man procession each year on the Fourth of July. This former slave donned a cocked hat, red breeches, and colonial coat to remind townspeople that he had served a master in the Revolutionary army. Evans also referred to himself as a "hero of the Revolution."[49]

Common whites shared the concerns articulated by these groups. They admired Virginia's heritage as much as any planter and could become incensed at the lack of respect on the part of northerners during the sectional crisis. The common folk had a stake in the territories beyond one of taking slaves there. The western lands provided hope that a place remained to start over if the economy worsened once again in Virginia. The North's attempt to limit slavery in the territories also appeared as an attack on property rights and an attempt to limit southern economic growth in favor of the northern political economy. It seemed unfair, to say the least, that northerners wanted to dictate the rules that should apply to the territories—especially when New England had protested the war and southerners had spilled their blood in acquiring the land.[50]

The raid at Harpers Ferry in 1859 presented a more personal concern that cut across class lines. Servile insurrection struck at the deepest fears of all white people. Although at first white Virginians were relieved when a general uprising failed to materialize, they became alarmed when northerners endorsed Brown's actions. Abolitionists had elevated sectional discord to a new level that many feared might lead to future incursions. Militia activity increased noticeably. Even in a Unionist area of Augusta County, citizens in Mt. Solon formed a military company of men aged 17 to 50 because "the outrage enacted at Harpers Ferry by a murderous band of fanatical emissaries, has at length aroused us to a sense of the great wrong and injury we are constantly sustaining at their hands."[51] Farther west, citizens in Putnam County along the Kanawha River watched their border anxiously. Militia units collected in May 1860 to meet a phantom force of 500 northern troops rumored to be crossing the Ohio River. Slave owners feared for the safety of their property and discussed whether to send their human chattel to secure areas. Banding together in militia companies was in itself significant. These units represented a cross section of the community, providing another way that planters and plain folk understood their social ranking and expressed their political allegiance.[52]

Yet this anxiety did not propel Virginians headlong into secession when the opportunity permitted. The Old Dominion watched as the cotton states parted one by one from the North and formed a southern Confederacy. Some of the same factors we have seen operating in the agricultural movement played a role at this time. The same state pride that could unite white Virginians against the North also caused some to hold on to their attachment to a Union that their ancestors had founded. Rival visions existed as to which best protected the Old Dominion—union or disunion. Highly contested, two-party politics played a role by reinforcing these alternative courses. Unionists stalled secession by claiming that the border states should hold their own convention because the Upper South had special needs and problems. Slave owners, for instance, needed reassurance that the new Confederacy would not resurrect the international slave trade to compete with the state's ability to sell slaves to the Lower South.[53] Overall, Old-line Whigs remained strong in the Upper South and their followers retained faith in the U.S. Constitution as the best protection of the South's political economy.

Numerous practical reasons supported this conservative stand. Economic ties and physical proximity to the North weighed on many minds, especially in the western half of the state where commerce depended on northern markets. And more than the economy complicated life on the border. Unlike the Deep South, war presented an immediate threat against the state, bringing armies into Virginia with disastrous consequences. "She is so far south," one Virginian noted about South Carolina, "and it is almost impossible to invade her coast, that she is perfectly willing for Virginia to receive all the calamities, and misfortunes of a war carried . . . upon Virginia's soil."[54] Unionists also feared that secession would cause slave owners to move in order to protect their property, draining slaves from the Upper South and leaving the region more vulnerable to an

influx of nonslaveholders. Through the emotional chaos that typified the secession winter, they could see clearly that the war might
cost the South the very treasure it meant to protect. One delegate
from the northwest in fact proclaimed that his Unionism was fostered by a desire to protect slavery. He asked his colleagues if secession would not "make a hostile border for Virginia, and enable slaves
to escape more rapidly. . . . Will it not, virtually, bring Canada to
our doors?"[55]

The turning point came on April 15 when Lincoln called on
troops to put down the rebellion. The request smacked of coercion
against a people who had democratically decided to go their separate
way, just like the Revolutionary forefathers. The Old Dominion
went with the Lower South rather than remain a border state in an
antislavery Union. The slave trade with the Cotton South, northern
agitation over abolition, disregard for southern wishes in the territories, a shared sense of southernism shaped by a slave society, John
Brown's raid, and finally Lincoln's call for troops had tipped the
scales toward secession. It appeared that the North had mounted a
consistent effort to deny southerners not only liberty but also life
and property. Even for conditional Unionists the United States was
worth saving, as one historian has explained, "only so long as the
cost of its preservation did not include a palpable threat to the stability of slavery."[56] Continued aggressive action by the Union settled
matters and kept providing a focal point for unity under the Confederacy. Looking back seven months after secession, Sarah Fife mused
about what made the Old Dominion separate from the Union. She
noted that the South had been cheated out of its rights, then explained more specifically what she meant: "The North has always
been the gainer, we have no share in the territories; we have to pay
them double the duty on goods that we do foreign nations; yet not
satisfied with this, they must attack our social system; incite our
slaves to rebellion circulating abolition volumes. . . . Either the
territories or the slavery question is sufficient to cause war, & both
are perfectly unendurable."[57]

Finding common cause for separating from the Union meant
one thing; fighting the war was quite another task. The savviest
leaders recognized the need to put behind differences and special
interests. Alexander H. H. Stuart, a slaveholder from the Shenandoah Valley who had voted against the secession ordinance at
the convention, hoped that a united front might prevent Lincoln
from sending troops into Virginia. "If we show divisions among our-

selves," Stuart reckoned, "the enemy will be encouraged by them, and make them the pretext for sending armies into our borders for the purpose of sustaining the bands of the disaffected." He counseled everyone to hold feuding in abeyance until after the contest.[58]

It was a fine wish but an unrealistic one. Free, white Virginians agreed on the most important facets of their way of life. They shared the assumptions of a society oriented primarily around small rural communities led by a slave-owning elite. They would expect planters to continue to shoulder the burden of caring for the poor and interceding on behalf of constituents at crucial times. State pride, revolutionary heritage, and notions of liberty gave them a basic consensus for fighting. To a person, Confederate Virginians believed they had been forced into the conflict because the North had left no other choice by advancing armies into sovereign states. Yet this was also a contentious society of outspoken individualists who would not hesitate to voice their discontent with the management of the war. They would have plenty of opportunity to do so as the people faced enormous strains while mounting modern warfare against a persistent, and destructive, Union army.

2

Problems of Labor and Order, April 1861–April 1862

The Southern worker, black and white, held the key to the war. . . .
—W. E. B. Du Bois, *Black Reconstruction in America*

By the summer of 1861, even Solomon might have needed advice. The volume of mail coming into the Confederate War Department in Richmond exhausted Albert T. Bledsoe. A career as professor at the University of Virginia and proslavery ideologue failed to prepare him as a bureaucrat. In the pile of correspondence he tossed into an armchair at day's end lay an array of competing concerns requiring instant decisions. Some letters contained relatively routine requests for military or political posts. The occasional crank also contributed, such as the "inventor" who asked for $1,500 to build a machine to move air at 100 miles per hour, ostensibly to aim at the enemy. Dominating this correspondence were petitions from communities for the return of the local miller, or tanner, or blacksmith. Occasionally there appeared individual pleas from women for the army to return an only son, a husband, or a provider because the household faced hardship and possible ruin. How should a public servant decide these matters? And which choices promised the greatest chance for Confederate success with the least suffering among the people?[1]

These questions highlight the problems that faced state and national authorities in the first year of the war. Within a few months the home front began to suffer from the loss of men vital to their economies. Areas with fewer slaves felt this loss the most: with white farmers and mechanics away serving in the military, the labor did not always exist to fill in the gaps. Each neighborhood had developed close-knit economic relationships over generations. The same families tended to own mills, tanneries, and other shops that kept communities running. When these men left home, problems other than economic ones occurred as well. The people in these communities increasingly had to find their bridles, shoes, grains, and other supplies in regional markets rather than close to home. The war also created a heightened sense of insecurity because of disorderly troops, suspected traitors, and speculators. Within the tobacco belt, residents worried about the possibility of a slave uprising as most young men went off to war. To local folks, the solution to all of these problems was simple: they wanted the military to exempt key personnel to preserve the neighborhood's way of living. To national authorities, of course, the answers were more complex. With perhaps 180,000 men of military age in Virginia—and little more than one million throughout the Confederacy—the southern war effort required a delicate balance of man power with woman power, soldier power with civilian power, and slave power with free power.[2]

The public's concerns did have an impact, although not always in the intended way. Government began to expand. Locally, officials organized supplies and provisions by authorizing community funds and group purchasing. Nationally, the Davis administration invoked martial law and established provost marshals to control spies, deserters, and disorderly troops. In April 1862 the Confederate Congress enacted the first national draft in American history, which not only put men in the military but also designated laborers who would be allowed to stay at home to maintain production. The kind of exemptions written into law matched those requested in the petitions that besieged bureaucrats like Albert T. Bledsoe. Trying to protect the community demanded certain controls over people's lives—not all of them unwelcome.

Few could foresee this development as most free Virginians rushed to support the war effort. As news of the April 17 secession ordinance reached the interior, people fired cannons, paraded in streets, and prepared for conflict. When the state turned out to vote for ratification on May 23, the balloting overwhelmingly favored disunion. Communities displayed their unity with a 130,000-vote majority for secession, although the margin tells a slightly deceptive story. Persons who harbored doubt remained at home rather than face the harassment experienced by those who openly declared Unionist sentiments. Some Unionists voted for secession because of pressure from neighbors, some of whom threatened to hang the uncooperative. In Fredericksburg, the community forced the *Christian Banner* to shut down after May 9, 1861 because of the Unionist sentiments of its editor. Even Unionists who quietly went about their business drew suspicion. One Campbell County woman told her husband: "I would not trust those strong Union men—none of them can be relied on—especially a Whig for if they think they are working against Democrats they will do all kinds of unprincipled things."[3]

Actions by the Lincoln government reinforced this enthusiasm. Danger from the Union army seemed imminent. Troops amassed in Washington to invade the South. By May 1861 they had entered Maryland and seized control of civilian life, further convincing southerners that Lincoln intended to deny people their rights through military force. The next target would be Virginia. Invasion could come from at least four directions: along the coast, near Norfolk, where the James River provided access to Richmond; in northern Virginia; in the Shenandoah Valley, from the Federal armory at Harpers Ferry; and from the Ohio River, up the Kanawha, eventually to threaten Staunton in the Valley. Delegates to the secession convention, which served temporarily as a de facto legislature, overwhelmingly chose Robert E. Lee to organize defenses.

Shortly, Union generals tested each avenue. The northwest fell fairly quickly as Unionists formed a new government and the northern army defeated Confederates at Philippi and Rich Mountain on June 3 and July 11, respectively. Governor John Letcher sent Lee and two of the state's prominent politicians—Henry A. Wise and John B. Floyd—to reclaim the region, but they failed badly. In the Shenandoah, militia and Confederate forces seized Harpers Ferry but evacuated the town after stripping it of equipment as Union troops arrived from the north and west. From Washington, northern soldiers prepared the advance into Northern Virginia that culminated in the battle of First Manassas on July 21. Along the southeastern coast, Union gunboats traded fire with Confederates at Gloucester Point, and northern soldiers reinforced their toehold on the state at Fort Monroe.

Although enthusiasm ran high the first couple of months, not everyone could afford to leave home. The first wave of volunteers consisted primarily of young unmarried men who had yet to establish themselves. The majority of the Lynchburg Rifle Grays were under age 30, and only fourteen of the 112 members were married. Units from Orange County looked about the same, with a study of that region concluding that "sons of the large slaveholders could afford to leave home for the army because they contributed relatively little to the household economy."[4] Areas with fewer slaves contained farmers who could ill afford to leave chores without finding someone to take their places. When an editor of a newspaper in Staunton worried that too few citizens responded to meet the emergency, he realized that the reasons had little to do with patriotism. "Professor J. Hotchkiss," he noted, "is also raising a company to go into service after harvest. It will be composed principally of our farmer boys, who are necessarily detained at home until the crops are gathered."[5] Faced with the losses in western Virginia and increasing pressure from the Union army, Governor John Letcher called out the militia in the second week of July, establishing a quota of 10 percent of the white population for each county. It was a controversial move, but he had to do something. The situation, however, was not grim enough for him and other southerners to accept help from an unexpected quarter. Black people in some areas volunteered to fight. In Lynchburg, for instance, free blacks attempted to form a company of soldiers. Welcomed at first by the press, the gesture quickly dropped from public sight.[6]

Volunteers steeped in a militia tradition found it hard to accept that they could not freely come and go. The victory at First Manassas only exacerbated this attitude, sending men trickling from the army. The Yankees had been defeated, went the rationale, so men should not have to stay in camp until another threat materialized. Why drill or perform other camp routine when crops needed tending at home? General Joseph E. Johnston recalled about this time: "Many, therefore, in ignorance of their military obligations, left the army—not to return." Some went home while others accompanied wounded friends to hospitals in the state's interior. "Exaggerated ideas of the victory, prevailing among our troops," Johnston added, "cost us more men than the Federal army lost by defeat."[7]

The war spirit had not died; rather, the men followed a local kind of patriotism in keeping with the militia tradition rooted in American life since the colonial era. Local militias performed much like volunteer fire companies in which members responded to emergencies and then returned to civil life. Few volunteers in the first year of war intended to adopt a different mindset. One bemused fellow wrote home when his unit arrived in Jefferson County that the women "call us Soldiers here—*not militia,*" and his emphasis underscored the novelty of the concept. In a similar vein, a Campbell County man told a friend: "I'm afraid George if I should come out of this war alive, that people will continue to call me 'Captain'—There's nothing half so genteel as 'Mr.,' and I don't like to give up the title—would you?"[8]

At this point in the war, the men remained more citizen than soldier, which created quaint but vexing problems in the military. Discipline was hard to inculcate among enlisted men and sometimes company officers. Because communities often used militia groups to form these early regiments, more complicated relationships existed within units than simply officer to enlisted man. There might also have been personal relations: uncle with nephew, merchant with miller, or planter with day laborer. In line with the antebellum tradition, community leaders were to heed the wishes of men who expected to hold on to the rights of a democratic society. The bottom line was that enlisted men should have some say in their fate: that officers should consult them in important decisions; that they could choose the units in which they would serve; that they could elect company officers. They also preferred to fight at home rather than perform guard duty somewhere else. A man from Botetourt County near the boundary between the southwest and the Valley noted that patriot hearts beat within his mountain wilds, but of a particular kind. While offering his "Blue Ridge Scouts" for service with the regular army, he added: "It would be impossible to get these men into service in any other way, except as militiamen."[9] Whenever action stopped, it seemed ridiculous to expect them to perform picket duty while their communities faced a Yankee threat. Members of the Wise Legion hailed from a part of the northwest that had fallen to the Union. Fifty-two of them voted to return to western Virginia, protesting that the enemy possessed "our homes and fire-sides." The petition added that the enemy was encroaching "still farther in to the bosom of our beloved Commonwealth." Consequently, the men could not understand why they "should be compelled to turn our backs upon them and our homes, to repel invasion in another quarter." Higher authorities, of course, denied the request.[10]

Local orientation also characterized civilians, who tried to keep the war a community affair by supporting their "boys" with minimal help from outsiders. Residents expected state and Confederate officials to supply arms and equipment, but accepting this aid did not mean relinquishing responsibility for *their* troops. Instead of turning to the national government, communities in Virginia and throughout the South conducted campaigns to gather food, clothing, and equipment. Women were especially prominent as they formed associations to sew uniforms, package foods, or present flags to local companies. Like Lucy Wood Butler of Albemarle, they believed that "our needles are now our weapons, and we have a part to perform as well as the rest."[11] Masters offered to send slaves to construct defenses, provided that the state would pay for transport and food. Men too old or too ill to fight funded local companies or donated provisions. County courts passed legislation for similar purposes. When a bank board in Lynchburg authorized $200 for each local unit, the cashier noted, "There is wonderful liberality displayed—Eighteen of our citizens have given $500 a piece for the purpose of equipping troops and maintaining their families in their absence."[12] This support became vital as winter approached. Virginians donated an estimated $3 million worth of overcoats, shoes, socks, and blankets, raising funds through floating bonds or finding money from other government pockets. The Lynchburg City Council, for instance, set aside $2,800 in surplus funds from the public water committee. Secretary of War Judah P. Benjamin noted the efforts overall in his annual report, indicating that without community cooperation the Quartermaster's Department could have supplied neither shelter nor other essentials for soldiers in time for winter.[13]

The Confederacy's victory at First Manassas also awakened civilians to the problems of running a modern war through local resources. Supplies proved entirely inadequate. Medical facilities could not handle the wounded who suddenly swelled the populations of towns. Charlottesville found itself caring for about 1,200 of the wounded from Manassas. The town contained a total of only 3,000 people, with hospital space for 300 patients. Residents scrambled to find room in public buildings and at the University of Virginia. Private homes absorbed the overflow, with each taking from two to twenty soldiers. Women volunteered as nurses, cooks, and seamstresses, but the institutions needed more of everything. Repeated elsewhere in the Confederacy, these conditions accelerated the establishment of hospitals that quickly turned to slaves and free blacks for staffing. By 1862 the number of African Americans working at the six hospitals in Lynchburg totaled 420, or nearly 14 percent of the town's black population in 1860. Hospital officials also needed soldiers to police the convalescing men who might not be ready for battle but felt well enough to cause trouble.[14]

By the autumn of 1861, three kinds of scarcity confronted people. The loss of the Kanawha Valley had cost the state one of its most important regions for producing salt—a necessity to preserve a family's bacon. The supply of leather from the North and from South America also dwindled because of the blockade. With so many tanners in the army, leather sometimes rotted from inexperienced handling or lying unprocessed in the tanyard. Finally, communities suffered from shortages of currency. The need for cash increased as the Confederacy adopted new systems of banking and currency. Women wrote to their husbands in the army for money because little circulated on the home front. In Augusta County, a wife could no longer pay tuition for her boys' schooling, saying, "I am out of money, have been for some time, so you see my darling husband I am in a dreadful fix." Another Virginian could not loan a friend $50 "as I have no money by me at all, and cannot collect enough to pay pressing demands. The wealthiest men in the county here have no money and consequently are not paying anything."[15]

Like most southerners, Confederate Virginians blamed the shortages on extortioners and speculators—often called "Yankee southerners"—who capitalized on the suffering of others by purchasing items for resale instead of their own use. It was quickly apparent that this could have an impact on morale. One Virginian indicated that a Union general attempted to erode loyalty among the populace by offering to supply them with salt at 75 cents per bushel, along with coffee and other goods. "To some," he continued, "these may appear but weak efforts to conquer men's patriotism, but to men who have wives and large families of helpless children surrounded by enemies—and suffering for the necessities of life—they are more powerful than armies." He added that families could not purchase salt for a month's worth of a soldier's pay. Shortages affected planters, farmers, and poor people alike, although the rich had the means to stockpile salt and other goods from the beginning of the war. No one, however, had stored enough to last the entire conflict.[16]

People who lived in towns felt these early shortages the most. From Lynchburg in particular came cries to do away with a free market by having local government step in to control transactions. A writer to a Lynchburg newspaper, identifying himself as "One of the People," suggested that salt dealers be licensed like the hucksters in Richmond. "Why may not our Hustings Court make out a table of prices and require all who are licensed to sell in the city to conform thereto, under certain penalties. Something must be done by our constituted authorities or the people will take the subject of redression into their own hands." The writer hated seeing good southerners behaving like Yankees. "If salt be scarce," he added, "its market value straight away goes up from 2¼ to 6 or 8 dollars a sack; no matter whether poor people can buy it or not."[17] Charles Button, the editor of the Lynchburg *Virginian*, carried on perhaps the most vocal campaign for government regulation of the marketplace. He did so with the understanding that any measures would be temporary. "Under ordinary circumstances," he wrote, "it would be impolitic, perhaps unjust, to interfere with the laws of trade; which, it is concluded, should be allowed to regulate itself without legislative interference." But in war, he added, "the laws, to a certain extent, are suspended." Under the circumstances, he pondered, was it right for government to suspend the liberties of individuals by forcing them from their homes and into the army while it respected the liberty of those on the home front who profited from the absences?[18] What Button suggested would become a reality in impressment legislation enacted by the Confederacy in 1863.

For the moment, however, local governments bore the burden of solving this problem. Lynchburg residents by late November 1861 had decided to control salt extortion by purchasing in bulk with community money. It took a week or so for a committee of merchants and key townspeople to work out the details. The committee calculated that the price of salt could be set at $3.50 a sack at a time when Governor Letcher claimed it sold at $20 to $25 per sack.[19] As communities throughout Virginia resorted to similar measures, the state finally endorsed these procedures in legislation enacted May 9, 1862. There was little coordination of these efforts. Counties negotiated individual contracts rather than cooperate statewide. Typically, magistrates on county courts established agents to secure the commodity with public funds raised through bond issues. Salt was then distributed throughout an area at the purchase price, plus the costs of transportation and commission for the agents. Richmond began this procedure in the summer of 1862 with the council providing $5,000 for the purchases. Petersburg did likewise. Thus, as early as the winter of 1861–1862, the trend had emerged for citizens to call on government to influence the market, although this expansion of powers occurred through local people administering a specified commodity.[20]

Communities could not solve all the challenges of mobilizing for war. State and Confederate help would be needed. At the end of the summer, Virginians began to realize this and complained to Governor Letcher and the Confederate War Department about the inequities they observed. This was especially true for regions containing fewer slaves than the tobacco belt. Alexander H. H. Stuart of Staunton spoke for the Shenandoah Valley when he warned against the governor's levy en masse for the militia order on July 15. Stuart explained that "men go to the battlefield with very little alacrity when they feel they may leave their wives & children exposed to horrors to which their own perils are as nothing—The call ought to be modified or the people may be driven to desperation."[21] Members of the Seventh Brigade, Virginia Militia, described the Valley's dilemma thusly: "The Valley of Virginia is a wheat-growing country, in which slave labor is scarce; consequently the larger proportion of the labor must be performed by white men between the ages of eighteen and forty-five years. The time for sending the wheat crop has arrived, and unless at least a considerable proportion of the men new here can be returned to their homes to attend to putting that crop in the ground we will be unable to raise supplies sufficient for our own subsistence." Valley people in general believed that the east could better withstand the demands for troops because of their slaves.[22]

Planters east of the Blue Ridge had their own worries. Those who hired out slaves for government work discovered they had entered uncharted terrain. It took time to clarify who should bear financial responsibility for slaves who escaped, died, or became disabled from the grueling work of building fortifications. The Confederate government at first wanted no part of this liability. In November 1861 the attorney general ruled that the government bore no obligation to reimburse owners because the Confederacy assumed the position of an individual hirer, whom the law absolved from paying damages unless expressly stated in a contract. Because work placed slaves near the frontier, many also escaped. Gloucester Point and Westmoreland County in the southeast became two areas through which slaves routinely fled. This stunned planters such as Edmund Ruffin whose proslavery views had not anticipated that "happy" slaves would leave of their own accord. Equally frustrating was the exposure of slaves to dangerous ideas. John Spiece of Albemarle County complained about impressed slaves sent to the Valley because "whilst there they get to talking with Union men in disguise, and by that means learn the original cause of the difficulty between North & South: then return home and inform other negroes."[23]

Planters began to withhold slaves, move them toward more secure areas of the interior, or demand their return from military work.
The Union success at Roanoke Island in March 1862 escalated these
trends in the southeast. Major General John B. Magruder claimed that
he could not send reinforcements to Suffolk in southeast Virginia because "notwithstanding all my efforts to procure negroes, I have received but 11 from the counties in my district, the presiding magis-
trate referring the calls in some cases to the district attorney, who
decides that it is illegal, and in other cases no response is made."[24]
Adding to the problem was a belief among slave owners that not all of
the community bore the war's burden equally. The teamster of Robert
C. Mcluer, a slave owner in Rockbridge County, died from typhoid
while working for the government. "I don't feel," Mcluer wrote the
governor, "that it is just that I should sustain such loss whilst my
neighbor who did no more lost nothing."[25] Planters unwittingly added
to labor shortages by hiring slaves to send to the military instead of
their own chattel, which quickly tapped out the available pool.[26]

To relieve the shortage of labor, local and state authorities first
turned to the free black population. Similar to the way World War I
stimulated demand for African American labor, free blacks in Virginia found opportunities at higher pay as workers of both sexes ne-
gotiated with soldiers to cook for company messes, wash clothes, and
perform other domestic chores. Within communities, mechanics and
artisans found increased demand for skills that would grow more
precious to the military as time passed.

Still, for many free blacks the story was not a happy one because
they faced coercion into military work. The state convention helped
by authorizing the enrollment of black men between ages 18 and 50.
Many would go to work in hospitals or be used as teamsters. Magistrates of county courts selected workers from the registry that free
blacks were required to sign each year. Local sheriffs then prodded
the workers into service. This method eased the demand for slaves
from planters and pleased mechanics as well. A Lynchburg mechanic indicated to Jefferson Davis that the Confederacy should put
the black bricklayers, carpenters, and stone masons to better use: "I
want to know, if that degraded and worse than useless race could not
do something in the way of defending the South such as throwing
up Breast works Building tents or any thing els [*sic*] that would be of
advantage to us. and take the hard portion of labor off of the Soldiers
who has to drill 6 or 8 hours every day besides work."[27]

As the demand for workers grew, Virginians experimented with convict laborers. The superintendent of the state penitentiary in Richmond sent seventy-nine inmates to work on fortifications in response to an order by the Confederate government on June 1, 1861. When he lost ten runaways, he resisted sending more, although he dispatched another group later that year. All of the thirty-two convicts in this second group were black—nineteen slaves and thirteen free men. A soldier detailed to work on the railroad reported to his family in December: "They are working negroes on it, all convicts."[28] The state needed such coercion because free black people often turned down dangerous work with the army. For instance, an official asked the government to impress workers because he could secure none at any price to build winter quarters.[29]

By the autumn of 1861, authorities recognized that the system for mobilization served neither front nor home front very well. Virginians led the Confederate states in numbers of volunteers, but there was a disturbing side to the statistics. By February 1862 only 1,500 had formed companies enlisted for three years, while the terms of 53,950 others expired in April. Many of these men found military service incompatible with either their physical abilities or their appetites. Even the healthiest and most patriotic felt the need to return to families undergoing difficult times. Someone had to do something to avert a crisis as enlistments expired.[30]

Letters to the secretary of war from the Augusta, Albemarle, and Campbell regions during calendar year 1862 reveal the stresses on communities and the delicate task facing state and national authorities. Consisting of 168 letters, the correspondence fell into three large categories: the need for labor, military questions, and personal security (table 2.1). As a whole, the communication shows that local communities were changing in ways that forced more regional orientation and expansion of government.

The need for labor was the leading reason for writing to the Confederate government. Correspondence of this kind constituted 67 letters, or 40 percent, of the total from these three regions. Many followed the pattern of the antebellum era by taking the form of petitions endorsed by local leaders who passed them on to the administration. Typically, the petitioners asked for the exemption from military service of a skilled artisan, professing that the neighborhood could not function without the individual. Communities missed millers and shoemakers the most, although tanners were also in demand. As usual, the Shenandoah Valley expressed these needs more than the tobacco belt, where slaves helped to fill artisan positions.

Table 2.1 Community Needs Expressed to the Confederate Secretary of War, 1862

Type of Request (N=168)	Augusta/ Staunton	Albemarle/ Charlottesville	Campbell/ Lynchburg
Labor Needed			
Tanners	3	2	0
Shoemakers	7	2	0
Millers	5	5	5
Smiths	3	0	1
Metalworkers	0	0	5
Laborers	4	0	1
Confederate Work	1	0	1
Slaves	0	1	5
Other	8	3	5
Subtotal	31	13	23
Military Questions			
Conscription	7	9	1
Substitution	3	1	4
Assignment Wanted	5	2	1
Exempt for Health	5	5	2
Exempt for Religion	2	0	0
Goods Impressed	4	2	3
Subtotal	26	19	11
Personal Security			
Deserter Problems	1	2	0
Liquor Problems	1	2	1
Exempt Overseer	0	2	1
Law and Order Fears	5	4	1
Disloyalty Suspected	8	1	1
Speculation Concerns	3	1	3
Household Needs	2	5	1
Subtotal	20	17	8
Totals	77	49	42

Source: Letters Received, Confederate Secretary of War, NA

The letters in this category emphasize the small radius in which local economies operated.[31] Almost immediately, war disturbed the fragile network of the neighborhoods. Petitioners on behalf of a tanner, blacksmith, or miller often complained that they could not find a substitute for these services within three to five miles. This might strike today's reader as a distance scarcely worth noting, but it illustrates the orientation of rural life in the mid–nineteenth century. Tobacco, wheat, and other crops involved transactions beyond the community, but the commodities of daily life—shoes, barrels, milled flour, leather goods, and so on—typically came through neighborhood resources in which custom dictated the cost. Cash played a role in the economy, but more often with external exchanges such as when merchants purchased supplies from the North. Internally, trust rather than cash characterized transactions. Merchants forgave debt or carried a customer until payment came, sometimes accepting services in kind.[32] The next village might lie only five miles away, but the journey covered a far greater distance into a different network of exchanges. And individuals often had no prior experience to guide them as to whether the seller would charge reasonable prices or whether the buyer would be trusted to pay a debt.[33]

War disrupted these long-standing arrangements, forcing many for the first time to confront prices established primarily through demand, and leaving them without the ability to conduct a transaction with little or no cash. Also, resentment built within communities when their valuable food was shipped beyond the neighborhood to help others.[34] Under such circumstances it was easy to feel as if one were being gouged by an extortioner. Undoubtedly some people were. To make matters worse, as the winter of the first year of war came, merchants tightened their lines of credit and demanded cash payment even from long-standing customers. In Lynchburg, merchant George M. Rucker announced that he would sell goods for cash only, making no deliveries before receiving payment "in view of all the troubles of the country." By February 1862, the town druggist in Culpeper began forcing people to settle their accounts.[35]

The second largest group of concerns involved military questions. Although constituting fifty-six, or 33 percent, of the communications from the three regions, these letters were less remarkable. They primarily asked questions about conscription laws and a host of issues surrounding substitutions and exemptions. The Shenandoah Valley residents were tremendously interested in these issues. As will be discussed below, the region contained large numbers of pacifist families associated with the Mennonite and Dunkard churches who hoped to secure religious exemptions. Other letters in this category came from men wanting a particular military assignment—promotion, transfer, and so on. Nine of the correspondents complained about the lack of regulations for impressment, which left civilians at the mercy of military officers who wanted goods.

The final grouping of letters to the War Department expressed anxieties about personal security or asked what to do about deserters, slaves, Unionists, speculators, and loss of providers for the household. Forty-five letters from the three regions, or 27 percent, dealt with such issues. Perhaps because it was early in the war, complaints from households about emergencies requiring their menfolk did not yet dominate: the total of eight that spanned the three areas appeared as frequently as those dealing with disloyalty, law and order, or speculation.

The Confederacy had tried to deal with "tories" in a more systematic way than the persecution that characterized early treatment of Unionists. Residents of the southern states were forced to declare their loyalty or leave the new country. An act determining alien enemies act adopted in August 1861 required persons who were not citizens of states in the Confederacy to evacuate by forty days after the president's proclamation of August 14. A sequestration act allowed authorities to seize property of the alien enemies who remained. Passed on August 30, 1861, this act responded to the Union government's confiscation of the property of Confederates. When enforcement began in October, the government seized Monticello because it was owned by Captain Uriah P. Levy of the Union navy. The government also granted passports to the 300 people in Lynchburg who had registered as alien enemies and asked to leave for northern territory. By October, provost marshals in Richmond had begun publishing the names of aliens and processing passports to lead them out of the country through Fort Monroe.[36]

The home front also worried about controlling slaves—a fear more strongly felt in the countryside than in the towns. Many in the tobacco belt east of the Blue Ridge spent the first months of the war anxiously watching for incipient rebellions. Petitioners to the government justified the exemption of overseers on the basis of shoring up the police powers of a community rather than protecting labor, an attitude mirrored by the Congress. The home front had reason to worry. In a petition calling for the exemption of an overseer, Thomas J. Randolph of Albemarle explained that the mountains and a river framed an area of roughly nineteen miles in which 270 slaves and seventy-nine white people lived. Of the latter, twelve were in the service, two had volunteered, and several had moved. Randolph estimated that thirty women and thirty children remained. Of the males, only two were eligible for service.[37] Similar circumstances would have applied to much of the county in which roughly 60 percent of the households had slaves. Rural areas of the tobacco belt, in which slaves often outnumbered the free, contained the greatest number of residents desiring overseers' exemptions.

Concern for law and order arose over the friction created by refugees, soldiers, laborers, mechanics, and others who flocked to towns. Fighting broke out daily and thieves routinely entered homes. Soldiers on furlough or awaiting orders challenged civilian watchmen. Charlottesville's jail overflowed with soldiers who proved so destructive that the jailer refused to accept more prisoners. Here and elsewhere, town leaders targeted drinking as the root of the difficulties and tried to ban the sale of liquor. They achieved mixed results. Because of the enormous profits from selling alcohol, farmers often wanted to turn their surplus corn into liquor. A woman in Campbell County told a friend it was no use quoting the price of corn, for it increased weekly "on account of so many stills being put up in the country." The local editor lamented the Confederacy's failure to prevent the distilling of valuable grain. The mayor attempted to halt the flow of alcohol by closing saloons but later rescinded the action because of the revenue that liquor generated for hotels and saloons in the city.[38]

When disorder showed no sign of abating, people petitioned the national government to declare martial law. Jefferson Davis issued a proclamation in late February for Norfolk and Portsmouth because the Federal army had landed in that vicinity. Davis and Congress had been reluctant to go this far because of the potential political backlash throughout the Confederacy. Southerners had rallied to the cause because they saw Lincoln directing military force to accomplish Yankee abolitionist goals. To calm concerns about the loss of liberty within the Confederacy, Davis vested civilian authorities—not the military—with the power to enforce martial law. The president had read the public's mood well. Within communities, tension existed over the extent of martial law and who should enforce it. Charles Button, editor of the *Virginian*, was among community leaders calling on Lynchburg residents to demand complete military rule, but a public meeting failed to support this position. Residents preferred to give local people the power to handle disturbances. In Lynchburg's case, this meant expanding the night watch and police powers in general. Richmond followed a similar course, with its council arming local police with shotguns, placing a curfew of 10 P.M. on the sale of liquor, and banning sales on Sundays. When none of the measures worked, the council finally invited the Confederate government to establish martial law. Brigadier General John H.

Winder took command on March 1, 1862, with city authorities at first welcoming the help.[39]

As spring neared, the Federal army commanded the attention of most Virginians and propelled Confederate authorities toward conscription as the means to resolve the most pressing problems of both home and front. In February and March 1862 enemy soldiers crossed the Potomac River into northern Virginia. By early March, Joseph Johnston retreated from near Washington and shifted defenses to the Rappahannock River. Union soldiers under officers marched into the vacuum. Much of the area fell under quasi-Federal control, costing Virginia resources for processing flour and fattening cattle. By March, George B. McClellan's Army of the Potomac shifted from Washington to the Peninsula. The base in southeastern Virginia offered the perfect position for a thrust toward Richmond. Outside of the state the picture looked bleaker. Ulysses S. Grant had captured Forts Henry and Donelson in Tennessee. The Union navy, in conjunction with the army, had begun sealing off the coast by seizing Port Royal, South Carolina, in November 1861 and Roanoke Island, North Carolina, in early February 1862. Everywhere one looked, momentum lay with the Union as the Confederacy faced the prospect of enlistments expiring among volunteers.

The military situation affected morale minimally in the Old Dominion, but in conjunction with events in the eastern theater it bolstered the argument for centralized controls over the war effort. This, of course, was not a unanimous sentiment; however, a segment of the population believed that lack of momentum occurred from mismanagement by leaders and too much democracy. One Virginian relayed sentiments common in a portion of the populace when he stressed to a relative that the time had come to employ stronger measures at home to defeat the enemy. Volunteers, he argued, should be enlisted for the duration of the war instead of limited terms. "There are many who will reenlist for the war & many who will have to be forced to go—all this from our mobocratic please-everybody institutions, the prostitution of the ballot box, and the 'liberty equality & fraternity' feeling that has been pervading all classes in this country until the government has gone to decay. . . . For my part I prefer the excess of power to the excess of liberty, and when the war is over I hope we will have a government that will stand the test of time, and keep the rabble quiet."[40]

Virginia authorities reached similar conclusions and placed the home front on a stronger wartime footing. Before McClellan's advance up the Peninsula, the Union threat had not quite hit home. A Richmond editor complained that the people remained apathetic despite the enemy's being within several days' march. The governor and General Assembly felt compelled to take action. On February 8, the legislature enacted a conscription act for the Old Dominion that established enrollment in the militia for all males between 18 and 45. Sheriffs and other local officials supervised the process. Through this procedure, the state hoped to answer the Confederacy's call for 65,800 men from the state for three years of service. Several days later Letcher used his executive powers to designate two classes of militia: males from 18 to 45 would serve as part of the first class; those from ages 16 to 18 and 45 to 60 would constitute the second. Both would be used for home defense and other purposes as needed, with the first-class militia assigned to trouble spots beyond the immediate community. In times of Union threats, businesses were to close at 2 P.M. so the second-class militia could drill. Letcher worried about Richmond because of the city's manufacturing capabilities, which, he noted, "are doing so much to uphold the Southern Confederacy that its loss to us would be well nigh irreparable."[41]

In one way or another, Letcher's action placed all white males from age 16 to 60 in the military, although these were state units. To protect the economy of the home front, the legislature subsequently adopted exemptions, emphasizing public officials, local civil servants, ministers, doctors, and officers of businesses essential for communications in the state—telegraph, canal, and railroad companies. The legislation was vague about which occupations would be judged essential to the economy, choosing to establish three-member exemption boards that would oversee these decisions in communities. Once drafted, men vital to the economy could be detailed for essential work and receive the monthly wage for a soldier, rather than the going rate for civilians. It was a more expedient plan than the national conscription that shortly followed, and it anticipated features to which Confederate officials would turn.[42]

The volunteers finally came, helped by Letcher's call in March to mobilize 40,000 militia members to defend the state. From Lynchburg to the lower Shenandoah Valley, officers and civilians noted the infusion of soldiers into the army. In his correspondence with the War Department, Stonewall Jackson, in the Valley, mentioned the influx. Jed Hotchkiss reinforced this impression by observing to his wife: "The men are in good spirits & many of those that at first ran away have concluded that it is best to come on & not wait to be drafted for the war." By March 19, 1862, the adjutant general for the state reported that three-year volunteers had increased to 27,898, up from 1,500 the month before. Although Virginia needed to raise another 13,045 to bring the companies up to the requisite 100 soldiers each, he noted that "so many have volunteered that there is a fair prospect of the deficiency being filled up without a draft, or by a comparatively small one." Without exemptions for students, the University of Virginia lost a number of people that spring. Professor Socrates Maupin noted that when the governor threatened a state draft in February, students went home to consult with families "in regard to the expediency of volunteering and thereby escaping what they deemed the ignominy of being drafted into military service." Seventeen took leave from the university through March 3 and another twenty or so were on leave or withdrew by April 12.[43]

The turn of events angered planters and manufacturers who feared the state had stripped the home front of men essential for war-related work and for preserving law and order. Proprietors of various manufactories filled the governor's mail with lamentations about the shortage of labor. The Langhorne mills in Lynchburg already had lost a number of millers, and its representatives hoped to hold on to the remaining three. At stake, the manager argued, was a government contract for 25,000 barrels of flour. In Albemarle, W. T. Early joined those protesting the lack of exemptions for overseers. He argued that the state draft depleted plantations of white males. Leaving operations in the hands of slaves, he continued, would produce disorganization, reduce production, and increase the chance of insurrection. A man from Lynchburg proved remarkably prescient when he told Letcher that the government ought to resolve a situation on the home front in which able-bodied males of military age worked on the railroad as commissaries, and in depots as ticket agents, while gentlemen over age 45 and disabled soldiers searched for work. He advocated switching these men, adding that most of the people were behind Letcher's measures for meeting the crisis.[44]

Perhaps the strongest response against turning most of the male population into soldiers came in the Shenandoah Valley, home of a significant number of the state's pacifist religious sects. One study estimates that roughly 400 families of Dunkard and Mennonite faiths lived in the Valley. Resistance in this region in early 1862 fed notions that the Valley harbored Unionist sentiment, although the underlying motivations probably were more complex. Sectarians would support no cause, whether Union or Confederate, that conflicted with religious principles. In March, Confederate cavalry captured at least two groups of Mennonites and Dunkards—one numbering more than seventy and another nearly twenty—as the men attempted to flee through Union-controlled northwestern Virginia into Ohio. Soldiers marched them to prison in Richmond. While spending one night in the Staunton courthouse, the group elicited more sympathy than hatred. "Some, if not all of them," one onlooker remarked, "are simple-hearted, inoffensive people, belonging to the Dunkard church, whose tenets forbid going to war." He added: "There is something pitiful in the case of these people, flying as they were to escape conscription, and being taken like partridges on the mountains. The whole crowd had a pocket pistol between them and no other arms."[45] This incident caused little alarm, for people understood the religious principles motivating such men. Even so stern a patriot as Stonewall Jackson treated religious objectors leniently by removing them from the front line and using them as teamsters or aides.[46] One result of this discord was that Virginia led both the Confederacy and the Union in crafting legislation for conscientious objectors. By March 29, 1862, the General Assembly authorized exemptions for religious reasons at the price of $500. Few at the time objected to what amounted to a tax on faith.[47]

Not all resistance was so tame. A more serious incident in April involved a group estimated at several hundred that staged what newspapers called the "Blue Ridge Rebellion." Political rather than religious reasons appeared to cause these men to band together, although at least one person believed Dunkards formed part of the resistance. Their methods, however, argue against interpreting this as a religious protest by pacifists because these rebels were "well armed with rifles, shot guns, and one instance with a pike." Stonewall Jackson crushed the rebellion with troops under Lieutenant Colonel J. R. Jones, who shelled the region, broke the resistance, and placed the leader in irons. Jed Hotchkiss revealed nothing about the person other than that he was "a tigrous looking fellow."[48]

Despite pockets of discontent, a number of factors cheered those who fought for the Confederacy. A critic of the Davis administration, Edward A. Pollard nonetheless crowed that the conflict proved the strength of slavery, because "no servile insurrections have taken place in the South, in spite of the allurements of our enemy; that the slave has tilled the soil while his master has fought."[49] The state also appeared to survive its first year of secession in fairly good shape. There were, of course, cases of disloyalty. The worst occurred with the loss of northwestern Virginia to the Union, which the remainder of the Old Dominion rationalized as resulting from a combination of a small group of malcontents and the Union army's interference. In the rest of the state, only the southwest contained a Unionist enclave worthy of note, and military strategists had dispatched John Floyd, a native of the region, to protect the railroad line there from further damage by tories. In the Tidewater, planters resisted sending slaves to the Confederate army, and both they and common tradesmen appeared far too willing to transact business with the enemy. But their reasons—while annoying—were understandable and not causing overwhelming difficulties.[50]

In general, common sacrifice was beginning to forge a new identity, partly helped by the army that had been assembled and had won a major engagement at Manassas. That organization had the unintended benefit of linking civilians to the cause. Each soldier was the husband, son, brother, or cousin of family members who avidly followed the progress of local units. William Blackford had been a staunch Unionist but by April 17 found himself being tugged toward the Confederacy as his son became among the first to enlist. "So I have a deep personal interest in the strife," he noted in his diary.[51] With a personal stake in Confederate success, these families might support measures to force the young men who loitered about town to contribute to the war effort.

A much more complicated process was occurring than the expansion of central government at the expense of local autonomy. In many respects the two goals were beginning to merge in the Old Dominion, especially because of the presence of Federal troops. Local and national interests intersected at other points. The breakdown of portions of the economy and the need to protect property fed support for the expansion of Confederate authority. This began typically as a cry for intervention by local officials for specific goals, such as buying salt or increasing the number of police. Leaders countered those who protested the loss of personal liberty by justifying such measures as being required only for the emergency: temporary inconvenience for the individual could result in the permanent improvement of society. When local efforts fell short and citizens requested national aid, Davis's use of civilian leaders to implement martial law helped ease the transition.

Some philosophically opposed centralized power, but more complaints centered on questions of fairness—whether the government exacted contributions equally. People accepted hardships and loss of liberty as long as they were convinced of the necessity and could see that most shared the suffering. And inequities did exist. For the moment, Governor Letcher believed the war fell hardest on the planter and farming interests, adding that mechanics—tanners, shoemakers, blacksmiths, wagon makers, and lumbermen—prospered because they were exempted from service and could realize profits. He also identified inequities in the boards of exemptions. The governor complained to the Confederate Congress that the system led to abuse by allowing men to schedule physical screenings with family doctors, who were paid by the applicants. Letcher came to the unremarkable conclusion that a surgeon mustered into the military would be a more appropriate examiner and urged national officials to reject current rulings on disabilities. When the state conducted medical screenings at courthouses in early January, some complained that the doctors were "quite partial toward the rich[;] they could get a discharg[,] a poor man did not stand any chance . . . they would not let them off on no circumstances[.] the poor people has got the fighting to do and the rich can take their pleasure[.]" Because of this, one man swore he would not go into the military until forced.[52]

Competition between state and national systems for raising troops also created confusion and gave men the chance to play one against the other. For example, if planters lost a company election or suffered other slights, they could resign from the Confederate army, raise a regiment for the state, and find themselves happily leading another unit closer to home. To build these new companies, local elites plucked men from the army whose enlistments had expired and who volunteered more readily if they could serve near families. Not surprisingly, this vexed Confederate officers. Colonel J. M. Brockenbrough of the 40th Virginia complained about the "worthless, intriguing, politicians, and those who have been defeated in company elections" who induced men to enter new regiments by "using bribery . . . and arguments which any worthless demagogue is capable of making." In other words, men of influence in a community—rivals perhaps of the very officers who complained about this interference—courted the foot soldier using methods commonly seen at every Virginia barbecue before the war. Most acknowledged the need for reform, which would result in future conscription legislation.[53]

For the moment, Confederate Virginians remained committed

to the cause, blaming privations or other problems on inefficient or corrupt public officials. Like people in most societies, citizens saw no contradiction between loving a nation while loathing its caretakers. "That our cause is just & the motives of the people are patriotic I am persuaded," wrote a woman in Richmond, "but whether we are to share the downfall of the designing, selfish men who precipitated the war, is a question which weighs heavily upon my heart, if pure men were in power I would feel more sanguine."[54]

The first year of war ended with the needs of labor and of law and order driving a shift in authority from community autonomy toward more centralized decision making. Conscription legislation would begin this transition. Better administration would end confusion and force people to choose Confederate service; however, it remained to be seen where the Old Dominion would find the labor it required at home without subtracting from the pool of potential soldiers. Secretary of War Judah P. Benjamin wisely noted that legislation could not solve all problems. "Laws cannot suddenly convert farmers into gunsmiths," he told President Davis. "Our people are not artisans, except to a very limited degree."[55] Difficult times lay ahead for balancing the needs of the home front and the army.

3

A Growing Sense of Injustice,
April 1862–April 1863

[T]here are indications of a widespread feeling that people, even the most humble members of society, ought to have enough resources or facilities to do their job in the social order, and that there is something morally wrong or even outrageous when these resources are unavailable.

—Barrington Moore, *Injustice*

Because of the military crisis in the spring of 1862, Confederate Virginians generally accepted conscription and other intrusions of government in their lives. Continued tolerance depended on how political leaders administered the new systems and met the challenges that lay ahead. As the year progressed, shortages of food and other goods eroded faith in the government. Popular resentment increased as hardships worsened—especially as planters and other wealthy persons avoided military service by hiring substitutes or seemingly capitalized on the misfortune of others by charging exorbitant prices for goods. The belief that the rich benefited while others suffered caused civilians to riot for food and soldiers to leave the army, actions that the state and national officials could not ignore. Officials responded first with a heavy hand, employing measures that tightened discipline in the army and drew clearer lines between front and home front. As desertion and discord continued, however, authorities realized that they also needed a softer approach and increased the efforts to administer charity for the needy. The emphasis on public welfare still focused at the local level as leaders statewide scrambled to prevent more sweeping changes. Given the chance, the consuming public would have instituted price controls on food, with either the state or national government regulating the procedure. Producers—typically planters and owners of large farms—succeeded in fending off these attempts, but only for a time. An important signal was sent, with the public describing the levels of support that it needed to continue fighting.

While the reaction of public officials helped to mitigate the worst of the discontent, several other factors contributed as well. First, the war went fairly well in the East. Despite its retreat after the battle of Sharpsburg, R. E. Lee's Army of Northern Virginia was establishing a reputation for invincibility that would fortify Confederate spirits. Second, the dissent expressed through desertion, food riots, and complaints to the War Department had a very specific goal—to improve conditions. Public discontent would ease if officials conquered subsistence problems or exacted contributions more equitably from all classes. Finally, the war itself added its own dynamic as the Union army became an unwitting ally in building Confederate loyalty. Until late 1864, the violation of personal property in Virginia helped to fire the will to resist by showing what was in store for southern property if the Yankees won. The effects of the destruction were felt by all classes and struck at a sensitive area: nineteenth-century Americans considered productive property as the means to ensure their liberty. The Union army, in short, provided a more formidable enemy for Confederate Virginians than their own government.

While the first year of conflict awakened Confederates to the problems of fueling the war effort, the second featured a time of adjustment for civilians and soldiers. This involved getting used to the discipline of the army, community sacrifice, and expanded government. Conscription had wrought considerable change in communities, dictating who went into the army and who stayed at home. Passed on April 16, 1862, the draft evoked emotions in Virginia ranging from relief to anger. Legislation restored method to the mobilization madness by eliminating duplication between the state and national systems. A frequent critic of the Confederate administration, Richmond newspaper editor Edward Pollard found himself in the unusual position of praising the Congress. He welcomed better organization and believed that the law "came not a moment too soon." Less satisfied, Governor Letcher believed that the draft was unconstitutional but supported it because of the crisis. "When the war is ended," he told the General Assembly on May 5, "we can discuss these questions and so settle them as to preserve the rights of the state." He did not oppose a draft per se, merely the administration of one by national instead of state authority.[1]

Within communities, reactions were similarly mixed. In only a few places, especially near the Tennessee border and in the Shenandoah Valley, enrollment officers faced active resistance that now and then turned violent. On the whole, Virginians accepted the draft more peacefully than other parts of the South and far more than northerners did in 1863. Grumbling occurred in private letters, but most men went quietly, if not happily, into the service. Invasion by Federal soldiers justified this drastic change in people's lives.[2]

Unhappiness, however, continued over certain elements of the national conscription act, but in this case Confederate Virginians complained about sins of omission rather than commission. Wealthier individuals welcomed Congress's retention of substitution, but the legislation failed to exempt overseers, which complicated management of plantations and raised concerns about security in the countryside. Dunkards and Mennonites from the Shenandoah Valley also complained because the legislation contained no provisions for religious objectors. Those who already had paid a $500 exemption fee to Virginia remained eligible for the national draft. Finally, the exemptions enacted by the Confederate Congress on April 21 failed to specify a number of occupations important to communities. Ironworkers and factory employees were protected, but communities did not know if the artisans on whom they relied would retain their exempt status. Even physicians kept from state service had to reapply for exemption from the Confederate army, with no guarantee they would receive one.[3]

Decision making was migrating from state to Confederate hands, except for one area that eased the transition. National authorities at first administered the national draft through the local boards instituted by the state of Virginia. When enrolling the militia in mid-February 1862, the governor and the legislature had established boards of exemption consisting of people from the community. On Campbell County's board, for instance, sat three presiding magistrates, the enrolling officer of the 53rd Virginia militia, the sheriff, and the county clerk. Familiar faces thus decided who should remain at home. The Confederate conscription office eventually did away with this in 1863, replacing local men with Confederate officers.[4] But a newspaper editor believed that having local people participate in the initial selection meant that the draft respected the principle of state rights. Not all, of course, went smoothly. As with any new system, trouble occurred, usually from overzealous officials. Conscription officers in the Wytheville area, for example, abruptly seized men working in the fields and would not permit conscripts to return home even for a change of clothing.[5]

In October 1862, the Confederate Congress issued new exemptions from the draft that corresponded to the petitions that flooded the War Department. Dunkards, Mennonites, and Nazarenes were released because of religious faith, provided they paid $500 or furnished a substitute. This repeated Virginia's law but required pacifists to dig into their pockets once again for the fee. Shoemakers, tanners, blacksmiths, wagon makers, and millwrights also were exempted, but with the proviso that they sell goods for no more than 75 percent above the cost of production in an attempt to control speculation and extortion. The twenty-Negro law also took effect at this time, allowing one male on plantations with twenty or more slaves to be excused from service to maintain police powers in the countryside and lessen the fears of a slave uprising.[6]

When put into place, the exemption law predictably favored the wealthy, yet it also answered concerns in communities by shielding artisans and skilled workers. Substitution led all exemptions by a considerable margin; however, exemptions granted in Albemarle, Augusta, and Campbell counties from November 1862 through October 1863 indicate that skilled workers and artisans received most of the actual exemptions for occupations. (See table 3.1.) Of the 812 exemptions granted to men from these communities (including towns), substitution accounted for 513, or 63 percent. Skilled workers and artisans came next with 128, or 16 percent of the total. Dominating this category were the shoemakers, millers, and blacksmiths who had been the focus of community petitions. Next in line came overseers: forty-seven were excused, but here the numbers favored the tobacco belt, which contained more slaves and the people most concerned about insurrection. Only three overseers hailed from the Valley. On the other hand, religious exemptions favored Augusta County, where nineteen Dunkards and two Mennonites paid the tax on their faiths. Of the professionals exempted, fourteen of the thirty-nine were physicians. When examined in total, the twenty-Negro law that exempted overseers was among the categories with the smallest impact. Complaints about a "poor man's fight" originated in connection with the widespread substitution

Table 3.1   Leading Exemptions Requested for Key Regions in Study

Category	Number	% of Total (N=812)
Substitutions	513	63
Artisans/Skilled Workers	128	16
Twenty-Slave Law	47	5.8
Professionals	39	4.8
Laborers	31	3.8
Religious (Mennonite and Dunkard)	23	2.8
CSA Government Work	10	1.2
Teachers	7	1.4
Local Government Officials	3	.3
Excused for other reasons (Sick, etc.)	10	1.2

Source: Record of Exemptions, 1862–1863, RG 109, Ch. 1, vol. 251, NA.

that prosperous people engaged in, with the overseers' exemption as bitter icing on this rich cake.

The aggravation that would result from substitution seems so apparent that it makes one wonder how officials could have allowed the procedure. Confederate Virginians, however, greeted the continuation of this customary practice with less hostility than one might think. Not all of the people who pursued this means for staying out of the army were looked upon as unpatriotic. A number of them had served in the army, believed they had done their duty, and did not want to enlist for three more years. Providing a substitute seemed the patriotic thing to do—an example used by Abraham Lincoln in the North. West of the Blue Ridge, substitution provided a means for pacifists to remain true to their principles until the Confederacy adopted religious exemptions. Prosperous Virginians also believed that the "best men" with a direct interest in the war should remain at home where their leadership could be used. That these men often were the largest producers enhanced their value (at least in their own minds if not always in fact) for the Confederate war effort. Abner Anderson, a soldier, counseled a friend still at home to remain a civilian unless a suitable position opened, adding that "nothing less would justify you in leaving your business at home. You can do the government and the country more service where you are than in a *subordinate* position in the army."[7] Substitution also probably enjoyed limited support among the needy because of the money that could be earned. The rate for a substitute in Virginia quickly settled at $1,000, escalating by the fall and winter of 1862 first to $1,500 and then to $2,000. Despite inflation, this represented a tidy sum for laborers who otherwise had little opportunity to earn comparable money, especially if they could desert while pocketing the cash.[8] Resentment of the practice would build only toward spring of 1863 as privations worsened and conscription forced more people into the army.

Conscription officers, though, took an instant dislike to the practice. Only a person who was ineligible for the draft could serve as a substitute, creating a demand for men too old, too young, or "foreigners"—people who had not established residency in the Confederate states. Conditions were ripe for fraud as men signed affidavits that they were older than the age limit. Complicity among local officials contributed to the success of these cases, although these instances declined as supervision tightened. More troublesome were the men who took money and deserted on the way to camps of instruction or soon after arriving. J. C. Shields, the chief of bureau for Virginia, reported that desertions from Dublin Depot in the southwest "have been about 140 up to this time; four-fifths of these have been substitutes deserting within twenty-four hours of their being received as such. I have endeavored in every way to protect the Government in this matter of substitutes, even to retaining the money until they are assigned, but with no success. Either some example should be made of them or the principal be in some manner held responsible."[9] Even when faithfully fulfilling their contracts, substitutes older than 45 often could not march twenty miles under a hot sun. Because officers enjoyed leeway in accepting substitutes within companies, they preferred boys between 16 and 18 to older men.[10]

Common men had no similar recourse to getting out of the army; they resorted to straggling or deserting and in the process helped compel authorities to redress problems in communities. Men left the ranks from a range of motivations beyond disaffection with the Confederacy or a loss of will. Virginia's experience, in fact, calls for modification of the standard explanation of desertion as demonstrating a lack of will to fight. Although some studies have allowed for desertion as a response to hardships without necessarily signifying renunciation of the Confederate cause, more often scholars interpret leaving the ranks as evidence of the fragile nationalism, class antagonism, or a collapse of will to fight.[11] Desertion, however, contained multiple meanings that changed over time: men leaving the army in 1862 strained against new government controls or reacted to privations in camps and households, while those abandoning the ranks in late 1864 more clearly had lost hope in the cause.[12]

The records also fail to lend credibility to the impression that desertion increased steadily through the war, escalating after 1863 and becoming a torrent by 1864. Desertion in Virginia regiments ballooned early in the war and slowed as time went on before probably escalating in 1865. Analysis of ten regiments from the key regions of the state indicates that some of the worst instances corresponded to the implementation of conscription in 1862 (table 3.2). Excepting the southwest, desertions in 1862 outpaced those of 1863. Three of the regiments showed increases between 1863 and 1864 but only one (the 22nd Virginia) significantly. Valley units experienced the most dramatic increase in desertion during 1862. The number of men who left the 5th Virginia between March 1862 and April 1863 accounted for nearly half of the unit's total for the entire war: 171 versus 352. Roughly one quarter of the regiment's total desertions came within the four months, March through June, in which the Confederacy exerted the greatest pressure to force men into enlisting for three years. These figures support a previous observation that absenteeism in Mississippi, east Tennessee, Arkansas, and Virginia, had largely disappeared by the middle of 1864. In fact, commands in those regions were increasing through the addition of deserters. Even more startling, the total figures show that while slightly more than 12,000 Virginians deserted from the Confederate army overall, about 8,500 returned to the ranks.[13] Better controls by conscription

Table 3.2   Desertion in Selected Virginia Units

Regiment	Location	1861	1862	1863	1864	1865	Total	Total Enlisted
17th Va.	Tidewater	22	65	53	25	11	176	N/A
13th Va.	Piedmont	39	131	23	28	22	243	1537
24th Va.	Piedmont	N/A	37	39	59	36	171	1302
30th Va.	Piedmont	?	15	21	9	21	66	1340
5th Va.	Valley	7	210	105	30	?	352	2010
33rd Va.	Valley	21	235	89	8	2	355	1382
52nd Va.	Valley	11	97	95	91	30	324	1506
51st Va.	Southwest	19	34	58	12	12	135	1839
63rd Va.	Southwest	N/A	34	254	129	?	417	1535
22nd Va.	Western	179	95	47	130	59	510	2473

Source: H. E. Howard Series of Virginia Regimentals, Lynchburg, Va.

officers and provost marshals accounted for some of this phenomenon, but other factors contributed. Kevin Conley Ruffner has argued persuasively that one reason for the decline lay in the hardening of the troops. Men unsuited for war rushed to the colors in the early going. Conscription legislation provided the opportunity to discharge those most likely to desert: the infirm, the old, the young, and those who had yet to establish residence in the state. The soldiers who remained after this initial period retained greater commitment to the cause and had the greater ability to withstand the rigors of campaigning.[14] Discipline within the army also improved. So did attention to the complaints of the soldiers, especially the need for furloughs and taking care of families at home. All of these things helped the transition of men from citizens to soldiers, which took a while to effect.

As noted earlier, recruits retained their notions of democratic relationships with officers, which had been formed in the militias before the war.[15] Enlisted men believed they had a right to choose the branch of service, location for duty, and officers. Civilians at home supported these opinions. A newspaper editor in Lynchburg praised the Davis administration for allowing the men who formed regiments in 1862 to elect their officers; it was only right that citizens who subjected themselves to military discipline should select the men who enforced it. "As citizens," he reasoned, "they have as much at stake in the issue of armed conflict as any other class of persons, whilst their lives are thrown into the scale also, and may be sacrificed by incompetent officers." When officers ignored the wishes of the men, soldiers invariably grumbled about the "arbitrary and despotic nature" of leaders. Together with the poor record of the government in caring for its soldiers, these breaches of the antebellum social arrangement provided volunteers with the moral authority to circumvent military restrictions.[16]

Anger extended to drill and discipline, which many believed unnecessary and which fostered resentment for officers who failed to grasp this point. Southern soldiers, one scholar has noted, believed strongly in their own free will and were used to obeying people who offered good reason for the orders.[17] Some officers lost the chance for reelection by being too strict and ignoring the wishes of the regiment. Even fellow officers might criticize a severe colleague, claiming he was "used to commanding Regulars & not Gentlemen."[18] Whenever officers denied furloughs or other favors to men whose responsibilities at home seemingly deserved special attention, the rejection created hard feelings. Those receiving better treatment recognized their good fortune. "The soldiers in this company," wrote J. A. Sutherland, "are not held in strict servitude as it is said of soldiers but are as free spoken to the officers as they were in Howardsville [in southern Albemarle County], in fact they do right smartly as they please."[19] Rules chafed the most whenever campaigning ended and the army settled into quarters. Soldiers saw no good reason why they should remain in camp.[20]

State and national officials unintentionally encouraged illegal absences through their handling of furloughs during the first winter, 1861–1862. The Davis administration intended to capitalize on the desire of men to visit families by reserving this privilege for soldiers reenlisting for three years. When General Johnston protested that the number of men granted this leave placed the army in jeopardy, Davis acknowledged the problem but encouraged the general to respect the policy because "the eager desire for a furlough during the inclement season will form the strongest inducement for your men."[21] This approach backfired by encouraging soldiers who remained, and who considered themselves equally deserving, to take "French leave" or "run the blockade." With many furloughs falling around the Christmas holidays, Virginia troops assumed they were not needed at the front and believed it appropriate to circumvent regulations to tend to business at home. Lax punishment reinforced this practice. Most punishment involved paying fines or spending time in the guardhouse, both reasonable trade-offs for a visit home. After noting that an acquaintance sat in the guard house for going home without permission, G. E. Crist told his cousin: "There is about Twenty Five men in the guard house, most of which have (run the *Blockade* as we call it) went home without permission."[22]

Officers contributed to the discipline problem through their own poor leadership. Restrictions on furloughs applied specifically to enlisted men and noncommissioned officers. Officers, as usual, received preferential treatment. One man explained to his wife that he had failed to secure a leave because "no furloughs are granted at this time to Privates or *non commissioned officers*, only to those that support the gold lace." Other officers sided with the men against the policies and thus encouraged continued absenteeism. While a colonel in the 52nd Virginia, future Congressman John B. Baldwin complained about the delay in permission to send home a man whose third child had died and whose wife was prostrate with grief. "Cannot this man have a furlough," Baldwin asked, "or is his case to be subjected to the general rule referred to?" Earlier he had warned the secretary of war that volunteers had rushed to war with little preparation for long absence. Restricting furloughs only to reenlisted men, Baldwin maintained, produced a sense of injury among those remaining in the ranks. Ultimately, complaints must have registered with the Confederate Congress. Lawmakers passed legislation that clarified furlough privileges for those sick or with family emergencies, although Davis vetoed the bill.[23]

Popular support thus built within the army for certain kinds of absences, particularly after battles when contact with the enemy appeared less iminent. As the winter of 1862 neared, soldiers expected a repeat of the prior year when numerous men had gone home. The Confederacy had canceled furloughs for reenlistments the prior spring because of the emergency from the Union invasion. The men still believed they were owed these visits, but the army subsequently limited furloughs. Miffed at the change, a man from Alabama stationed near Fredericksburg thought he could make it home but cautioned his wife not to tell anyone. If he could not secure a furlough, he wrote, "I will turn something up to get home."[24]

If the men left the army to try to save their homes, their comrades often understood and tacitly condoned the action. An Albemarle County man, Micajah Woods, stationed near Saltville in the southwest wrote his father in March 1863 that desertion there was "still on the wing," with at least 116 men leaving on one night. Woods indicated that the men were "from the border—a region occupied or at the mercy of the enemy. Their wives and families in the majority of cases are helpless & destitute of the absolute necessities of life, and worse than this, are subject the insults and depredations of the marauding parties of each side that infest their whole country." Even such an unforgiving Confederate as Jubal A. Early after the war could remark that "some palliation was to be found for the conduct of many of those who did desert, in the fact that they did so to go to the aid of their families."[25] That soldiers left for family reasons gains weight when considering that most deserters at this time appeared to go home instead of fleeing to enemy lines. Virginia had perhaps no more than two to four regiments of men defecting to fight for the Union.[26]

No matter how understandable, absences from the army vexed military leaders. Major General James Longstreet revealed the extent of the problem before the Seven Days' Battles around Richmond in late June. Of the 32,000 Virginians supposed to constitute part of the right wing of the army, Longstreet had roughly 20,000; of that number, about 7,000 were absent. "That is to say," Longstreet noted, "while I ought to command 32,000 Virginians, I do not really command 13,000.[27] Absentees averaged roughly 40 percent of the aggregate number for the twenty-four regiments from the Old Dominion in Longstreet's wing. It did not console generals that the absences fit the typical pattern of men straggling after a battle and trickling back to the army.

After assuming command of the army in Virginia in early June, Lee brought harsher methods to bear on this problem. At the first lull in campaigning, the general instituted ritual executions to drive home the point that men could not leave the ranks. These began in earnest in August 1862 before the army advanced toward Maryland. Invariably a regiment or brigade assembled to witness the execution and then march by the fallen body. These scenes provided gripping details for postwar reminiscences but received matter-of-fact acknowledgment in some contemporary accounts. A North Carolinian, for example, wrote home about a man executed "for crimes which I suppose deserved death." A squad of eight or ten carried out the sentence, which sounded horrible but, the witness added, was not as terrible as he had expected. Officials selected for these examples the worst cases involving the clearest breaches of conduct. It would serve little purpose to kill a man whose plight evoked sympathy. Indeed, most deserters were not executed but were absolved, jailed, fined, shamed, or otherwise punished. No more than three of the deserters from the 52nd and 5th Virginia combined received a death sentence. Edward Porter Alexander, noted artillerist in Lee's army, emphasized after the war that men understood the difference between those who deserted for justifiable reasons and the lowest grade of men—the bounty-jumpers who enlisted for money and left at the first chance.[28]

Poor delineation between home and camp exacerbated the absentee problem. Civilians and soldiers mingled with each other, blurring the boundaries between their lives. Towns provided natural meeting points through such government installations as hospitals and quartermaster depots. Camp discipline in the early going also was hardly tight. Women's diaries attest to how soldiers stationed near homes continued to live in communities and participate in socials or religious services. Whenever armies moved, one woman noticed a corresponding emptiness at church and other venues as men rejoined their units. Officers more than enlisted men enjoyed this ability to retain community ties, but even privates roamed the countryside in large numbers in the first two years of war. With armies nearby, visits to civilians from soldiers looking for food occurred nightly with hospitality extended at no cost as long as supplies lasted. The reverse also held true: in the first year of war women and children often visited relatives in camps, turning military installations into transplanted homes as children played with men in the regiment. "We often drive out to the camp [of Jackson's men near Winchester] to see our friends," Cornelia McDonald remembered about October 1861, "and they were near enough often to slip into town to see the girls or get a good supper."[29]

To reduce fraternization with civilians, Lee instituted strict orders in late September 1862 requiring soldiers to have passes before leaving camp.[30] The stern efforts worked to some extent, although not perfectly. A South Carolinian who returned to the army in January 1863 noted that discipline had improved, straggling was down, and desertions were comparatively rare. Only eight men out of 2,400 had been under arrest since the first of the year, and those for misdemeanors.[31] A Virginian noticed something similar when he wrote home on February 2, 1863: "Our government instead of following in the footsteps of last winter, seems to be putting forth new efforts to keep our army up to the maximum." Authorities had sent his cousin on special service to round up stragglers and deserters.[32]

Desertion, however, was not a problem that could be solved solely through focusing on the army. To keep men in the ranks, officials were required to address problems within communities because the public often tolerated absences by soldiers for family reasons.[33] As usual, the first efforts to police the home front more thoroughly involved punishing transgressors. Only later would authorities target charity for soldiers' families to keep the men in the ranks.

In the beginning, though, military officers were outmanned on the home front and had to rely on community members to police themselves. Conscription officers at first published lists of deserters in newspapers and offered rewards for return of the miscreants— typically $30 to anyone delivering a prisoner. Most advertisements proved fruitless: a list of 181 men ran for five months in Augusta County with only minor revisions. Bureaucratic inefficiency to some extent overstated the problem. People understood that the lists could be misleading by including soldiers recuperating from wounds or on furlough. In Lynchburg, the editor of the *Virginian* corrected an advertisement for deserters from the 2nd Regiment Virginia Cavalry because it contained two soldiers on surgeon's leave, one of whom had been discharged from the army. In the Shenandoah Valley, a carpenter in the 52nd Regiment Virginia Infantry published a rebuttal to the charge he had deserted, stating that he had received sick leave and then a furlough. "I intend to do my duty as long as I am able to bear arms," he added, printing his location as proof that he hid from no one.[34]

Commanders supervising military affairs in a region could not patrol the countryside effectively and had to ask the War Department for help. Because of its hospitals and location along a railroad, Charlottesville collected men who drank at the local grog shops, fought with citizens, and defied a guard composed of elderly men. Although Commander of the Post John Taylor had forced 182 men from the 19th, 45th, and 55th Virginia back into service, he could not keep up with the numbers of absentees. A month later Brigadier General W. H. C. Whiting confirmed as much when he reported that 1,200 officers and men from Jackson's and Ewell's divisions skulked about the town. Worse yet, many carried passes for furloughs issued by company officers, indicating the need to change attitudes within the officer corps itself. Large numbers of deserters from Jackson's army continued to pass through the town in August, reportedly on their way to North Carolina. Squads of five to ten men daily traversed the region, avoiding the thickly settled areas. A Confederate officer had arrested ten deserters from North Carolina but they escaped. He was given authority to use a portion of the 19th Virginia Infantry, a regiment from the region, to help police the area.[35]

These circumstances led to the replacement of community-based civilian authority with national military police. The Confederate government inched toward this solution first by authorizing partnerships of military and local authorities before resorting to national intervention alone. On June 18, General Samuel Cooper urged military officers to enlist county officials to catch deserters and stragglers. Word went out to sheriffs, sergeants, and constables to arrest anyone without an approved furlough, but the scale of the problem defied easy remedy. By July, about fifty deserters, stragglers, and convalescent soldiers were being collected each day in the Staunton/Augusta County region and returned to the army. The Confederacy next established provost marshals in communities, with the express mission to police the home front and return men to their units. These officials settled into posts in Virginia in August as ritual executions increased in the army.[36]

The Confederacy had begun to control aspects of life previously beyond reach of government. Confederate officials patrolled the home front as well as the army. By the autumn of 1862, provost marshals maintained pass systems and other restrictions on individual liberty to catch stragglers. In November 1862 Chief of Bureau J. C. Shields had begun to replace local authorities with officers from the Confederate army to enforce conscription—a transition effected by early 1863. Military officers controlled exempting civilians in war-related work, assuming this duty from the employers who had filed affidavits to proclaim a person's eligibility. In February 1863, this procedure tightened further by allowing only the chief of bureau for a state to certify the workers required for an establishment. Slowly, the tendrils of national military authority stretched throughout communities.[37]

Because of continuing disorder in towns, the public greeted increased control by the military with resignation if not acceptance. "This petty annoyance should be patiently borne," wrote one editor, "if, by its endurance the object had in view by the Government may be even measurably secured."[38] Some grumbled, as when John B. Baldwin wrote on behalf of a constituent from the Shenandoah Valley, but these instances typically involved cases in which military personnel blatantly ignored civil rights. For example, Baldwin complained that a man whom soldiers arrested in Rockingham County on charges of disloyalty actually had defended his wife from harassment by those same troopers. In general, property owners welcomed the increased supervision because they felt powerless to stop the disorder instigated partly by friendly soldiers. When authorities in Danville arrested convalescent soldiers who had upset the wagon of a civilian for undisclosed causes, the comrades of the accused gathered at the jail, bent on tearing it down if the defendants were not freed. The mayor stood firm and officials weathered this crisis by telegraphing Richmond for support.[39] Instances such as these caused officials again to target whiskey as the problem, and provost marshals did their best to limit the flow. Most arrests under martial law involved the sale of liquor by civilians to enlisted men, usually in army camps. By the spring of 1863, the Virginia General Assembly authorized expanded powers for the city councils of Richmond and Lynchburg to shut down gaming houses and taverns. The legislation also empowered Lynchburg to arm its police.[40]

An emphasis on whiskey-drinking soldiers as the root of a community's problems obscured changes in the nature of crime. The earliest disorders featured personal assaults among soldiers or between troops and civilians. But in the winter of 1862–1863 community leaders complained of a growing number of thefts and burglaries. In Lynchburg, thieves broke into stores, homes, and churches— sometimes during daylight. A backlash came in January when a crowd marched on the town jail and threatened to hang a man named Brown who reportedly had taken 200 watches from a silversmith. Municipal nativism had infected the townspeople, who viewed any outsiders as foreigners and prime suspects for criminal acts. The accused thief in this case had been found in the Washington Restaurant, known as a gathering point for refugees from Maryland. Cooler heads defused the lynch mob but residents still called a meeting to discuss getting rid of "foreign thieves and scoundrels." Similar concerns plagued Staunton, where a citizen bemoaned the neglect of the town by public officials, especially the inefficient police who "witness the numerous robberies and thefts which are nightly occurring and no clue to the culprits." In a letter to the newspaper, this citizen called for an "indignation meeting" to discuss these issues and achieve better enforcement.[41]

Public outrage failed to connect disorder with the obvious causes—widespread shortages and escalating prices of provisions. Any plan to preserve order or help to keep men in the army eventually would have to include a way to make food more available. Prices in the first year of war had increased steadily but moderately; suddenly, the cost of goods shot up. In the six months from August 1862 to March 1863, prices of most foodstuffs increased on average nearly threefold. Family flour that had cost $7.50 per barrel in 1860 went from a low of $10 per barrel to $30. Bacon soared from a low of 35 cents per pound to $1.10 per pound.[42] While enemy depredations contributed to this index of misery, Virginians felt more inclined to blame farmers who, they alleged, withheld crops from towns or sold them at outrageous prices that buyers termed extortion.

Angry denunciations of these conditions frequently appeared in the usually discreet Virginia press. Resentment more often focused on large-scale farmers because of their visibility and impact on prices, but all growers shared common problems. Prices on farm implements, seed, and services from town merchants and artisans increased. Horseshoes that cost 25 cents in 1859 now cost $1; slave shoes had risen from $1.50 per pair to $15. Attempts to recover these higher costs of production by charging more for food inevitably prompted allegations of extortion. Townspeople suspected that suffering came because greedy farmers—or southern Yankees—withheld crops or manipulated the market. An editor claimed that well-to-do farmers "were grinding the faces of the poor, and destroying the cause of their country." He added in another column: "Things are going wrong, in this respect, all round. We need a fresh start and a better one." Hundreds of personal exchanges that constitute a market had moved beyond the ability of local people to control.[43]

Another figure occasionally surfaces in this tale of speculation and extortion—the poor man with the wits to take advantage of the situation. The rise to power of some of these individuals angered people on a variety of levels, particularly when a man formerly beholden to the planter became an agent purchasing for the government. John Marshall McCue, a community leader from Augusta County, called on the secretary of war to stop the "infernal cormorants" who fattened themselves on the Confederate treasury. He was upset with a person who could not secure credit worth $10 before the war riding "with pockets stuffed with Confederate money buying horses, cattles & *swindling* the government. 'Tis doing more to dishearten our people and *sour* them with out cause, than you can imagine." This situation at least disheartened McCue, who complained probably because the agent also took the best horses and harnesses.[44]

From those bearing the worst of the hardships came pleas for greater help from the government through financial support and price controls on goods. A Shenandoah Valley woman asked the governor why families of soldiers could not receive aid to help them through the hard times. She had four sons in the army, lived in a home rented by her children, and carried wood for herself throughout winter. Aid through county or town officers had existed in many Virginia communities since the start of the conflict, although the efforts were haphazard at first and scarcely enough to cover the need. Augusta County, for instance, had a form of social security through weekly payments to widows ($1) and children (50 cents each) of soldiers. But no one accounted for mothers whose husbands were in the ranks, and this mother of four indicated to the governor that the magistrates who supervised charity for the poor did nothing for her. In the meantime she counted twelve or fifteen young men who should be in the service but instead vacationed at the springs after securing medical exemptions. This especially vexed her because her youngest son—aged seventeen—could not get a furlough to visit her.[45]

The crisis over provisions escalated during the second winter of the war, hitting nonproducers especially hard. R. G. H. Kean in the War Department noted: "The most alarming feature of our condition is the failure of the means of subsistence." His concern was echoed by a young man in the army who encouraged his family to grow wheat, corn, peas, and other foodstuffs, "as the great thing to be feared as likely to cause us to have to stop the war, is want of provisions."[46] Local officials continued to fund solutions with public money or use government to supervise purchasing. Salt crises occurred now and then, but these were coming under control through programs such as Lynchburg's, where the city in November promised all taxpaying residents a four-month supply at prices lower than the market rate. Confederate authorities cooperated by allowing army wagons to transport the commodity. Prices on other goods—especially foodstuffs—continued to spiral upward, and hunger prevailed in many portions of the state. This problem required broad solutions to restore faith in the currency, resolve transportation difficulties, and adopt adequate taxation. Instead, the Confederate Congress enacted impressment.[47]

It was easier to take this route: popular support existed for impressment because of the problems with so many friendly soldiers—one of the factors that made Virginia different from sections of the South with fewer troops at home. On March 14, 1863, the Virginia General Assembly had instructed its senators in Congress to adopt the impressment law already passed by the House "so that the burdens of this war should be to some extent equalized between the citizens of the states."[48] Ever since the war began, many portions of the state had served as a military camp for friendly soldiers who often seized whatever they wanted from civilians. In this instance, country folk suffered more than townspeople. Farmers in all but the most isolated places had reason to support better regulation of this practice. Until 1863, reimbursement varied because of a tedious and confusing claims procedure. Virginia's legislature tried with little success to curb these tendencies. Confederate impressment made the process more certain by establishing limits to what the military could seize—surplus goods and crops grown for market rather than family use.[49]

Growers and wholesalers recognized the need for impressment but wrangled with the government over whether prices should be uniform for the country or float according to their market value in communities. Make no mistake, the issue was not about controls versus no controls but about who would set the prices. Two camps formed in congressional debates along the age-old lines of centralized power versus local: those led by Virginia Senator R. M. T. Hunter, who favored uniform national prices, and those who wanted market value in communities to rule. Hunter strongly believed that impressment should establish uniform prices, and he opposed "vicinage appraisal," or the alternative of having assessors from each locality set prices according to market value in a community at a particular time. Local persons, Hunter argued, would collaborate to appraise prices at higher levels, allowing the speculator to dictate what government paid. Senator Gustavus Adolphus Henry of Tennessee supported Hunter, using Shakespeare to highlight the fallacy of relying on market value as determined by local conditions. When downed at Bosworth field, Richard III had offered to trade an entire kingdom for a horse. With no other bid on the table, the senator quipped, a kingdom became the market value of a horse at that time.[50]

Hunter and his allies could not persuade Congress to adopt uniform price controls. The needs of constituents rather than ideological concerns of party seemed to motivate representatives. Congressman John B. Baldwin, for example, had been a Unionist Whig who now championed Confederate independence. Yet he repudiated the central controls that Hunter advocated because of the experiences of people in the Shenandoah Valley. Baldwin claimed to know a miller who had lost $80,000 when the government impressed wheat in Richmond. The purchase price had been about half the market value in the Valley. Although Baldwin supported feeding soldiers, he believed it dangerous to do so at prices lower than it cost poor people to feed wives and children.

Although the resulting legislation did not regulate prices nationally, it did attempt to control speculators who either grew crops for the market or bought foodstuffs for resale. Impressment offficers who dealt with farmers growing food for the table were to be controlled by vicinage appraisal, or arbiters picked by the government agent and the farmer. In this case, the referees would not only come from the community but these local people also would serve as the last word on the subject. With speculators, however, army officers enjoyed more latitude. If the military was unsatisfied with a price, for example, and believed others in the community conspired to boost the cost of goods, officers could take the case to state and national authorities, or beyond the reach of local influence. No one at the time appreciated just how much this legislation could favor the poor instead of the rich. For one thing, the law obviously targeted large-scale farmers who grew for the market. More importantly, the commissioners of impressment who every two months set the government prices that the military would pay for selected goods would provide a stabilizing force for prices in general and would become one of the chief ways to help the poor and families of soldiers as time passed, goods grew scarcer, and inflation worsened.[51]

Few citizens could foresee these consequences as civilians adjusted to a new national nose in their affairs. Instead, these policies—and the usual confusion surrounding implementation of a new plan—contributed to the bread riot in Richmond on April 2, 1863. Food shortages had plagued residents before national impressment took hold. One soldier had noted wryly in March: "They say that the price of looking at foods in Richmond is five dollars."[52] Increased population from refugees, poor transportation, a heavy snowfall, and destruction of crops by Federal soldiers had slowed the flow of food into the Confederate capital. Zealous national officials worsened matters by quickly employing the new authority to impress goods, sparking resistance among farmers who wanted to wait until they could assess the act's implications.[53]

Tobacco speculation hit its peak in the Old Dominion at the same time, further reducing the food supply and leaving the impression that the wealthy stayed home to increase their coffers. The General Assembly in March restricted the amount of tobacco that could be planted, but even a reduced yield earned enough to entice people into production. One man made $8,000 trading tobacco on two trips to Baltimore. The Piedmont remained the location of speculation fever, with a focal point at Lynchburg. A disgusted former judge advocate for the army wrote in March: "Lynchburg has gone mad—running stark mad—men, women & children—gamblers, doctors, niggers, preachers, lawyers—all tobacco—tobacco—from morning till night from night till morning. It's still rising."[54] Profits such as these were vital to families as depreciating currency and other circumstances drained their fortunes. Civilians such as John B. Minor at the University of Virginia had invested in Confederate bonds and would remain committed to the cause but sold tobacco to supplement his salary as a professor. Even under those circumstances, speculation failed to win unanimous sympathy among planters. Citizens in Amherst, Buckingham, and Nelson counties registered disgust through public meetings that called on the legislature to ban tobacco growing completely. A glimpse into the records of Lancelot Minor's plantation in Amherst confirms that at least some major growers quit producing tobacco at this time, converting production to wheat, corn, hogs, and turkeys.[55]

To hungry people, this speculation, no matter how understandable, confirmed the suspicion that greed, rather than nature or war, lay behind their suffering. On April 1, several hundred women from a working-class neighborhood in Richmond met at a Baptist Church to discuss what to do about their plight. Part of their anger occurred because the city council had taken a hard stand and refused to increase help for the poor. Led by a woman who sold meat in the market, and who was married to a prosperous painter, a crowd formed the next day and grew to 1,000 or so active participants. Most were women, predominantly wives of workers at the Tredegar Iron Works and working women from a clothing factory, although some came from the upper classes. Joined by men and others as they marched through the streets, the participants ransacked stores for food. As usual in such circumstances, the targets expanded to other goods, but by no means did people loot and pillage as broadly as alleged by authorities, who hoped to discredit the crowd as consisting of thieves taking advantage of the riot. Neither threats by police nor fire hoses broke up the crowd. Finally, Jefferson Davis dispersed them by urging the rioters to fight Yankees and not their own people, backing up his words with the promise to fire on the participants.[56]

The food riot alone may have achieved little. After all, only one erupted in the Old Dominion, and smug elites could blame Yankees, public mismanagement, Irish rabble, foreigners, or the tendency of the indigent to pillage and loot rather than work as reason for the disturbance. But authorities could not ignore the context in which this protest had occurred. Besides food riots elsewhere in the Confederacy, signs of worker unrest sporadically surfaced in towns, such as a successful strike by draymen in Lynchburg to prevent the city council from fixing prices for their services too low. Worse yet, voices could be heard from portions of the tobacco belt that the time had come to seek an armistice. Merchants and professionals in Albemarle County held a public meeting to form resolutions urging the Davis administration to negotiate for peace with Union states from the northwest. They reaffirmed their loyalty to the Confederacy but added that it would be wise to see if the conflict could be stopped, to prevent further loss of life. The proponents of this strategy had been misled about the extent of unrest in the Union, especially in what is today the Midwest where the Copperhead movement had grown increasingly apparent. Actions by northern Democrats fueled false hopes that peace overtures would be accepted and would break the back of the Union. This movement in Albemarle, however, died from lack of support, and no other effort gained momentum.[57]

An increase in charitable measures on the part of counties and towns became the immediate, widespread by-product of the agitation. As early as 1861, communities conducted relief programs for families of soldiers. County courts run by local magistrates oversaw these efforts, which in some cases included money stipends to those in need, a local form of public welfare.[58] For a while, local governments also issued small notes, in increments of as little as 50 cents and 25 cents, to increase the supply of money in circulation—a practice banned by the legislature on September 22, 1863, although notes in circulation continued to trade indefinitely. For the most part, the early campaigns were small and less structured, with neighborhoods relying first on contributions from residents for voluntary care for the needy. When those well-intentioned measures inevitably fell short, local government stepped into the void, nudged along by humanitarian concerns and the need to contain the "rabble."[59]

Within two weeks after the Richmond food riot, the council that earlier had refused to help the poor enacted an ordinance for "the Relief of Poor Persons not in the Poor House." Council members set up a free store and handed out tickets entitling the bearers to goods at no charge. Communities also continued to employ group purchasing with public funds, expanding from salt to subsistence and fuel. While these measures can be considered efforts by the privileged to maintain their power, the gestures also contained other impulses— military, to preserve the chance to defeat the enemy by retaining a loyal army, and humanitarian, to address complaints seen as just.[60]

Whatever the motivations to aid the poor, the campaign appeared to stave off the worst cases of starving. At no other time in Virginia did public anger erupt into a food riot. When she toured a poorer district less than a year later, Judith McGuire found that most of the people could avoid starvation, although admittedly not live very well, through aid from the city.[61] Ultimately, measuring the impact of these charitable efforts is difficult because observations came through the eyes of elites, some of whom were smugly convinced that the "rabble" deserved their fate by not working hard enough for their food. Yet the testimony suggests that life improved a bit in Richmond, perhaps partly because the desperate gesture of the city's women convinced farmers to part with their crops. At least one observer seven weeks after the bread riot found the city's groceries stocked with plenty of goods, although at "fabulous" prices. Conditions remained very difficult for people from 1863 through the rest of the war, less because of the amount of supplies than because the goods were priced beyond reach of the less affluent. If persons lived on self-sufficient farms beyond contact with the enemy, Confederate army, or impressment agents, then they stood a chance to live comfortably if not ostentatiously. The rest struggled to put meat on the table, with aid likely preventing starvation for the poor who chose to overcome pride and accept charity.[62]

Yet this was not an insignificant effort. Charity sent a signal that elites in the community understood the problems of the citizenry and maintained the mutual obligations between planters and the poor that had been built during years of antebellum paternalism. From this point in the war, officials turned increasingly toward finding solutions that not only featured police or punishment but also benevolence. This escalation of charitable efforts would consume increasingly substantial portions of community budgets, taxes, and resources. When those fell short, the Confederate government would help the cause in its own peculiar fashion. For the time being, though, charity began and ended in a person's hometown, which continued the traditional responsibility of neighborhoods to care for their poor.

If commitment to the cause were measured only by the struggle over privations, then the Confederacy would have had at best a mixed record in Virginia; however, the war itself fed the public's heart and mind if not the belly. Actions by the Lincoln government and Union soldiers fortified the will to resist and helped to define the Confederate cause. As Barrington Moore has observed, "Especially in times of political crisis a very important part of the way people decide who they are is to decide who their enemies are."[63] In this case, Confederate Virginians identified the enemy as a vandal who preyed upon helpless civilians and ignored the Constitution by waging war on property, both real and slave.

They had reason to think so. Secession itself had come because of actions by the Lincoln government that many Virginians deemed coercive and unconstitutional. They also noticed the infringement on civil liberties against Maryland residents to keep the border state in the Union. In March of 1862, however, the war turned more personal as the Union army crossed the Potomac and, except for brief respites during Lee's offensives into Maryland and Pennsylvania, controlled northern Virginia for the rest of the war. Union soldiers immediately burned fence rails, robbed hen houses, and entered homes. To some extent, they were held in check by a core of officers, traditional Democrats like Irwin McDowell, John Reynolds, and George B. McClellan, who waged a limited war for reunion without the loss of slavery. By treating civilian property respectfully, they hoped the Confederate populace would realize their betrayal by a slave-owning aristocracy and return to the Union fold. To residents in northern portions of Virginia who suddenly found Union soldiers on their doorsteps, this policy offered little consolation. Few relished serving as host to an enemy army even when the officers tried to police their men. And not everyone did. Brigadier General John W. Geary typified another group of northern officers who encouraged men to punish the secessionists and prided themselves on earning the hatred of Confederate Virginians.[64]

As the Federal army pushed its way into northern Virginia, two streams of Virginians formed, heading in opposite directions: white refugees going south and escaping slaves heading north. "We live in continual excitement," a young woman in Charlottesville noted as she watched the white migration from her window, adding that "the road is thronged from morning until night with people running horses, wagons, carriages, cattle, sheep & everything from the Yankees, who have taken possession of Fauquier[,] Loudoun & all those upper counties." Some of the refugees remained in Virginia's heartland while others pressed on to Richmond.[65] Word of federal transgressions in the occupied areas reached home through letters from family members in the military who witnessed the results of the destruction or from relatives who noted the way soldiers broke into larders and pawed over goods. In Fredericksburg, Union soldiers occupied the town, instituted martial law, and attempted to install Unionists in prominent positions. Small wonder that Jed Hotchkiss cheered the death of a Union cavalryman during an engagement in the Shenandoah Valley, adding: "I am not vindictive, but I really did not feel sorry to see the horse & his insolent rider laid low, it seemed a just retribution for the evils they had inflicted on an innocent people." And a man who had been a proud Unionist only a year before now felt compelled to comment: "The re-establishment of the Union under the old Constitution is an idea which I suppose no sane man indulges. The whole character of the government must be changed before the North & South can be held together."[66]

The Union soldiers appeared interested in upsetting the entire southern social system as they presented escape-minded slaves with a golden opportunity. The incidents of runaway slaves reached a visible height between the spring and late summer of 1862. Confederate Virginians had attempted to limit such occurrences by shifting their human property from portions of the state near the coast to the interior. But enemy incursions into northern Virginia exposed new territory to the enemy and provided fresh avenues for escape, especially as white refugees took to the streets. With the occupation of Fredericksburg, slaves from across the Northern Neck and upper Piedmont used the town as a safe harbor on their journey through Baltimore and on to Washington. On April 25, a Fredericksburg woman noticed the parade of slaves and then recorded her worst anxiety: "I am afraid of the lawless Yankee soldiers, but that is nothing to my fear of the negroes if they should rise against us." She added the next month, "Matters are getting worse and worse here every day with regard to the negroes. They are leaving their owners by the hundred and demanding wages." Citizens attempted to band together in refusing to hire out their own slaves or contract for others, but nothing slowed the migration. By midsummer as many as fifty contrabands each day were sent from Fredericksburg to Washington by the provost marshal.[67] The problem extended deep into the state as the Union lines offered an enticing target. Six slaves fled works on the James & Kanawha Canal Company on Daniel's Island near Lynchburg in July 1862. Nine more left three weeks later. All but one were from Loudoun County; they were apparently trying to return home, which was behind Union lines. When Superintendent James M. Harris reported that twenty-one slaves escaped within a three-week stretch, he added "a guard will have to be employed if we keep the negroes on the canal."[68]

Masters grew more wary, if such a thing were possible, about holding on to slaves, but they were frustrated about how to accomplish this. The problem was exacerbated as the state, acting on behalf of the Confederacy, issued quotas to counties for slave laborers to dig entrenchments and perform other military work. Shielding their property from impressment officers did not always work because slaves had a habit of taking matters into their own hands and bolting. Besides, as one slave owner wrote in a Richmond newspaper, only a minority could afford the escalating costs of transporting slaves to other areas. Even if they could, planters were uncertain about where the safest place would be. In one sentence, a slave owner captured with dramatic clarity the personal damage that the fleeing slaves caused: "Men went to bed rich and got up poor."[69]

Life worsened for Confederate Virginians as northern policy toward civilians hardened in the summer of 1862. Union Major General John Pope's appointment as commander of a new Army of Virginia coincided with the demise of what one scholar has termed the Union's conciliatory policy toward the South. McClellan's failure on the Peninsula and the attitudes of southern civilians fed momentum for stiffer prosecution of the war. Wherever Union soldiers had advanced in Virginia they had found some Union sympathizers but more often confronted a hostile public, except among the African American population.[70] When Pope assumed command, he ordered his men to subsist on products seized from Confederate households, force civilians to swear oaths of loyalty or leave their communities, and take retribution on the populace for guerrilla activity. Federal troops almost immediately implemented Pope's order to subsist off the countryside and began taking loyalty oaths when Lee's army defeated Pope's at Second Manassas in late August. The damage, however, had been done. Much of Northern Virginia became a wasteland. Because of Pope, one citizen clamored to raise partisan units in the Valley to halt the destruction.[71] Another Virginian commented about Pope: "Of all things in the world that I hate it is fighting. but it would afford me the greatest pleasure to thrash that contemptible scoundrel, but we will pay him up for it yet." He was not alone. A soldier reaffirmed to his brother: "Sir if it was not for us here the Yankees would take everything your Father is worth, and it would be right with them. They are Great Rascals[.] I hate them worse than I did at White Hall [his home] drunk. I will kill them if I can." Women expressed similar wishes. Lucy Buck blamed Lincoln for the seizing of property and exclaimed, "Oh I'm so tired of tyranny!"[72]

The shelling and sacking of Fredericksburg in December provided a rallying point for these attitudes. On December 11, Union artillery shelled the town to silence soldiers who picked off engineers bridging the Rappahannock River. The next day, Union soldiers sacked the town in an orgy of destruction that astounded even some of the participants as they rifled abandoned homes, took what they could use, and smashed what they could not.[73] Confederate Virginians were deeply affected by the plight of civilians, as revealed in charitable donations. During this time of statewide scarcity, a total of roughly $170,000 in contributions flowed to Fredericksburg residents. Occasionally, donations came from other parts of the Confederacy but most originated from within the Old Dominion.[74]

Union depredations solidified the portrait of an enemy who

threatened all citizens, slaveholders, and nonslaveholders alike. These images supported the notion that the Lincoln administration waged war to subjugate the South and deprive Confederate Virginians of their property. A number of themes along these lines appeared in public and private accounts: the Yankee motivated by money and greed; barbarians and vandals who had no compunction against seizing private property; abolitionists who hoped to upset the social and economic order; and heathens who shelled churches and stole family Bibles. Gender images drove home the ravages of the enemy in a way designed to inflame a man's sense of honor. Newspaper correspondents stressed that the home front was filled with helpless women open to violation—not sexual assaults per se but violation of personal space by the enemy pawing through wardrobes. Accounts invariably depicted Union soldiers rifling a boudoir, donning women's garb, and parading in drag in the streets. Editors added to this concern by playing up the impact of Union occupation of the racial order, with white women bearing the brunt of this affront. An editor noted that in Union-occupied Norfolk he had heard that a mother and daughter walking down the street met two Afro-Virginians, one of whom reportedly told the mother that "when white women see a coming gentleman, they must get out of their way." The men then shoved both women into the street. Whether true or embellished, the account provided compelling images to drive home the consequences of northern victory for planters and plain folk.[75]

By the spring of 1863, then, Confederate Virginians lived in a delicate situation. On the home front, the public experienced growing privations. Planters lost slaves, with repercussions for production of crops. Resentment grew among soldiers and civilians against the people who avoided military service or prospered while others went hungry. Yet the picture was by no means bleak. Confederate spirits rebounded as battles went fairly well in the eastern theater. The slaughter of Union soldiers at Fredericksburg raised spirits, and the enemy had provided a definition of the Confederate as the antithesis of the Yankee who preyed upon civilians. Unhappiness with the government did not overlap into disenchantment with the cause—especially as the success of Lee's army made continued sacrifice seem worthwhile and even, to some, a purgative from God to instill a new sense of strength and purpose in His people. For the time being, a fragile stasis had been achieved. But the war would not let it remain for very long.

4

Toward a Rich Man's Fight,
April 1863–March 1864

I think, under providence, *the whole question now turns on food.*
—Frank G. Ruffin, December 26, 1863

When Allen T. Caperton of Virginia urged his fellow senators to throw the wealthy men who had paid for substitutes into the army, he knew the matter interested people beyond the Senate chambers. Representatives at that session of December 29, 1863, understood the need to placate soldiers who complained that the poor man fought a rich man's war. Military fortunes had declined. Food shortages and inflation wracked the home front, hurting morale and stimulating absenteeism from the army. A few days before Caperton spoke, Congress had ended substitution. Now, members planned a further assault against the rich who were sitting out the war. Caperton proposed that Congress pass a bill voiding arrangements with substitutes as a New Year's present for the soldiers. On January 5, 1864, President Davis signed the legislation that placed into the ranks the men who had purchased these exemptions. Momentum had swung toward turning the war into more of a rich man's fight.[1]

Confederate policymakers during the third year of conflict began to pay more attention to the needs of small slave owners, non-slave-owning farmers, and soldiers' families. Even legislation to beef up the military in February 1864 included measures to help the disadvantaged at home. A change in exemptions for slave-owning, for instance, not only established government growers but also came remarkably close to nationalizing food prices for families of soldiers throughout the Confederacy. This transition came about because agitation on the home front, absenteeism by soldiers, and military reverses on the battlefield threatened the future of the fledgling nation. Survival demanded stern measures, including elimination of exemptions based on class. Congress followed its action on substitution with a new military bill in February 1864 that effectively turned all males aged 17 to 50 into soldiers. As the government purged its rosters of white men fit to fight, women and slaves moved into production of war-related goods, and free blacks faced conscription for military work. Increasingly, the Confederate cause became equated with a struggle for independence demanding of its followers sacrifices similar to those endured by their Revolutionary ancestors.[2]

Yet these desperate acts hardly seemed necessary as the third year of war opened. Despite problems with manpower, food, and war weariness, Confederate Virginians still had reason to cheer in April 1863. The Army of Northern Virginia under Robert E. Lee comforted the weary with the prospect that sacrifices actually might achieve success. Some made the obvious connection with Revolutionary Americans. One soldier wrote his wife from near Fredericksburg that "though I leave my children poor in worldly goods, it is gratifying to know they will be able to speak of their father as one of the soldiers of the Second Revolution for Independence." The battle of Chancellorsville only enhanced Virginia's love affair with Lee. A Richmond newspaper reported after the victory in May that everyone "feels entire confidence in our army and its able commander, and are convinced that whatever can be done will be done, and that in good time."[3]

The situation left the political leadership of Virginia and the Confederacy stubbornly committed to allowing the wealthy to buy their way out of service. Complex motivations bolstered the defense of substitution in congressional debates from March through April 1863, but the expressed reasons came down to two. The first concerned worry about the possibility of slave insurrection if all white males were forced into the army; the second, that without adequate supervision slaves would work too slowly. Additionally, many officials recognized that ending substitution would not solve manpower needs. Conscription officers reported that the wealthy who bought their way out of service included not only shirkers but a number of farmers, manufacturers, and mechanics essential for war-related production who would not be sent into the army anyway and who had sent a substitute as a patriotic gesture.[4]

Authorities, however, knew that something had to be done to defuse discontent over inequities in conscription. While clinging to substitution, Confederate lawmakers hoped to toss the public a bone—and eliminate obvious abuses—by modifying provisions for overseers. On May 1, Congress tightened the twenty-Negro law by eliminating automatic exemptions. To qualify for an overseer, a farm had to meet strict criteria. First, a minor, woman, lunatic, or man in the army must own the farm. Second, no white male eligible for the draft could qualify, a provision that prevented a planter who had contracted a substitute from winning an exemption for his son as an overseer. Third, the law demanded that overseers must have performed such work before the conscription act took effect in April 1862. Additionally, the overseer or owner of the property must pay a $500 tax each year to remain exempted. Congress also gave Jefferson Davis and the War Department latitude to exempt laborers whenever necessary—a clause vital for maintaining farm production in areas such as Virginia's Shenandoah Valley, where the size of the slave population did not automatically allow for exemptions of critical growers.[5]

Good news from the front helped perpetuate privileges for the wealthy. On the day the new overseer law took effect, Lee and Union Major General Joseph Hooker began a battle near Chancellorsville that ended in victory for Confederates and raised hopes that independence remained possible. The victory braced soldiers in the army as well, mitigating the shock surrounding the death of Stonewall Jackson on May 10, 1863. Officials attempted to maintain the better mood by applying lessons learned from overzealous enforcement of impressment a few months earlier. National authorities operating within the state effected the transition in the overseer law to protect the new crop. Orders to conscription authorities specified exemption for overseers who otherwise should report to the army whenever a farm's crops went to the government or fed the indigent. Officials hoped that increasing the supply of food would alleviate discontent on the home front and, subsequently, the pressure on soldiers to desert.[6]

Although conscription officers acted prudently by protecting crops when implementing the overseer law, their caution in forcing men into the army fed suspicion that the administration still favored large slave owners. After all, substitution continued unabated among the wealthy. Indeed, the recent legislation actually prompted Virginians to employ more substitutes, as men once protected by the law became exposed to the draft. These men hunted for substitutes in local defense units—the only remaining pool of possible substitutes—but the army quickly moved to close the loophole.[7] Localism also hampered volunteering. At the University of Virginia, John B. Minor balked against the plan of Secretary of War James A. Seddon to use local defense troops for more than ten days and for missions beyond the borders of the community. "I am persuaded," Minor wrote the secretary of war, "that the utmost they can be persuaded to *volunteer* for, is to protect their homes, & that not against the invasion of *armies* but against sudden & temporary incursions expected but to last for a few days. I fear it is indispensable to limit the service to a short time . . . and to objects which appeal to personal selfishness."[8]

Discontent among the broader electorate took a more alarming turn in May. Congressional and gubernatorial elections in Virginia subtly shifted political leadership toward former Whigs who had accepted secession slowly. Six of Virginia's sixteen seats in the lower Confederate house changed hands, with former Whigs or Unionists constituting five of the victorious. Being a moderate Democrat, Governor John Letcher hoped to continue public service as a congressman from the Shenandoah Valley but lost to the Whig incumbent, John B. Baldwin, who had opposed secession. Owner of eleven slaves, Baldwin had served as a colonel in an Augusta County regiment and proved to be effective in balancing support for the Davis administration with the needs of constituents, especially in gaining military exemptions for mechanics, artisans, and religious pacifists. In Albemarle County, the venerable William C. Rives returned to the Confederate Congress. He had emerged nationally in the Jacksonian era as a member of the U.S. House of Representatives and Senate. During the secession crisis, he had pushed for a peace conference. Like many Unionist Whigs, this owner of more than 100 slaves immediately supported his state when it seceded and served in the provisional Confederate Congress. He had bowed out of the First Congress and now would replace James P. Holcombe of Charlottesville, an avid secessionist and proslavery ideologue who dropped out of the race.[9]

Although installing a number of former Unionists, the election indicated no desire to end the war or return to the Union. The campaign in the Old Dominion had been a lackluster affair, suggesting a distracted public. A number of circumstances accounted for the results: the usual midterm ground lost by most administrations, the anger over conditions on the home front, and the restoration of voting patterns that existed before the war. Events had tarnished secessionists while reviving former Unionists, but only those who embraced the Confederate cause. Unionist Whigs tended to be the most nationalistic—or at least feared less than their Democratic opponents the consolidation of power in government, especially when in the hands of the "best men." They also held long-standing patrician notions that the rich must care for the poor. West of the Blue Ridge these men received support from the soldiers, while eastern Virginians resigned themselves to these leaders who infringed on liberties because their communities served as the seat of war.[10] Whatever the reasons, the elections resulted in no loss of support for the war as the winners favored strong measures for prosecuting it. But the balloting did send one strong signal. The soldiers had voted in significant numbers, a consideration that influenced future debates over mobilization. Leaders such as Senator Caperton recognized that they could ill afford to ignore the fighting voters.[11]

The impact of these elections on Congress awaited the session that opened in 1864, but other events helped push authorities into exacting greater sacrifices from the wealthy. Food shortages continued to affect civilian morale and the ability to keep soldiers in the ranks. The Federal army played a significant role in this scarcity by ravaging an area from Fredericksburg to the lower Shenandoah Valley—a key section of the state that had contributed vast amounts of grain and livestock before the war. By January 1863 Lee had trouble securing grain for the army from around Fredericksburg. Soldiers found some perishable foods locally but needed the railroad to haul goods in from Richmond and from outside the Old Dominion.[12] When the army began the Gettysburg campaign in mid-June, the devastation in the state struck British observer Arthur J. L. Fremantle as the men passed Sperryville near the foothills of the Blue Ridge. The land was "almost uncultivated, and no animals are grazing where there used to be hundreds. All fences have been destroyed, and numberless farms burnt, the chimneys alone left standing. It is difficult to depict and impossible to exaggerate the sufferings which this part of Virginia has undergone."[13]

Conditions forced the public living in or near zones occupied by the enemy to supplement subsistence in whatever ways possible, including illicit trade with the North. While this at first concerned officials as disloyal behavior, Confederate authorities looked the other way and eventually attempted to capitalize on the trade. When a Confederate enrollment officer complained about the extent of illegal trading in the Northern Neck, Secretary of War James Seddon cautioned against cracking down. All trade with the enemy was illegal, Seddon admitted, but "situated as the people to a serious extent are, beyond the power of active protection by us, and cut off from supplies through their regular avenues of trade . . . by the enemy, some barter or trading for the supply of their necessities is almost inevitable and excusable."[14] This activity flourished in the Fredericksburg area and in the southeast. Later, Confederate authorities licensed people conducting trade through the lines in cotton, tobacco, and other goods in exchange for food and supplies for the army.[15]

Ironically, the waste from the Federal army also provided a way to keep food on the table. After the war, a white Virginian named Elijah remembered that the military goods littering battlefields and abandoned camps served as a way to survive. A Fredericksburg resident, he regularly traveled to Chancellorsville to buy the clothing of northern soldiers, some of it stripped from the dead. He took the goods to Essex County to trade for corn meal. Upon returning, he exchanged the meal for two blankets and a coat. A mule provided the transportation that allowed him to conduct this enterprise. "Any number of families jest lived on what they got from the Union armies in that way," he noted.[16] Elijah's experience suggests that a sophisticated "market" in bartering, complete with unwritten rates of exchange, had established itself; that farming areas toward the interior had grain to spare, at least for individuals if not armies; and that a mule could mean the difference between hunger and a full stomach. This last fact in particular explains why the public might have found impressment officers who collected livestock for the army more than a casual threat to the pursuit of a livelihood.[17]

Lee mapped his military strategy partly in relation to the scarcity of provisions for soldiers and civilians. Food was not the only factor motivating Lee's raid into Pennsylvania, yet the general's correspondence with Jefferson Davis indicates that privations formed a critical component of his decision to head north. Lee understood the disparity in resources between the two armies and believed he must seize any chance to exploit growing divisions among northern civilians over the prosecution of the war. Supply concerns and the likelihood of a future northern offensive made it impossible to remain along the Rappahannock indefinitely. To stay meant the army would continue to drain a region already strapped for supplies. Lee had had to send a portion of the army under James Longstreet to Suffolk to find more food. One historian has noted that an offensive campaign was not the only choice—indeed, it may have been the wrong one in retrospect—but conditions on the home front strengthened the tendency within Lee toward aggressive action.[18]

The campaign, however, cost what the Confederacy could afford the least: the army sustained more than 20,000 casualties. Coupled with defeat at Vicksburg, the impact of Gettysburg struck Confederate officials almost immediately. In the War Department, R. G. H. Kean observed, "In this crisis of our affairs the prospect for recruiting our wasted armies is very poor. The conscription up to [age] 40 is about exhausted. Between 40 and 45 will not yield probably over 50,000 men and will take 6 months to get them out. We are *almost exhausted.*"[19] Davis shared this perspective and attempted to shore up the deficiencies. On July 16, the president ordered to camps of instruction all persons between 18 and 45 who had not yet enrolled. The next day, word went out to conscript officers in Virginia to obey Davis's order.[20]

The government also canvassed its own rosters to find employees eligible for conscription. Quartermasters, commissaries, and officers using detailed and exempted workers compiled lists of names, occupations, ages, and reasons for exemption. The quartermaster's operation in Lynchburg attests that officers acted when they found workers who could be of better use in the military. Of eight employees working for Captain E. McCormick, two had physical disabilities and four were over the age limit. Patrick Gregory, who worked as a mailer, had no good excuse. Next to his name someone wrote: "Has reported to the enrolling officer."[21]

To replace clerks, the government turned to some extent toward women. Unlike prior hiring that had tapped daughters of planters, this round targeted women from the working classes, soldiers' families, and the needy. In Richmond, officials visited homes to interview people requesting employment with the quartermaster's bureau. A list of ten women under consideration included wives of men in a variety of occupations: a carpenter, a stonemason, a member of the city watch, a soldier, and a worker in a government laboratory. The rest lived with children or other dependents without visible means of support. They constituted only a portion of the hundreds of destitute women who petitioned the government for work, often to no avail. A study of Confederate women suggests that favoritism of the upper classes continued in these selections and that the only poor women hired typically lived close to the offices where they sought employment.[22]

The measures to put men into the ranks worked in Virginia, at least momentarily. Before this, conscripts reporting to camps of instruction had declined from around 850 per month to about 600. After the prodding by Davis and the Conscription Bureau, the pace picked up again with September posting 833 newcomers and October 778 before declining once more to the 600 level. By late August, Josiah Gorgas of the Ordnance Bureau noted that Lee's army was increasing at the rate of 600 per day.[23]

Even this effort to place men in the ranks failed to impress the army's commander because of chronic absenteeism. A fairly organized march from Gettysburg back to the South turned into a haphazard affair as soldiers strayed from units when entering the Old Dominion. On July 13, for example, cavalryman Frank Imboden recorded that Ewell's division had waded the Potomac "and without a straggler marched to Martinsburg. No evidence whatever of demoralization is visible in Lee's great old army." Later in the month conditions changed. Imboden noticed that "evidence of demoralization are visible. More desertions than usual are occurring." A woman in Albemarle County supported his observations about absentees as she watched the roads at the end of July: "Stragglers in considerable numbers have been going down this morning."[24]

Some of this straggling represented little more than the typical pattern as armies moved through regions from which the men had been recruited. The lure of home proved irresistible, something that company-grade officers understood. Oddly enough, this kind of straggling probably helped the army by increasing the morale of men who returned to the ranks because they could ease their minds about how their families fared. In his account of the Stonewall Brigade, John Casler recalled taking unauthorized leave at this time to check on his family in Frederick County as the regiment passed Winchester. The company's lieutenant could not grant permission for the leave but let Casler go as long as the private understood that capture meant prosecution as a deserter. General officers on the whole tolerated these absences less, but even they sometimes recognized the importance of looking the other way. Jubal Early had done the same with troops under his command when the Confederate army seized Winchester on the way to Pennsylvania. When Nathan Bedford Forrest led his expedition into western Tennessee and

Kentucky from March through April 1864, he had in the ranks a number of men from the region. "I have as far as prudent," Forrest reported, "allowed my troops an opportunity of going home."[25]

While historians face insurmountable problems sorting out which men deserted or left for family reasons with the intention of returning to the army, people in the community and the army had no such difficulties. Elias Davis, a soldier in the army, noted, "Many of them I am truly sorry for, men who have large families dependent [on] their labor for supports. We have many ugly reports in the army of how illy treated are the wives and children of poor soldiers by the wealthy and speculators. Many have believed those reports and have applyed for furloughs which having been denied them, have been tempted to visit home regardless of the consequences." He understood that deserters constituted a different category of people. "The great bulk of deserters," he continued, "are worthless characters, whose consciences are no checks to their desires to do meanly."[26] Virginians blamed the most frequent desertions on North Carolinians, indicating that many left the army in bands of ten or more. State bias undoubtedly influenced these accounts; the army in general suffered from straggling regardless of the nativity of the men. Virginians may have looked more patriotic only because they enjoyed the advantage of geography—with home nearby they could more easily "straggle" while those leaving for homes farther away earned the label of "deserter." Yet the evidence does support that numbers of North Carolinians seized the opportunity to head home.[27]

Remarkable agreement existed among military commanders, Confederate authorities, and community leaders about the cause of the absences. All parties concluded that the behavior was linked to broader problems concerning the ability of government to feed its citizens and to stop extortionist prices. Instead of employing ritual executions and other harsh measures of the prior summer, military and civil authorities used leniency to stem the straggling problem of 1863. Perhaps officials had little choice. Faced with the staggering losses that summer of nearly 90,000 men throughout the Confederacy, they needed to muster every possible person. Evidence, however, supports that the reasons for leniency ran deeper: that officials understood that men remained away from the army because of the inability of the nation to care for its people.

President Davis offered this interpretation himself in a message to the nation on August 1, in which he issued a general amnesty for all soldiers absent from the army. He reminded the public that the North attempted to subjugate the South. Citing the enemy's destruction of property and other violations of liberty, Davis added: "Fellow-citizens, no alternative is left you but victory, or subjugation, slavery and the utter ruin of yourselves, your families, and your country." The president then excused the absentees, indicating he believed few of the men unwilling to serve their country "but that many have found it difficult to resist the temptation of a visit to their homes and the loved ones from whom they have been so long separated; that others have left for temporary attention to their affairs with the intention of returning, and then have shrunk from the consequences of the violation of duty."[28] The president followed his amnesty by declaring August 21 as a day of national fasting and prayer, his usual method of forcing the public to reflect on circumstances and renew commitment. Soldiers also participated, with a special exhortation from Lee to remember that all had sinned by cultivating a "revengeful, haughty, and boastful spirit." Holding its annual meeting in Nelson County, the Albemarle Baptist Association encompassing Augusta, Albemarle, Nelson, Amherst, and Fluvanna counties supported Davis's resolutions to use every means to return soldiers to duty and promised adherence to the day of fasting and prayer.[29]

Lee grudgingly accepted the necessity of an amnesty. He had grown so exasperated with absences from the army that he temporarily believed that leniency might encourage more men to return to the ranks and thus suggested a proclamation of mercy to the president. To alleviate the pressure on men who stayed in the army, the general instituted a system of furloughs in which soldiers proving their need to go home could do so at the rate of one man for every hundred present for duty. Within the army, the leaves were referred to by at least one soldier as "furloughs of indulgence." The duration of the leaves varied by the state from which a soldier hailed, with those farther from Virginia receiving longer time because of travel. The number of leaves granted depended on the season, increasing to two per company and then to no more than five per hundred during the Christmas and New Year's holidays. Implementation probably differed depending on the company, but in some Virginia regiments the officers allowed the soldiers themselves to vote on who deserved to go home. They forwarded the names of nominees to the colonel of the regiment who made the final selection from the popular choices.[30]

These procedures rationalized the furlough system, but predictably even this innovation did not console everyone. Soldiers felt slighted if they could not get a leave. When a soldier from Fluvanna County informed his wife that he could not come home in April 1864 because Lee subsequently had clamped down on furloughs, it seemed unfair because rain made active operations unlikely. "I have not had my deserts, during the war," he concluded, "and I sometimes feel sullen and almost unpatriotic because of it." Others objected to the system itself, which required passes that caused one to remark that "a Soldier is worse than a negro." However, most of the men enjoying furloughs probably deserved them. A man in the 49th Virginia complained that he could not visit home during the winter because only the old soldiers received furloughs. "If I had anything to base a furlough on," he wrote his father, "I would try it. If you can frame any excuse to base a furlough on I would be glad for you to write and let me try it."[31] On the whole, though, the complaints underscore the importance of leaves to the men and that the system relieved the most urgent cases.

Lee quickly changed his mind about the efficacy of mercy in handling absenteeism. Early in August he acknowledged that the general amnesty had helped fill the ranks but told the president that absences continued despite the concessions and that some men took advantage of the situation. According to reports Lee received, bands of Virginians joined partisan units near their homes. The Shenandoah Valley offered one region in which deserters hid. Others crossed the James River near a place called Balcony Falls to head south along mountain routes. Reports from the home front support the general's contention that deserters congregated in the Valley, at Scottsville in lower Albemarle County on the James River, and in the mountainous regions in the southern Piedmont. Between the amnesty and the furloughs, Lee wrote, "I would now respectfully submit to Your Excellency, the opinion that all has been done which forbearance and mercy call for, and that nothing will remedy this great evil which so much endangers our cause except the rigid enforcement of the death penalty." Months later, he urged the secretary of war to end pardons in these cases and to allow executions as the only effective measure for holding the army together.[32]

When supported by the government, executions took place. Soldiers had mixed feelings about the effect of the punishment. John Casler noted in his memoir that executions might have prompted men to desert to the enemy rather than risk capture at home. His assessment, however, came well after the war when it was clear that the means had failed to achieve the ends. During the war, at least some did not mind this grim solution. One Virginian serving in North Carolina wrote that among prisoners captured by his unit were two deserters: "They were hung a few minutes before we left Winston. I tell you there is very little mercy shown deserters now." About the same time, editors in Virginia once again featured accounts of ritual executions in which the accused calmly accepted their grim fate— likely a romanticized account to send a message that even these people would awaken to the harm of their crime, even if a bit too late.[33]

Ironically, communities began to help Lee with this problem. As privations continued, deserters became less welcome in communities. The men typically found sanctuary in mountainous regions deep in the central and western portions of the state. Deserters themselves aggravated tensions by preying on communities in the southern Piedmont. After men described as deserters burned barns on three farms in Franklin County, vigilantes tracked them to a cave eight miles outside of Franklin Court House, tried them on the spot, and summarily executed two of them, Robert and James Saul. Altogether, the vigilantes fired fifty-one rounds at the two men who constituted part of a band that had established itself in the region. Reports indicated that an escaped convict named Goodson organized the group that robbed farms to lay in supplies for the winter. The conscription officer for Franklin County placed guards at the passes and hunted down the deserters, at one point capturing sixty to seventy of them, killing two and sustaining wounds to four of his men. The leader managed to escape.[34] Tight administration of the home front was proving effective, especially when citizens had a reason to help.

To raise spirits during these difficult times, some officials conducted a propaganda campaign throughout Virginia. Senator Louis T. Wigfall of Texas played a prominent role in sessions that used the traditional means of creating public consent. As in the antebellum era, the leaders resorted to public meetings in which the participants voted on resolutions that were then publicized in local newspapers. One of the first sessions took place in Charlottesville, which set the pattern. Wigfall paired himself with prominent Virginia political figures (in Charlottesville with James P. Holcombe of the University of Virginia and in Staunton with Governor-elect William Smith). After listening to patriotic speeches, the audience voted on resolutions to which they signed their names. The "Albemarle Resolutions," as they became known, pledged that participants would promptly pay their tax-in-kind; they would set aside another tenth of their surplus to sell to the government at prewar prices, taking payment in Confederate bonds; and they would invest their surplus in bonds instead of land and slaves. To spread the burden on more than farmers, the resolutions called for merchants, mechanics, and professional men to pay taxes amounting to an additional tenth on their businesses. Wigfall visited Staunton, Louisa Courthouse, Orange Courthouse, Harrisonburg, and other places. Buckingham County also held a meeting, although it was unclear whether or not the senator attended.[35]

The impact of these meetings remains difficult to assess because no clear picture exists of who attended and how faithful the participants remained to their word. Community leaders consisting of the wealthiest merchants, mechanics, and planters clearly orchestrated these sessions, but they had done so for every important county and town gathering before the war. They thus acted well within the character of the political culture and should have retained at least some allies among farmers and workers. In Albemarle County, Thomas J. Randolph lent to these resolutions his considerable influence as a large planter. Joining him were prominent members of the town, including an important merchant and an owner of a hotel. Former Whigs attended the Augusta County meeting, including Alexander H. H. Stuart. Working men played no significant role in the sessions. Nor did anyone differentiate between small slaveholding and nonslaveholding farmers: accounts invariably stated only that a considerable number of agriculturists attended. The best guess is that these sessions bolstered the spirits of those inclined to support the Confederacy while proving less persuasive for farmers who withheld crops because of principles, disaffection, or selfishness. The meetings also placed men on record with pledges that neighbors might well hold them to.

One thing is certain: pledges by community leaders failed to resolve food shortages. Privations continued. The winter of 1863–1864 promised to be another hard one. Public resentment would grow to the point where more and more people called for price controls on food, which farmers strongly resisted. In the end, officials would have little choice but to eliminate privileges for the rich and increase the Confederate government's involvement in providing for the needy.

Prices within Virginia had stabilized briefly in June as a tax act and impressment temporarily slowed inflation. The costs for essential goods set by the state commissioners in Virginia ranged from more than one-half to three-quarters lower than the open market. Fall brought renewed inflation as people laid in supplies for winter. Flour in Lynchburg had settled in September at between $30 and $40 per barrel. By December, the price catapulted from $80 to $100 and then hit an astronomical $250 to $275 per barrel the following spring. Bacon, corn, and butter increased as dramatically, although corn briefly decreased by the spring of 1864.[36] Often in this volatile period the cost of goods and services could increase dramatically within a single day. In Charlottesville one October morning, Cornelius Dabney paid $1 for repairing the heel of his shoe. "When I carried the shoe to him in the evening," Dabney wrote about the cobbler, "he charged half dollar more."[37] Artisans and professionals sensitive to claims that they extorted money for services attempted at times to hold prices down or published explanations of why they charged so much. Physicians in Augusta County formed an association in 1863 with the stated goal of exchanging educational information and improving themselves as professionals. However, this group had the ulterior motive of establishing uniform prices for doctors' services, which increased their fees by linking them to costs not only of medicine but also of agricultural and mechanical equipment.[38] Other providers in communities worked toward less self-serving goals, hoping to make goods and services more affordable.

If extortion could not be controlled, the community at least could help the less fortunate. Key differences from prior relief campaigns were the scale of these enterprises, the extent of local government coordination, a trend away from cash stipends toward rations, and the sentiment in some quarters for setting maximum prices on foodstuffs. In late July 1863, officials in Lynchburg authorized a public store to supply the needy with necessities at cost. They raised the necessary $25,000 through non-interest-bearing shares, turning the operation into a public corporation, as had been done with railroads and canals constructed in the state. The council quickly implemented this system, stocking bacon, flour, corn meal, and other necessities, with the store furnishing to eligible persons a month's supply at a time. Managers accepted cash only, a provision that probably limited access to townspeople earning wages rather than poorer farmers who were more reliant on barter. The town stopped short of establishing a free store as Richmond had done after April's bread riot. In Staunton, the council doubled taxes on

September 5 to fund purchases of meat, flour, and wood for families of soldiers. This came at the behest of the mayor, who presented a petition signed by ninety-three people calling for the increases. To oversee the funds, the council appointed a four-person committee that worked two months before collecting enough money to purchase goods that were then sold at half their original cost to families of volunteers. Both Lynchburg and Charlottesville also helped pay the rents of the poor rather than have them become homeless.[39]

State officials did their part by clearing the way for local governments to conduct relief work and by easing the tax burden. On October 27, the General Assembly passed legislation to ensure that public stores served the needy and did not become avenues for further speculation and extortion. The law stipulated that communities could borrow up to $10,000 per 1,000 white population at no more than 6 percent interest. Communities could not sell goods for a profit but were required to distribute them to the poor at cost, plus expenses such as transportation. The act also authorized railroads to ship these goods as a priority over everything else except military supplies. Four days later the legislators passed another act specifically for the relief of indigent families of soldiers and sailors. Finally, the lawmakers empowered communities to use the tax-in-kind and local impressment to secure provisions, using the prices set by the Confederate law. For the duration of the war, county courts were to gather names of the indigent families of soldiers and refugees to administer to their wants. This process had begun randomly during the summer but escalated over the winter and continued for the remainder of the war, with communities such as Campbell dropping monetary payments entirely in favor of distributing rations alone. By September 1864, the county court of Campbell was issuing 25 pounds of meat or 20 pounds of flour per month for each eligible person, raising money through special levies.[40]

To ease the burden for these new costs, legislators eventually suspended the collection of state taxes. A sound budget—at least with paper money and bonds if not specie—presented authorities with the opportunity to look good for constituents. Jonathan M. Bennett, Virginia's auditor of public accounts, by November 1863 saw that the state budget would achieve a surplus, despite nearly a third of the state having fallen under Union control. The General Assembly used this happy situation to fund relief measures for people who came from Union-occupied regions of the state. When the lawmakers finally passed the act that suspended taxes on March 3,

1864, the treasury contained $9.3 million, which Bennett estimated would carry the state for at least a year. As late as September 30, 1864, Virginia still held $5.4 million in funds. It is not clear if state officials ever resumed collections.[41]

Overall, the local charity drives tallied impressive results, especially in communities with greater resources, such as Staunton, Charlottesville, Lynchburg, and Richmond. By December, Campbell County had appropriated $220,000 for soldiers and their families since the war began. Albemarle County Court collected $125,000, through which the county supported 1,200 wives and children of soldiers.[42] Richmond predictably mounted the largest campaign. Between April and December 1863, the city council established a free store for the indigent; set aside another $105,000 for the Overseer of the Poor; allowed use of the city's carts to carry fuel for the needy; appropriated $20,000 to purchase wood, coal, and other necessities for the poor; and authorized the committee on light to furnish surplus coke free as a source of fuel.[43]

The measures could not overcome all problems because resources rarely equaled good intentions. Communities such as Amherst County that tried to maintain subsidies for soldiers' families could not furnish the stipends regularly and whenever resuming them rarely issued back pay.[44] Confederate impressment agents also competed with local authorities for the same dwindling resources. By the spring, the chairman of the relief effort in Campbell County estimated he needed to feed 700 people but could find neither bread nor meat at any prices and turned to the commissary at Lynchburg for help. While Albemarle had enough breadstuffs to feed soldiers' families until August 1, relief agents could find neither corn meal nor meat. "This county has been exhausted of supplies and money cannot purchase them," a resident told the secretary of war, adding that unless aid came from the government "great distress and I almost fear starvation will follow."[45]

Throughout Virginia, momentum built for the national government to supplement local charity. Typically this meant gaining access to supplies controlled by the military. As early as October 1862, when people faced the first truly difficult winter of the war, Lucy Otey and Mrs. John Speed had petitioned the secretary of war to grant women working in hospitals the option enjoyed by officers to purchase goods from the commissary in Lynchburg. These two women had conducted a tremendous service for the government in establishing a Ladies Relief Hospital that functioned as efficiently as any Confederate installation, but the War Department denied the request. Other women wrote the secretary hoping that the government would issue rations to wives of soldiers.[46]

Others hoped for access to military supplies. Inside the War Department, John B. Jones recommended to President Davis that perishable goods paid to the government under the tax-in-kind be sold at reasonable rates to civil officials and the public to reduce discontent. Without relief for "non-producers," Jones believed that further riots might occur in the city.[47] This solution faced resistance from other parts of the bureaucracy. When a War Department official suggested that it was important to feed the city with government supplies, the commissary general of subsistence rejected the notion. The official supplied a chilling reason: "that the alternative was between the *people* and the army, that there is perhaps *bread* enough for both but not *meat* enough, and that we have to elect between the *army* and the *people* doing without." The department employed an "army-first" mentality: Virginia lawmakers were angered when impressment agents from the commissary bureau ignored their request not to impress goods in route to markets where the public might have access. The bureau seemed bent on steering goods toward the military no matter the impact on the home front.[48]

As they had during the bread riot, "the people" refused to accept the situation without comment, only this time the public sought legitimate political channels instead of the streets. Beginning in September, mechanics and working men in Richmond tried to eliminate the free market when it came to food. They had pressed representatives in the General Assembly to extend the price schedules of impressment to all necessities. Proponents of the bill believed the system functioned effectively and hoped it would expand to allow everyone to purchase necessities at regulated rates. The group held as many as four public sessions from late September through October 20 to demand that representatives to the General Assembly support regulated prices or step down from office. They succeeded in having legislation submitted, and for a time momentum appeared on their side. George Wythe Randolph, a former secretary of war now serving in the state senate, had softened from opposing the bill outright. Randolph indicated that he would follow the wishes of constituents as he delivered the group's memorial to the General Assembly. The stage was set to debate the most sensitive points of life on the home front: whether government should regulate prices for all or a free market should prevail, and whether legislation should favor the consumer or the producer.[49]

A meeting October 10, 1863, represented the apex of the battle for the group pressing for price controls. A mixture of persons attended the meeting in Richmond, although it is difficult to be precise about the composition of the audience. Refugees and a sprinkling of state and Confederate government workers joined the mechanics and skilled workers who formed the core of the movement, well represented by printers. One of the speakers, E. B. Robinson, was a typographer. The participants identified speculation as the most pressing problem on the home front, blaming state and national authorities for encouraging a combination of capital against labor that resulted in privations for families of soldiers. In their resolutions the group added that "as freemen we abhor and detest the idea that the rich must take care of the poor." The responsibility to care for the unfortunate, according to this manifesto, lay not with the rich but with the government. Otherwise, the relationship would perpetuate an unwholesome dependency that would corrupt the nation.[50] These persons saw less danger in being beholden to government than to planters.

From their first appearance the protesters took pains to portray themselves as patriots who shared a common bond with the soldiers. They did not want to disrupt the war effort but merely call attention to mismanagement by public officials. During one of the first meetings, on September 19, resolutions pledged loyalty to the cause, thanked the soldiers in the field for their work, and reassured that the group wanted to help families by relieving them from "the iron grasp of the extortioner and the money changer."[51] At the meeting on October 10, a refugee from Kentucky showed how low he considered the people who refused to do their part for the cause. He ranked with the speculators and extortionists persons who purchased substitutes (a practice the group officially opposed) as well as Maryland residents who had fled their state but who avoided service as aliens without Confederate citizenship. He called these people "parlor patriots" and the soldiers "kitchen patriots" who were "not afraid to go among the pots and kettles." The mechanics and working men wished to help the soldiers by easing life at home.[52]

Newspaper editors, legislators, and key planters mounted a vigorous campaign to quash this radical move. They dubbed the Anti-Extortion Bill "the Maximum," linking it to a similar law dur-

ing the French Revolution. Newspapers used large amounts of ink
to show that similar efforts in the past had failed, especially during
the French and American Revolutions. They also reminded that
when Richmond had fallen under martial law, an edict placing a ceiling on prices had resulted in a reduction in goods for sale. Editors
played on people's fears—still fresh from their experience with the
shortages seven months earlier—that regulation of prices would contract supplies once more. They and other opponents also pointed
out that this action taken on a state level would be particularly destructive if not adopted by the entire Confederacy. Goods and services, they predicted, would flow from the state as merchants and
craftsmen moved to find higher prices in unrestricted markets. Besides, they argued, most solutions would fall short because the underlying reasons for the high prices were a scarcity of goods and a
depreciated currency. As their solution, the opponents of regulated
prices advocated an assault on competition through voluntary associations of people who would conduct group purchase for communities and legislation that would tackle the currency.[53]

Whether or not he planned the strategy, Randolph's request for
direction from constituents provided a creative way out of the
predicament. To learn the sentiments of the constituency he asked
the Richmond City Council, on which he also served, to conduct a
special election to record public sentiments. Council members
agreed, setting the date for October 22. When the vote came in, city
residents rejected the measure by 867 to 292. The public may have
been skeptical that such a law would work or, as R. G. H. Kean in
the War Department noted, that regulations would curtail production so that there would be "great danger of famine here."[54] The bill
died quietly.

The small support for price controls reflected in the voting
might not accurately reveal public sentiment for price controls either
in the city or the state. Unlike general elections, soldiers did not
vote. Neither did refugees who filled the city and who maintained a
prominent presence in the protest meetings. A statewide referen-
dum that included all eligible voters might have resulted in a different outcome. In Amherst County, for example, residents that same
month urged the legislature to adopt the schedule of prices outlined
by impressment as the maximum on all enumerated goods sold in
the state. The newspaper account of this meeting also featured a letter from a soldier claiming that his colleagues shared the concerns of
mechanics and working men who supported the measure.[55] Even

more interesting, when William Smith issued his inaugural address as governor three months after the battle, he avidly supported setting a ceiling on prices according to the impressment schedule for Confederate goods. Patriotic citizen farmers, he claimed, established these prices, whereas prices set by sellers would result in driving the army from the field. While he admitted that history was not on his side in proving the effectiveness of this course, he believed the exigencies of war demanded stern measures because the problem arose from shortages of goods, not currency, as opponents of the Maximum alleged. Smith pointed out that no amount of money could conjure nonexistent goods.[56]

The Maximum died, but planters and political leaders in the state recognized that discontent would not. During the campaign against price regulations, the editor of the *Richmond Whig* understood that the meetings of mechanics, protests of landlords against tenants, and other actions indicated "that important reforms must soon be made to prevent serious disturbances of the social order." Jones had come to the same conclusion, although he was especially nervous that the city had come to a flash point as he observed that as many as 1,000 of the men involved in the meetings to push for the Maximum had been members of the militia and thus carried muskets.[57] Based on the way the issue died, he had overreacted, but the concern of Jones and others about "the mob" was understandable. Public discontent revealed itself around the state in activity ranging from crime to public criticism. Arsonists in Lynchburg targeted suppliers that seemingly benefited from shortages and high prices: a government bakery, a tobacco factory, and a cooper shop that also distributed flour to the government. As residents battled this last fire in late February, they were pelted with rocks thrown from an opposite hill.[58] The usually supportive press warned farmers to part with surplus provisions. "Of all things," a Staunton editor observed, "hunger renders men the most reckless. An angel could not bear its gnawing with patience, and but few men are so saintly or timid as to be deterred from wading through blood or fire to mitigate its pangs." He concluded that "no man will stand by and see his children cry for bread while his neighbor's garner is full. The man who thinks so is an idiot or a lunatic."[59]

Virginians found planters easy scapegoats for these hardships because a minority of slave owners brought attention to themselves by appearing to protect their own self-interest. Some had failed to distinguish themselves in responding to calls from the government to send slaves for military work. The greatest resistance came in the richest tobacco regions of the southern Piedmont where Campbell, Bedford, and Pittsylvania counties posted the highest deficits from quotas.[60] Substitution increased as an irritant when scandal rocked the system. It became known that men used forms forged with names of colonels and captains who had been killed in battle. A circular from the Conscription Bureau observed: "The evil of fraudulent substitution has grown to be of such magnitude that the utmost vigilance is called for upon the part of officers of conscription to correct it and to place in the military service of the country the large number of persons of whom the army has been deprived by the chicanery of the agents of substitution."[61] While the evidence does not indicate that slave owners were any less patriotic than the rest of the Confederate public, they nonetheless provided visible targets.

Some political leaders found the scandalous behavior within their own class unconscionable and likely to scuttle the war effort if it continued. In August Senator Caperton of Virginia had written the secretary of war to call for an end to substitution. The letter indicated that the sentiment was becoming widespread that the war had become a poor man's fight. Caperton believed it was time for all to fight or else the Confederacy faced destruction. He planned on soliciting support from the Virginia General Assembly and promised to advocate measures in Congress that would compel those who had hired substitutes to enter the army.[62] The *Richmond Whig* unwittingly corroborated the accuracy of Caperton's observations as it attempted to dispel the notion that it was a rich man's war but a poor man's fight. An item in November summed up the sentiment of those who clung to substitution by calling the critics who mouthed the slogan traitors and demagogues. The rich, this writer contended, suffered as much as anyone in the conflict, with many fortunes swept away by the Union army. This was close to the truth. The writer was even closer to the mark in reminding that thousands of artisans also remained at home where they "take advantage of their exemption to extort the most unheard of prices for their labor."[63] Most people, however, found it easier to blame planters rather than face the more difficult reality that the Confederacy required better-coordinated regional and national markets, supported by sufficient transportation and a currency that built confidence instead of suspicion. Sentiment was swinging toward the idea that attacking substitution would solve two problems with one solution: add more manpower to the army and eliminate the people who conducted most of the speculation and hoarding that drove up food prices.

The representatives who assembled for the fourth session of the First Confederate Congress in December showed that they had strong instincts for survival. The public outcry made it clear that the Confederacy had three problems to address: manpower for the army, food for soldiers and civilians, and a way to fund everything through a sensible monetary policy. President Davis reinforced these priorities in his annual address on December 7, in which he ranked the currency as requiring the utmost attention. Concerning manpower, the president asked for elimination of substitution, a new exemption law, and greater use of African Americans to free able-bodied Confederate Virginians for the army. He hoped Congress would enlist all men in the army so that the executive branch could decide who should serve as producers.[64]

The ax fell first on substitution, with legislation ending the practice in late December. Only two representatives reportedly voted against it. No one even remotely considered sending the mercenaries home: substitutes would remain in the service for the duration. Less certainty surrounded what to do with the men who had paid for their services, the so-called principals. Some planters and professionals (lawyers, editors, and doctors) openly and indignantly defended the right of these men to remain out of the service. Any change in the law amounted to a breach of a legally executed contract. Davis, however, had prepared for this argument by having the attorney general research the subject. He ruled that substitution was a privilege the government could revoke—that whatever contract existed occurred in private between the substitute and the principal and had nothing to do with the Confederacy. Congressmen such as Louis T. Wigfall used this ruling to help carry the bill to passage. Almost immediately, word went down to enrolling officers to accept no more substitutes and begin forcing the principals into the army. The action occurred just in time to head off protests growing within the military itself. A memorial had arrived in Richmond on January 7 from officers in Longstreet's army requesting that the government throw into the service those people who had hired substitutes.[65]

To the amazement of Charles Button, the measure provoked little outrage. The editor of the Lynchburg *Virginian* opposed forcing principals into the army as an unconstitutional act violating "a solemn contract between the Government and its citizens, well calculated to impair public confidence in the plighted faith of the former." However, instead of complaining as Button anticipated, most men wondered if the new act allowed them to select their branch of service. The Conscription Bureau gave principals until February 1 to make this decision; after that, they lost freedom of choice.[66] It is unknown how many took this course, but the number of arrivals at camps of instruction between mid-February and early March bulged dramatically in Virginia from the 526 of the previous month to 1,476, the second-highest total for any month during the entire war.[67] Few people other than former principals could have swelled the numbers because almost no one else remained on the home front. In a census of manpower throughout the Confederacy, a conscription officer on January 25, 1864, estimated that Virginia had enlisted 138,489 men between ages 18 and 45. With another 25,063 exempted, the total came to 163,552, or fully 93 percent of the eligible pool.[68]

On February 17, Confederate lawmakers completed most of Davis's agenda with a flurry of legislation that contracted the currency, conscripted free blacks into military labor, increased taxes, and limited exemptions. The currency law forced the public to trade notes for Confederate bonds or incur a fluctuating penalty based on the denomination of money kept beyond certain dates.[69] Free blacks between 18 and 50 would be drafted and paid $11 per month—far below what they could earn on the home front—to build fortifications, serve as teamsters, assist in hospitals, mine nitre, and perform other work determined by the secretary of war. The act also entitled the War Department to impress up to 20,000 slaves if the number of free blacks fell short. The tax bill significantly raised the burden on all civilians, although it softened the blow by including deductions for heads of households, widows, children, and sons in the army.[70]

Public reaction focused on the currency law. Ruffin praised the laws and noted that he encountered little dissatisfaction except among speculators. William M. Blackford, a banker in Lynchburg, admitted that the tax bill hit him hard, taking as much as $6,000 from his salary of $8,000. "Yet strange to say," he noticed, "no one grumbles. I think the currency bill [is] about as good as could have been devised under the desperate circumstances of the case." Not all shared Blackford's opinion. A man in Richmond counseled his wife to put the couple's money toward land and investments other than Confederate bonds, which he presumed would not be worth much after the war. "The world is up and down since the tax bill & currency act," he wrote. "Every body is crazy on the subject."[71]

A new military law, meanwhile, not only turned all civilians into soldiers but also expanded the powers of the executive branch to direct the economy. The new law forced Confederate men between 18 and 45 into the regular army and those from 17–18 and 45–50 into home units for emergency defense. In addition to government workers, ministers, physicians, and teachers, the act repealed most exemptions.

One remarkable exception to the repeal of exemptions concerned farmers who could supply food. Most scholarly attention has interpreted the fifteen-Negro law that came in under this military act as merely continuing the privileges of slave owners. Yet this portion of the law served the interests of the needy at the expense of the rich. True, the act allowed one male to remain home on farms with fifteen or more slaves. But this new regulation turned the exempted planters into government growers who had to supply crops not only to the army but also to the selected civilians in their neighborhoods at reduced prices. For the privilege of staying home, these exempted growers supplied 100 pounds of beef or pork for every slave between the ages of 16 and 60 (or an equivalent in grain), put up a bond in case of default, and maintained subsistence for their slaves. The legislation also made these producers sell goods to families of soldiers at prices established by the impressment commissioners in each state. With this extra detail, Congress had established a price provision less sweeping than the universal measure contemplated in Virginia but one that allowed families with men in the army to purchase foodstuffs at less than market rates.[72] With mobilization in the Old Dominion and the Confederacy running at better than 80 percent, this act affected a huge portion of the nation and came close to nationalizing prices for everyone based on the impressment schedules. The act, however, did place a premium on loyalty by specifically designating the families of soldiers as eligible to buy at reduced rates.

With the fifteen-Negro provision and other facets of the military bill, the Congress had recorded striking achievements. Representatives had struck at the heart of public dissent by wiping out the ability of large-scale slave owners to avoid military service. They also, through a very clever means, had begun to dictate the economic production of the nation. Planters still could grow tobacco or other cash crops, if they chose; however, they first had to meet their obligation to the government for supplying foodstuffs. The new legislation also subtly turned more control of manufacturing over to the government. As with the overseer law of May 1863, the president retained the authority to designate people he considered vital for agricultural or other work. This meant that Davis could exempt from service large producers with few or no slaves to keep production going in regions with more nonslaveholders.

For manufacturing, the act had the implications of turning everyone not specifically exempted into soldiers whose economic importance would be judged by the War Department. As an enlisted man in the Confederate army, a wheelwright or carpenter could be assigned to a quartermaster's shop and then quickly returned to a regiment when a situation warranted. It was a remarkably flexible and all-encompassing system that placed inordinate power over the home front into the hands of the War Department.

The public had watched the crafting of the military bill to see whether it merely replaced one mechanism favoring large slave owners with another. They worried about rumors that a planter could exchange his status of principal for that of government grower. John Baldwin and others west of the Blue Ridge, meanwhile, feared that the fifteen slaves needed to qualify as a government grower discriminated against the Valley. In 1860 only seventy-one of more than 800 slave owners in Augusta County had the requisite amount for the exemption. Staunton and other communities also had a large number of mechanics who feared they would be sacrificed to the military. Finally, Dunkards and Mennonites worried that the legislation eliminated their status as conscientious objectors. Baldwin protested such an eventuality, claiming "they are an honest & conscientious people who would suffer martyrdom before they would take part in war which they are taught from infancy to regard as a great sin." He added that if they remained exempt, "we will not lose a soldier by such a step & will keep a fine body of farmers—who are greatly needed."[73]

The worries came to naught as the executive branch took these community needs so much into account that the number of exemptions under this act favored farmers with fewer slaves. In Virginia, more than 500 slaveholders won exemptions under the fifteen-hands rule but the combined exemptions and details for agricultural production came to 2,932 by September 1864. Most of the exempted growers were farmers with five slaves to none, which included the yeomanry. This mirrored Virginia's economic picture of smaller farms with fewer slaves per agricultural unit than the Cotton South. This was not the case everywhere. In the Deep South, large slaveholders benefited the most from this same law.[74] While statistics did not list agricultural details by region within states, a significant num-

ber probably originated from the Shenandoah Valley, a fertile region
for grasses and grains. The act also preserved exemptions for religious reasons, which further helped the Valley.

Communications with the War Department indicate that the
system of government growers took shape fairly rapidly throughout
Virginia. By March, a woman who successfully petitioned to exchange crops for cotton to clothe slaves noted that her husband sold
only at government prices and that everyone around him "must go
naked & starve before he'd break his *oath* to the *Govt* & *smuggle* anything." Another exasperated planter complained to the department
in June that no one in Bedford County could sell crops to anyone
above the scheduled prices—a condition that discriminated against
the farmer while mechanics, doctors, lawyers, and merchants faced
no similar regulation.[75] As always, confusion over a new system
somewhat hurt its effectiveness. A woman from Guinea Station just
South of Fredericksburg had the notion that the government allowed rations for poor working families. The War Department responded that no such law existed, yet the woman might have been
able to get what she wanted through her county court, many of
which were offering food to the poor. The Confederate government
merely authorized purchasing of food from selected growers; local
communities continued to be the domain for relief programs involving free aid.[76]

Slave owners holding libertarian principles cringed at the migration of power to the president. Throughout the rest of the war, national authority could interfere with local power arrangements. This
fed fears about concentrated power, despite reassurances that these
channels of power would endure only for the war. Edward Pollard
decried transferring decisions from "proper constitutional jurisdiction" and the Congress "to the exclusive discretion, caprice or mal-
ice of a single official," by which he meant Jefferson Davis. However, even Pollard understood that soldiers supported this change.
He blamed part of the expansion of executive power on the army
because it "contained the great body of voters in the country, and
was destined to hold the balance of political power in the Confederacy."[77] More people than Caperton understood the potential of
the soldiers' vote.

Pollard's comments capture the magnitude of the shift in the
third year of war toward policies that distributed the pain among
various classes. Legislation ended substitution and exemptions for
overseers. Those who remained at home sold goods to the govern-

ment and to soldiers' families at fixed prices versus what they might secure on the open market. A number of the wealthy went into the army despite having paid for substitutes. Free blacks and slaves would become even more important to war-related industries. Conscription officers scoured the state and government bureaus for men to place into the ranks. Authorities on all levels tried to placate soldiers by attending to the needs of their families, most often through charitable efforts administered by county courts and town governments. Even if these measures fell short, the blame did not necessarily fall on local officials directing the distribution of goods. During the autumn of 1863 a woman in Richmond looked at her dilapidated shoes and the tattered sleeping gowns of her children and wished that a foreign nation would wage war on the United States to make refugees of its people and lay its cities in ashes.[78]

The Union army affected more than ideology. As always, enemy soldiers snapped the fragile networks for provisions. At the end of February and in early March 1864, Union cavalry destroyed mills stuffed with government flour and a depot containing 60,000 pounds of meat. This prompted even the heartiest souls to ponder the chance of Confederate success. "I think, *under providence*," a man wrote a friend as early as December 1863, "the whole question now turns on food. If we can get meat enough, or our Soldiers will do on less than enough, we can weather all the other blunders of Mr. Davis & the Generals." He believed that all depended on whether authorities managed the effort adroitly. "Whether they will or not is another question," he continued, adding: "I hope yes; I fear no."[79]

5

Between Privation's Devil and the Union's Blue Sea, March 1864–April 1865

The Masses cannot starve and yet maintain the spirit that is necessary to uphold this great cause, and fight through this bloody war.
—Lynchburg *Virginian*, September 22, 1864

Civilians watched from hilltops while the squad of eight to ten Union soldiers carried out the destruction. As wisps of smoke thickened into clouds, one observer acknowledged the passing of a familiar landmark with: "There goes Rockland Mill." The officer leading the men had stated matter-of-factly, "Go over there and burn that mill," and the grinding of machinery gave way to the crackling of timbers. In a five-mile radius around Dayton, soldiers exacted retribution on an entire community for the death of a Union staff officer. Families slept that night on open ground within sight of the flames that hours before had been homes. Here and elsewhere Federal troops destroyed a total of 2,000 barns filled with wheat, hay, and implements; seventy mills filled with grain; and roughly 4,000 head of livestock. No one counted the homes. This was not central Georgia in the winter of 1864 but a handful of counties in the Shenandoah Valley between late September and early October. Instead of the more flamboyant title of "March to the Sea," the experience won from residents a simpler but perhaps more descriptive name—"the burning."[1]

In the final year of war, the Confederate war effort in Virginia began to unravel because of the Union army. Through cavalry that knifed into the state in late winter of 1864 and the major incursions of the spring and summer, the war penetrated more extensively into the Old Dominion, wearing down the endurance of the populace physically and psychically. Wherever the men in blue went they left devastation and a new sense of vulnerability among civilians. When Union cavalry under George Armstrong Custer patrolled north of Charlottesville on February 29, 1864, some residents hid in the bushes with their most precious property—the livestock and slaves that would help to lay in a crop. Although few casualties occurred, and Confederate soldiers restored security the next day, the episode left Louisa Minor feeling "as if the war was *being brought to our own doors*."[2] Although belief in the Confederate cause never completely disappeared, a political event reduced civilian hopes for success. After President Lincoln won reelection in November, morale among Confederate Virginians plummeted, as it appeared that the North would press the fight rather than sue for peace.

No matter how much its powers expanded, the War Department could muster only so many resources to meet this mounting pressure. Conscription officers stripped men from the home front. A minister preaching in Charlottesville noticed that the pews contained only older men with gray hair, younger men who were maimed, and women dressed in black. Most white men between the ages of 17 and 50 were in the army, leaving slaves as the only sizable group left to put into the fight. Privations tested the limits of endurance and hurt morale among all classes, not just the small-scale farmers or nonslaveholders. Large-scale farmers on whom the burden of production now rested felt besieged by their own people, as nonproducers and the poor clamored for regulated prices on foodstuffs and the Confederacy demanded slaves for production and military work. Hope remained as long as the army held the field, although toward the end of 1864 the population visibly tired of the shortages and the lack of military success. "He must be a bold man, reckless of his opinions and wild in his conjectures," an editor cogently observed in September 1864, "who will undertake to say that we can stand this evil another year." Traveling to Richmond on the James and Kanawha Canal in December 1864, Cornelia McDonald rode with a mountain man who had been drafted despite being over age 45, losing two sons in the war, having another in prison, and leaving a wife alone at home. "Groups of murmuring men were all around," she wrote, "and I first began to realize that the patience of the people was worn out; that their long suffering and endurance was to be depended on no longer; that they were beginning to see that it was of no avail to deliver the country from her enemies."[3]

Yet it took a concerted effort by the Union to break the public's will. As the government proved unable to solve the massive problems of mobilization, the Confederate citizenry relied for its morale on the army, much as Revolutionary Americans had rested their hopes on Washington's men. Consequently, as the spring campaigns opened, few Virginians at home or in the ranks considered the war a lost cause. Soldiers had spent a relatively quiet winter and remained remarkably optimistic, given the hardships experienced and the prospect of more ahead. Religious faith helped renew spirits through revivals that swept through the ranks and, although more sporadically, behind the lines. John B. Jones noticed that revivals in Richmond in October 1863 began among the Methodists, but Reformed Baptists also participated. After Jones attended one of the revivals he prayed that the religious fervor would soften the hearts of the extortioners. Farther to the interior, Sarah Strickler recorded that a new outlook on life animated many of the young girls at the Albemarle Female Institute in Charlottesville. She resisted for nearly another year before she tired of "groping in the darkness for something that I felt the need of" and joined the ranks of the converted.[4]

Robert E. Lee was seen as a more tangible savior who increased his stature by fending off Ulysses S. Grant's troops at the Wilderness and the Spotsylvania Courthouse in early May. In a strange way, the greater resources of the Union backfired psychologically as southerners marveled that their country had resisted one of the most powerful industrial nations on Earth for so long. As May gave way to June and the end of war seemed no nearer, one soldier noted: "The whole army is pervaded by a calm confidence in the wisdom of Gen Lee's dispositions and in their own ability to repel any attack of Grant's army."[5]

An improvement in material conditions—albeit small and short-lived—also fortified spirits. Pork supplies declined, but the amount of beef in the South had increased. This could not have come at a better time. Soldiers had endured a grim winter with rations at one point cut from one-half to one-quarter pound of meat per day. Stronger measures by the government eased this plight as the commissary received permission to set aside passenger trains in favor of freight cars hauling subsistence supplies. This intercession spurred railroad owners to greater efforts to maintain the flow of provisions and to keep the government out of their businesses. Blockade runners also brought in more meat. All the factors contributed to slightly better conditions in the ranks. "They issue good rations to our troops," Jed Hotchkiss wrote home that spring, "better than ever before—but corn meal is the only bread stuff they issue now."[6] This infusion of provisions fed the soldier's soul as well. Even in bleak January 1864 a man in Jubal Early's command could feel warm about the cause. He told his wife that the enemy was deluded in thinking that the Confederacy tottered because of internal problems. "Our army is certainly better organized than it has ever been to my knowledge," he observed, "and it is prepared to stand a harder shock than ever. All seem to anticipate what is coming and to prepare themselves for it."[7]

Civilians shared in the slightly better times, although less consistently, depending on the area. The closer persons lived to the front, the less their lives improved. One impressment agent sent down the Valley from Staunton could journey only as far as Shenandoah County because of Union soldiers. He reported that flour in the region cost a great deal, corn could not be found, and bacon could be secured in North Carolina for $2 less per pound.[8] After years of occupation by an enemy, Loudoun County in Northern Virginia had little left to offer. On the other hand, deep within the southern Piedmont, prices in Lynchburg stabilized or declined for a brief moment in the spring of 1864. The cost of pork and beef held at previous levels, but the supply improved from early in the year. Sugar dropped from $8 to $7.50 per 100 pounds. Overall, the Confederacy was converting to growing food instead of tobacco and cotton. Parts of the Shenandoah Valley and central Georgia especially promised a bountiful harvest of grain, raising their importance as strategic targets by the federal command.[9]

Too many hands reached for the same goods to allow the home front to achieve an equilibrium for long. The Union army would not rest. In May and June, Union soldiers ripped up each of Virginia's four major railroad routes and destroyed 491,000 rations in one depot alone. Where the enemy failed to penetrate, local and national agents competed for the same food. In Augusta County in late April 1864, local justices revoked ceilings on prices in a desperate attempt to gather food for needy families by offering more money than the army's agents.[10] Impressment became the principle irritation on the home front for the last year of the war but not among the lower classes usually blamed for this discontent. The most vocal protests emanated from prosperous farmers and large slave owners who provided the biggest targets for government agents while the poor and the nonproducers supported impressment so that they could acquire food at regulated prices.

Tactful agents might have been able to reduce the friction, but good help was as hard to find as food. Manpower shortages left behind men of lesser abilities for bureaucratic positions. A quartermaster in Lynchburg lamented that while he tried to hire the best agents, he found none with the right combination of intellect and judgment. An officer in the Conscription Bureau echoed these comments. Answering allegations of deficiencies in the system to the inspector general's office, officer George W. Lay reminded critics that the personnel limited the systems that could be devised, adding that the bureau's agents worked hard but represented "the gleanings of material unavailable for other uses."[11] Abundant proof supported him. In one case, agents impressed the team of horses belonging to a detailed soldier who hauled materials for a foundry in Lynchburg that made military supplies. The War Department eventually ordered the horses returned to its own contractor.[12]

Agents and civilians wrestled a great deal over horses and mules. The military needed stock for the coming campaign. It was an insatiable appetite. Between October 1863 and February 1865, the quartermaster depot in Charlottesville alone had stabled nearly 7,000 horses.[13] Civilians required the same animals to plow fields or haul materials. To protect communities from overzealous or inept officers, the Confederacy appointed local assessors to hear appeals of impressments. When a citizen from Southampton County protested that an agent had taken horses during the cultivating season, the quartermaster stopped the process until a hearing could be held. In these cases, two disinterested citizens—one chosen by the local person and the second by the agent—confirmed the need for the animal and the price. In case of disagreements, the procedure called for the selection of a third party that both agreed upon. Assessors then publicized rulings through newspaper notices that described the animals and the prices granted. The advertisements also indicate that disputes occurred frequently: they routinely contained the names of three assessors instead of two. The procedure quieted complaints, although it never stifled them.[14]

Conflict over impressment did not always stem from expansion of government power. Sometimes, personality conflicts between local elite lay at the heart of friction. William Langhorne in Campbell County's district served notice on V. M. Epps to bring two mules to the courthouse for arbitration. After a hearing, the board ruled that Epps had to hand over a mule. He accused the board of biased treatment because persons from his neighborhood, named E. A. Rawlins and Mrs. Jones, did not contribute their livestock. Langhorne explained that Rawlins had furnished 500 bushels of corn and 100 stacks of fodder without compulsion and proposed to furnish a mule. Mrs. Jones apparently offered similar contributions. "I was informed that the said Epps had never furnished anything to the Government which he was not compelled to furnish," Langhorne told the local quartermaster in charge of these matters. "I therefore did not choose to propose any terms to Mr. Epps, preferring that his case should be decided by the tribunal provided by law." Langhorne then freely admitted that he had treated Epps with greater severity. "The only pleasure which I have in my present position is in being the agent of the law to force such men as V. M. Epps to do their duty to the Government."[15]

Epps refused to let matters lie. He charged Langhorne with shirking his duty as an able-bodied conscript, to which the accused replied that despite a medical exemption he had volunteered for government work that paid less than he could earn in private business. Neighbors and a quartermaster at Clarksville affirmed that Epps sold grain to the government in 1862 and 1863; however, the quartermaster's office backed the government's position and there the appeal ended, except that the quota against Epps was increased to two mules. The stubborn Epps argued that rival planter Rawlins had more slaves (thirty-seven as opposed to thirty-three) but only contributed one mule to the government. Epps received no satisfaction for his claims.[16]

Tensions between the Langhornes and the Eppses of Virginia may have continued prewar rivalries. Both sides in the above dispute appeared to have supporters. Langhorne moved in high circles, numbering among his friends Thomas Bocock, Speaker of the Confederate House, and Judge William Daniel. As the owner of thirty-three slaves, Epps had a less influential circle of friends who nonetheless supported him in resisting the government. Because of the willingness of friends to rally behind him, Epps might have had a case that he was unjustly discriminated against. However, the evidence makes it equally plausible that he cared primarily for himself.

The incident clearly supports studies that reveal factionalism within the planter class over the prosecution of the war and the nature of the Confederacy. Some men in Virginia assumed a libertarian posture in believing that government caused many of the Confederacy's problems by interfering with the market and preventing its "natural" inducements from functioning. These men argued that if farmers received market value they would produce more surplus, part with crops more readily, and earn funds for increased taxes that would allow the Confederacy to pay more for subsistence. Another group of planters had emerged with a greater commitment to what today would be called national goals, or those subordinating local, short-term interests. To accomplish their ends, they exacted sacrifices on their own class. This group had existed since the beginning of the war but assumed concrete form during the debates to eliminate substitution in late 1863. Many former Whigs assumed this posture, although not exclusively. In Charlottesville, William C. Rives and Thomas Jefferson Randolph provided key leadership and often led efforts calling for more sacrifice from leading citizens.[17] Members of this group, however, did not always subordinate local to national interests. John Baldwin in the Shenandoah Valley conceivably belonged to this class, yet he supported strong, centralized measures for prosecuting the war only until those policies collided with the interests of the mechanics, small slaveholders, and sectarians among his constituents.

Nowhere did these differences come to the fore more prominently than in the controversy during the summer of 1864 over the prices to be paid for impressed goods. The commissioners who set the state's impressment prices decided to increase what the government paid for enumerated goods beginning with the July/August schedules. Bowing to the wishes of large farmers—with a sympathetic push from Secretary of War James A. Seddon, who as a Virginian stood to benefit—the commissioners arbitrarily multiplied by six the prevailing price on key articles such as flour, wheat, corn, and hay. Wheat thus went from $5 per bushel to $30; family-grade flour jumped from $28 to $168. Planters and large nonslaveowning farmers believed that the boost was long overdue. Impressment prices had held steady for about half a year while the cost of goods had soared. Even with dramatic increases, the price of impressed goods lagged behind the marketplace by more than 50 percent, as flour in Richmond sold for $350 to $400 per barrel.[18]

Outrage greeted publication of the schedules. The Lynchburg newspaper called the prices "The Road to Ruin," and Charles Blackford of the same city deemed it "an official acknowledgment of bankruptcy" and "a deathblow to the currency." He noted that the farmers immediately would increase their prices, causing him to wonder, "How are our people to live?"[19] In Charlottesville, the *Daily Chronicle* echoed these concerns, particularly that the price schedule caused farmers to lose confidence in Confederate bonds. Congress in February 1864 had contracted the currency to curb inflation, but the state commissioners wiped out any gains. Just as Virginians had less money to pay for goods, the schedules raised the costs of commodities essential for subsistence. Because the schedules acted as an anchor on the free market, the new level meant that everyone would pay more for everything with less money in circulation.[20]

Throughout Virginia people protested the decision in county meetings that gained vigor the farther west one traveled. The Albemarle County meeting consisted of "the very largest and most intelligent producers." It included Thomas Jefferson Randolph; E. Coles, from one of the leading slave-owning families; Slaughter W. Ficklin, a planter famous for breeding livestock; and Dabney Minor, a large-scale planter and agriculturist who had contributed articles to farm journals. They understood the danger to public loyalties that would come through allowing the prices to rise. In Augusta County, John M. McCue and state legislator Hugh Sheffey chaired the meeting. Although these men were small slaveholders who conducted some farming, their lives revolved around towns, the law, and politics. Their focus thus was not surprising when they noted: "The schedule may swell the nominal profits of a few large landed proprietors, but its effects on the non producers, and middle classes, will be sad indeed." "What the farmers need," they stressed, "is not exorbitant prices, but a sound currency—exemption from unnecessary interference with their labour—protection from the lawless conduct of petty officers and a proper regulation of the rail roads so as to afford them early access to market with their crops."[21]

Economic interests provided only one reason to oppose the new schedules: humanitarian concerns added moral furor to the backlash. Opponents noted the impact on the poor and the families dependent on community aid. County courts raised relief by purchasing goods based on prices set by the impressment schedules. With the schedules increasing, communities would have a greater tax burden to support the needy. In Henrico County near Richmond, the County Court went from appropriating a mere $4,000 for relief of soldiers' families in March 1863 to $172,000 for the fiscal year 1864–1865. Without accounting for the new schedules, taxes to support this charitable effort had increased one hundredfold, from

$20,605 to $206,058.[22] The new prices also hit soldiers in the pocketbooks. Effective June 9 Congress had boosted the pay of soldiers, but an increase of $7 per month paled against the escalation of flour and corn prices by 500 percent.[23]

At best, the new schedules struck many as unpatriotic, but the public soon had evidence that collusion within the Confederate government had created this situation. When a congressional investigation reported on the persons who had benefited from the new schedule for wheat, Secretary of War James A. Seddon led the list of fifty-five producers who garnered $30 to $40 for their wheat. For his 430 bushels, Seddon received $17,200. Under the old schedules at $5 per bushel, his same crop would have earned $2,150. Pressure had built in January, before these findings became public, for Davis to overhaul his cabinet. When Speaker of the House Thomas Bocock, a fellow Virginian, began to feel the same way, the pressure increased and Seddon resigned on February 5, 1865. The public subsequently learned about how the secretary of war had sold his wheat at $40 per bushel, but his departure, along with larger concerns over the end of the war, served to defuse their anger.[24]

Adding to the public's dissatisfaction was that certain civilians, despite "talking poor," made conspicuous examples of their prosperity. A blacksmith in Nelson County who owned 4,000 acres of land in the tobacco belt amazed a visiting cavalry officer. The soldier wrote home that this civilian "is very much down in the mouth—talks of subjugation & said he *was starving*." The blacksmith told this sad story amid gulps of ham and cabbage, cold roast beef, baked potatoes, batter bread, biscuits, milk, and butter, washed down with coffee and a few pitiful swigs of apple brandy. This did not win any sympathy from the soldier who watched him.[25]

Outrage again was not relegated to the poor. Within the army, men from wealthier families had adopted the perspective of nonproducers dependent on their pay and community relief to help families. Charles Blackford came from a prosperous family in Lynchburg that typically had identified with planters before the war. Inside the army he sided with nonproducers against the large-farm owners who manipulated regulations for their own ends. "The producer has everything," he wrote, noting that most of them were exempted from military service because of their productive capabilities. "He exchanges his corn and wheat for coffee and sugar, prates about the hardships of war and the high prices, brings nothing and complacently asks the starving wife of his friend who is in the army $100 a bushel for wheat, $4 a quart for tomatoes, and if he does not get it he locks the wheat up for higher prices and feeds the tomatoes to the hogs."[26]

Faced with a persistent vocal challenge from all ranks of society, the commissioners repealed the prices in August and returned to the previous schedule. They did so reluctantly, honestly dumbfounded that the deference granted them by the masses had limits. Like many of the wealthy, they assumed that planters knew best and reasoned that their own personal fortunes as large-scale farmers determined the success of the Confederacy. Upon recovering from the public furor, they took umbrage over having to bend to popular will. William B. Harrison, one of the state commissioners who set the prices, wrote a colleague that "the clamour against us in order to make us put down the prices in the schedule is nothing but a nefarious scheme to deprive the agricultural class of their rights." He complained that his position as a commissioner was compromised by having "to fix prices to suit the public will" and not the dictates of his judgment. He also bemoaned the loss of support from Secretary of War Seddon, who had caved in quickly once controversy arose.[27]

That the conflict over prices occurred at all attests to the effectiveness of the fifteen-Negro law in restricting sales of crops. Passed in February 1864 by the Confederate Congress, the legislation forced farmers (with the usual few finding alternative markets) to sell goods at stipulated prices. These growers noted that this was not fair—that they sold in a regulated market while buying in a fluctuating one. The costs of leather, wagons, and agricultural supplies escalated without government controls, causing farmers to demand regulation of the services of mechanics, doctors, and merchants.[28] They tried to fix prices on their expenses but failed to win limits on iron, leather, and other goods. An increase in impressment prices provided the one way to address their predicament.

The trouble was that by this time the poor, the government workers, the families of soldiers, most townspeople, and nonagricultural workers in general had grown dependent on the prices fixed by impressment. If anything, this group wanted increased government help of a certain kind. More people, not fewer, were trying to gain permission to purchase foodstuffs at reduced rates. When machinists of the Virginia and Tennessee Railroad struck for higher wages in the summer of 1864—threatening, ironically, to report for military duty if their demands went unmet—officials placated the men by allowing them to buy provisions at government prices. By August 1, the government headed off further unrest by authorizing all civilian employees to enjoy this benefit, and bureau chiefs began taking a census of applicable employees.[29]

As the war continued, the Congress debated about opening this privilege to all citizens. Further depreciation of the currency and continuing problems with food supplies caused a bill to be introduced in the Senate to grant all civilians the ability to purchase goods at the army's impressment prices; however, the measure was a desperate move that lacked a clear champion. Even the bill's sponsor, Senator Edward Sparrow of Louisiana, voiced concern about its constitutionality. The legislation also met with the usual complaint that it discriminated against the farmer. In a matter of weeks it was clear the effort would go nowhere, although a handful of Virginians mounted a last-ditch effort in December to push the matter down to the state level and have legislatures set maximum prices on all articles, agricultural and mechanical. Led by Fayette McMullin of Smyth County, even this maneuver failed as another Virginian, John Baldwin from the Valley, spoke against the bill to protect the artisans and mechanics in his constituency from price controls on their products.[30]

These controversies diverted the public from the more complicated factors undermining subsistence. It was easier to blame the large agriculturists exempted for production and public officials who supported fraudulent ventures rather than a host of problems that caused the shortages plaguing the Virginia home front. County agents combed the countryside for food to supply the poor, either a step ahead of or behind purchasers for the Confederate army. Competition for those goods increased as civilians shouldered their way onto the list of citizens who could purchase food at government prices. Even nature conspired against Virginia as a wet spring delayed corn planting and a subsequent drought lasting until August hurt the crop. Transportation broke down more frequently, hampering distribution. As money lost value, Confederate impressment agents found that farmers would not accept government money. For those who would, the government often did not have enough funds to pay. An agent who purchased for the region east of the Blue Ridge Mountains had no funds and remained behind in payments. Growers in general preferred gold but accepted treasury notes for their products.[31]

Making matters worse, the Union army increased its activity west of the Blue Ridge where precious crops were maturing. In

June, Major General David Hunter pushed a force up the Shenandoah Valley and deep into the Piedmont, but this thrust was checked at Lynchburg by a detached force under Jubal Early. Hunter had burned homes and conducted other depredations in the Valley but, inexplicably, had passed over the crops. Hopes among the citizenry rebounded, especially as Early's men pushed their way north into Maryland. Life, however, shortly turned worse for Virginians. The Union army returned with a vengeance to the Shenandoah Valley as Major General Phil Sheridan carried out his orders to inflict massive destruction.

Sheridan's three victories in the Shenandoah Valley in September and October 1864 finished a process that years of war had begun. The invading enemy disrupted supply networks, compelling more and more Virginians to seek basic foodstuffs beyond their communities. Civilians rarely dealt with neighbors anymore but had to find goods anywhere they could. When they did, they had to beg permission from the government to transport supplies. The military in 1864 monitored all shipments to crack down on speculation. Army officers regularly turned down requests to send materials across the state, keeping goods where commissaries needed them. The practice also blocked the flow of supplies from areas of abundance to those with scarcities. Even if a farmer had provisions, neighbors might not be able to buy them. The owner of the Albemarle Female Institute in August unsuccessfully petitioned to secure goods from another portion of the state because the crops of local farmers had been committed to the government.[32]

Under such conditions, the suspicion built that communities withheld goods from other regions, heightening friction between town and country. Rumors circulated that county courts in Virginia prohibited shipments of grain outside their jurisdictions. This may have been an overreaction to a petition by residents of Albemarle County who asked the government not to take more crops from their community. Whether true or false, the news upset the editor in Lynchburg where refugees had increased the burden on the city. The Campbell County Court had established 25 pounds of meal or 20 pounds of flour as the monthly stipend for indigent families, with more allowed depending on the number of children. By late September little wheat could be found. "Between Confederate and county impressing agents," a local editor commented, "the people in the towns are in a fair way to suffer."[33] His lament was not unique. Across Virginia communities struggled to meet their obligations to the nation and their own needy. In the Valley, the justices in Augusta County had to grant extensions for paying county taxes because of property lost to Sheridan's men. At a time when more help was needed for civilians, fewer resources existed.[34]

Some families could not receive even the meager relief supplied by their communities. Living in Union-controlled areas, Confederate civilians faced grim choices. Some left home to become refugees in the South. Others headed north. Still more remained, forcing them to live off rations they could beg from the Union military. Joseph Barton, who lived near Winchester, made such a request. He petitioned Major General Sheridan for fodder to feed his cows so they would produce milk. The youngest of his five children was starving because the child was too young to take anything else. Sheridan never answered the request, despite endorsement by a Union officer. The child passed away.[35]

In these circumstances, the Confederacy mounted impressive efforts to feed the military—but at continual cost to the home front. In December 1864 and January 1865 not enough meat could be found in the Old Dominion for both civilians and soldiers, even though orders had been given in October to impress all necessary supplies. Meat was available in North Carolina and Georgia, but Sherman's raid complicated transportation. To avert a crisis, it took repair of the rails in Georgia and a concerted effort to ship food in from North Carolina. Miraculously, the commissary was able to gather enough supplies for the army in Virginia up to the end of the war. By April, when the military evacuated the capital, rations remained on hand at Richmond, Lynchburg, and Danville. The countryside, however, was exhausted, and a desperate Congress finally lifted all controls to let local conditions determine prices in the hopes that greed would stimulate more production. The measure came too late to have any impact.[36]

Food was not the only declining resource that affected the spirit of civilians. The continual quest for soldiers sent the government on a downward spiral of desperation until, by March 1865, the Congress disbanded the Conscription Bureau, returning responsibilities for this effort to individual states.

Authorities began by targeting free blacks for factory work and military labor to release white men for combat. Some Confederate contractors preferred the free blacks to white labor. The superintendent of the harness shops at Clarksville begged his Richmond superiors to let him pay these workers more than $75 per month, to keep them happy, and recruit more. He reported that they were "carpenters, blacksmiths or blacksmiths helpers, and selected as the best of that class of mechanics to be found in the neighborhood, some of them in fact superior workmen to many white men."[37] African Americans served as conscripts in quartermaster shops, nitre mines, ordnance departments, railroad companies, and hospitals, among other organizations crucial to the war effort. While helping the military, the draft of free blacks hurt the local economies of artisan-starved Virginia. Conscription during 1864 accounted for anywhere from 60 percent to 72 percent of the remaining 2,500 eligible males. Figures for Albemarle, Augusta, and Campbell counties illustrate what these men meant to their communities. The draft claimed 107 free blacks. Most were farmers and laborers, but fifty-two listed work as mechanics or small shopkeepers. The leading occupations included twelve blacksmiths, nine tanners, seven shoemakers, five carpenters, and five coopers. Everyone recognized their importance: the General Assembly protested the draft, fearing the men might desert to the enemy and their skills would be lost forever.[38]

Slaves provided a larger pool of workers than free blacks but they became as precious as food, with planters, government contractors, and military bureaus competing for their services. Quartermaster depots in particular had become large operations. The shop in Lynchburg that fixed wagons, harnesses, and other transportation equipment contained fifty-four white workers, four free blacks, and 260 slaves. The quartermaster depot at Staunton employed roughly 120 African Americans, considerably less than Lynchburg but probably the most in the Shenandoah Valley. Nitre and mining operations also used large numbers of black people, while ordnance shops, which paid the highest wages, favored white laborers.[39] The demand only increased in the autumn of 1864 when the government tried to replace potential soldiers with slaves for manufacturing work. The policy hurt regions with smaller slave populations. In the southwest neither nonconscripted free blacks nor slaves could be found in November 1864 to fill jobs in an iron works in Wytheville.[40]

Resistance among planters frustrated the efficient deployment of slave labor. Never warm to the idea of sending slaves to workplaces from which many escaped, planters became downright hostile in the final years of war.[41] State and national authorities interpreted these actions as a lack of patriotism; however, the story was more complex. Some large-scale farm owners obviously cared more about themselves than the Confederacy and deserved condemnation. But planter resistance arose from several factors: long-term experience with impressment, much of it negative; communities pulled in multiple ways to furnish labor; and the Union army's impact on helping slaves to escape.

All told, Virginians faced seven requisitions for slave labor—the first three through March 1863 for state service and the remainder for the Confederate government. On county courts fell the responsibility for implementing the procedure. Augusta, Campbell, and Albemarle counties answered the first calls as honestly as one could expect, although with some complaining. Communities first compiled a census of slaves, then quotas went out to individual slave owners with the sheriff sent to enforce compliance and levy fines. Few furnished more than one slave per call. Eventually the legislature dictated that no more than one-fifth of a region's slaves would be taken. Anyone who had lost a third of his slaves would be exempt.[42]

By the fall of 1863 cooperation diminished. Augusta and Campbell counties failed to comply with calls for slave labor, although the reasons varied. In the Shenandoah Valley, the justices themselves disobeyed the order while the magistrates in the southern Piedmont tried to comply but produced pitiful results, eventually fining at least 17 slave owners who resisted. Local leaders in either case expressed a number of legitimate complaints about the process. Augusta magistrates noted that conscription had taken so much white labor that the community could not function without slaves. All three regions also contained hospitals, supply depots, quartermaster shops, and government businesses that drained the local labor supply, circumstances the Confederacy failed to consider when setting quotas for impressment. Most important, authorities complained that the government did not compensate slave owners adequately for losses from death, dismemberment, or escape of slaves. Although in agreement with slave owners, the Confederate Congress had not yet set an appropriation for the expense.[43]

Adding to the problem was the fact that slaves ran away, especially when Union soldiers entered a community. At least 30,000 escaped to Union-controlled areas by 1863; an untold number fled in the last 16 months of the conflict. Out of an 1860 population of nearly half a million, this still left a considerable number at home—perhaps as many as 90,000 males between the ages of 18 and 45.[44] Although seemingly a large figure, the Confederate war machine consumed huge numbers for work on plantations and in hospitals, quartermaster shops, commissary depots, munitions factories, teamster wagons, and field units. Every loss hurt, especially late in the war when Union raids provided more opportunities for escape just as slaves were needed most.

Because of the enemy's impact, the government tended to use free labor in areas Stephen Ash has termed the Confederate frontier—regions held by the South but penetrated sporadically by federal soldiers.[45] In Virginia's case, important mining operations for gunpowder lay within the frontier. An inspector of a nitre manufactory near Staunton reported that the mines had experienced two raids, which prevented "the employment of slave labour to any extent; were it not for this difficulty I should think slave labour ought to be substituted for four fifths of the men now employed." Nestled within the more secure hills of the southern Piedmont, Lynchburg's nitre operation depended primarily on African American workers.[46]

Matters worsened after the Union army stepped up activity in 1864. Henrico County near Richmond illustrates how thinly the war had spread slave resources. This county had cooperated with the seven requisitions for slaves, but by January 1865 magistrates finally protested the quota for 130 slaves. Federal soldiers occupied areas of the county containing the largest slaveholdings. Magistrates scraped together 102 slaves but only by taking them from hospitals and government facilities. They could not raise enough by tapping individual farmers as in the past. The Westham Iron Works yielded fifteen slaves; Camp Winder Hospital, another eleven; Chimborazo Hospital, ten; and Camp Jackson Hospital, eight. No one said how these positions would be filled.[47]

Governor William Smith, however, believed that the lack of response was due to poor patriotism among the agricultural interests. In February 1865 the governor met the situation head-on by calling for legislation that would impose more stringent quotas. Smith ignored the fact that conditions had deteriorated to the breaking point. Entire communities, and not just individuals, resisted the calls. Bureaucratic channels had collapsed as desperate military officers requisitioned supplies and workers regardless of conflict with other impressment activity. For instance, as state officials prepared quotas that communities received in March 1865, counties in the interior of the state were still trying to comply with earlier demands from Brigadier General Raleigh E. Colston. When receiving a third requisition from the state, the clerk from Campbell County Court just about gave up. He responded that the area still had thirty slaves to furnish from the prior calls. "We are then, you see, between the devil and the deep sea," he reported. "With two requisitions from the Gov. and one from Genl. Colston, we are likely to be *overtasked*. This last request of the Gov. should be revoked, else we will suffer unduly."[48] When the magistrates subsequently discovered that the community already had 198 slaves serving as government employees—exceeding the quota for the most recent impressment—they declined to send more, saying the community had fulfilled its obligation. The governor was not impressed with this reasoning.[49]

These final calls for black labor came as the Confederacy considered using slaves as soldiers. Planters themselves were divided in their opinions about the issue. R. T. Hubard told his brother, the commissioner who set impressment prices, that he adamantly opposed using slaves to fight. He believed that slaves would desert, adding, "Those who advocate this plan have probably no negroes of their own."[50] Hubard miscalculated in thinking that no slaveholders supported the measure. Some masters pressed for using slaves in the ranks for practical reasons. M. G. Harman, one of the larger slave owners in Augusta County, pushed President Davis in January 1865 to use Afro-Virginians in the Confederate army. Harman had lost about half of his slaves already and knew that they might be put to use by the Union. Nationalists such as Edmund Ruffin also preferred to lose some slaves rather than face subjugation by the North that would be worse, he predicted, than the colonists had suffered under English rule.[51]

The debate gained momentum over the winter of 1864–1865 as military defeats and Lincoln's election rocked the Confederacy. The administration tested the idea in Richmond newspapers friendly to the government. State lawmakers passed resolutions prodding senators in Congress to reverse themselves and support the position. General Lee helped the cause by declaring that he favored slaves as soldiers. Some planters never could accept the decision. A slave owner from Campbell County recorded his disgust, saying, "I think we have disgraced ourselves and besides I think we are whiped[;] the idea of having negroes fighting to enslave their offspring is more than ridiculous." Yet he noted that a vote within Company B, 11th Virginia Infantry, revealed that most soldiers favored the bill with only six opposed.[52] On March 13, 1865, the legislation passed, although national authorities never clarified whether the slaves who fought would go free, leaving the decision to state officials and individual planters. The measure came too late to have an impact on the fighting.[53]

Something this drastic needed to be done because the Confederacy was running out of able bodies. Early in 1864 officials in the Conscription Bureau recognized that eliminating substitution and tightening exemptions would not produce enough fighting men. Virginia had roughly 93 percent of all males of military-age either in the army or committed to war-related work. John Preston of the Conscription Bureau reported on April 30, 1864, that the military had so depleted the farming class that future enlistments risked hurting production of food. Some opportunities remained in Georgia, Alabama, Mississippi, and Florida, but the bureau had exhausted Virginia and both Carolinas. Only a few alternatives existed: to revoke all details, appeal to patriotism, or hope that enough boys came of age. "For conscription from the general population," he gloomily predicted, "the functions of this Bureau may cease with the termination of the year 1864."[54]

Preston believed one group might yield results—the nonproducers: bankers, clerks, police, magistrates, overseers of the poor, sheriffs, and public functionaries. Getting these men into the ranks would not be easy, Preston warned, because communities used these positions to shield some men.[55] Elections for local officials in May indicated that the offices attracted men hoping to hide from military service. Candidates in Lynchburg were "as thick as leaves; as plenty as blackberries; as busy as bees; as importunate as beggars." This observer added, "the dear people cannot go amiss now for public servants. Every fellow wants to be his servant."[56]

Shirkers could gain only limited sanctuary through holding local office. The exemption process left it to governors to decide which local community and county officials were a necessity. As people heard that he planned to force all magistrates under age 45 into the army, Governor Smith's mail filled with petitions from officials attempting to hang on to their exemptions.[57] Under some pressure, Smith reluctantly admitted it was necessary to keep some men home for these tasks but certainly not all. By July he announced the criteria for gaining exemption from military service. First preference went to men over age 45, then, in order of importance, re-elected justices; those who had served in the army; family men; those in feeble health; large-scale producers; those managing estates of widows and orphans; and finally men approaching age 45. By December 1864 he had reduced the number of justices of the peace allowed in communities from four to three per district to force more of these officials into the army.[58]

Smith policed these offices fairly well. When a Confederate inspector general audited public officials in Virginia in September, fifty-one of fifty-three justices in his jurisdiction were over age 45. The other two were 17–18 years old. Younger men performed police duties, but 90 of the 94 between the ages of 18 and 45 presented nothing out of the ordinary. The total number of Virginians assigned at this time to community offices and to work with railroads, telegraph companies, foundries, mills, and other essential industries amounted to 2,731—1,711 of draft age.[59] Although this was a small number, the practice nonetheless irritated Smith because many justices retained exemptions even though hailing from parts of Virginia occupied by the enemy. On December 7, 1864, the governor spent a significant portion of his annual address urging the legislature to close this loophole.[60]

Drastic times continued to demand drastic measures. After Atlanta fell and Jubal Early's command lost twice in the Shenandoah Valley in September, the Confederacy needed more men. The result was General Order No. 77 of October 8, 1864, which revoked all details and temporary exemptions. All men between 18 and 45 years old had to report to camps of instruction, no matter if they were mechanics, millers, or farmers. "Experts," or soldiers with technical backgrounds related to ordnance and munitions, constituted one exception. These men would remain in their jobs until bureau officials could assess their importance to maintaining production. For a short time, exempted agricultural workers also remained at home under the fifteen-Negro law.[61] In effect, there was no such thing as a white male civilian within military age, except for the infirm and those needed to produce food.

This final sweep of the home front resulted in 4,538 men reporting to Camp Lee near Richmond, a number that exceeded by more than three times any other month for the entire war. The numbers were too large to process. The conscription officer for the state begged volunteers to forego physical exams to expedite assignments within the army.[62] Lynchburg alone lost roughly 150 men in this call. Two in particular caused a minor fuss because they operated the gas works, and citizens complained about potentially being plunged into darkness. The enrollment officer, Captain E. J. Anderson, would allow no exceptions; the commandant of post had to intercede on behalf of the gas workers and the town. Even four bank officers from the city who filed habeas corpus complaints to prevent their going found themselves on the way to Richmond with the promise that they could return when their cases came up at the next term of court. Less than a month after the general orders came down, Jed Hotchkiss noticed the impact. "The reserves & detailed men," he wrote his wife, "are coming in rapidly and being examined & assigned either to the army or light duty, as they are found capable or not." He added that little could be done to prevent an acquaintance from reporting because "the Government is determined to have *every one*."[63]

To ensure that men could not hide from the order, the War Department sent inspectors into communities to find able-bodied conscripts. These agents from the offices of the adjutant general and the inspector general determined the experts who would remain with government contractors and shops. One of the inspectors, Thomas Y. Peyton, covered much of central Virginia. In Lynchburg, he found approximately 117 men working with quartermaster, commissary, ordnance, and other departments. Fourteen had been turned over because of the order in October. When visiting Charlottesville, Peyton identified only seventeen men working in war-related work and concluded that eight should be retained while the rest would go into the military.[64]

These last efforts increased disenchantment with the war and sparked resistance among the people targeted by the draft officials. The action had fallen heaviest on mechanics, laborers, and farmers with fewer slaves than the fifteen necessary to earn an exemption. Areas of smaller slaveholdings such as the Shenandoah Valley stood to lose most of their laborers to the military. Some refused to go. An inspector from the adjutant general's office reported as delinquent ninety-two detailed workers in Augusta County, including forty-one farmers, twelve millers, nine blacksmiths, eight shoemakers, and four millwrights. Not all had resisted the order revoking their details; some had entered the army directly, by-passing Camp Lee. Others, however, went to Rockingham County, which had been spared from the call because of Sheridan's raids. Still others had deserted, presumably to the enemy. In another report, the inspector referred to the 291 detailed soldiers working in nitre operations throughout nine counties in the Valley as "brush men." Without guarantees that they could continue working, he explained, the men headed for the brush: "An attempt to arrest one, is but the signal for the whole to take to the woods or desert to the Enemy." A woman in the Valley observed about this time that "Davis is robing the cradle & grave, this last call the most of the men went to Yankeedom."[65]

The orders of October also began to signal the death knell of the Conscription Bureau. It would take four more months, but the government's latest actions renewed the struggle for power between the Congress and the president. Representatives were angry because the executive branch made all of the decisions. Libertarians were the most unhappy with these circumstances, but a number of people had grown disgusted with the Davis government's management of the war. For the most part, the public viewed the decisions in October as placating rich landowners at the expense of nonproducers: mechanics, laborers, and government clerks. The all-out effort severely crimped production for the home front while resulting in little gain for the military: it quickly became apparent that the new men were among the first to desert. Upset by the "unwise and faithless policy which has been adopted in regard to detailed farmers, & the reserves," Alexander H. H. Stuart planned to pressure Senator R. M. T. Hunter and Representative John B. Baldwin to prevent stripping the area of laborers.[66] When these traditional political channels failed, momentum grew in the Confederate Congress to disband the Conscription Bureau and turn its function over to states, effective on March 17, 1865.[67]

Two factors aided this transition. First, the public turned its back on the bureau, which had lost credibility in the final months of the war. This could not be helped. There were not enough people or resources to go around. In this climate, resentment grew whenever civilians saw *any* able-bodied men remaining at home, even if some of them were essential to administering government programs. Any man of draft age working for the Conscription Bureau, the Commissary Department, a quartermaster, or a provost marshal carried a double stigma. His function alone angered an increasingly war-weary community. But the public also resented him because of his ability to avoid combat. In his columns in a Lynchburg newspaper, editor Charles Button singled out the men attached to government service who guarded train depots, checked passports, or otherwise aided the provost marshals. "Every village and hamlet in the Confederacy abound in these men," the editor wrote, "nearly all of whom are able-bodied soldiers who are kept from the front by means unknown to outsiders."[68] Within the War Department, Jones derisively referred to the Conscription Bureau as the "Bureau of Exemption," although his hostility was heightened by the news that government clerks would no longer be sacrosanct from the draft. As the end of the war neared, the public vented its frustration on the visible agents of the government, especially conscription officials who represented the national arm that affected so many lives.[69]

A second factor helped make the Conscription Bureau expendable. Administration of conscription, the public believed, could be conducted at the state level through the Reserve Corps. Established in 1864, these units consisted of men who remained at home doing government work—the detailed workers and exempted agricultural workers. They doubled as emergency troops to protect key agricultural and manufacturing operations from raids by Union cavalry and also patrolled communities for deserters. It seemed to many that the generals in charge of these Reserves—in Virginia's case James Kemper—could assume responsibility for conscription. This contained two advantages. It would keep community considerations in state, rather than Confederate, hands and would eliminate duplication with the Conscription Bureau. The number of men gained by collapsing the bureau would be minuscule, but the public just did not care anymore.

Within the army, life was equally bleak during the winter of 1864–1865. Absenteeism ballooned during this period after the reverses in the Shenandoah Valley, Lincoln's re-election, and Sherman's march through Georgia. Many lost hope and left the army. "The reserves of which you speak," a soldier wrote a friend back home, "will but ill supply the place of veterans. Since last fall 2,200 of Longstreets Corps has deserted." Absenteeism generally increased over winters as men attempted to go home; however, these men headed in a different direction that signified a new meaning to their departure. "I am certainly not overstating the number," this soldier continued, "when I tell you that the average per night is 100 men and in most cases they desert to the enemy." He believed that every casualty henceforth constituted cold-blooded murder, then concluded: "I would be as glad to see the independence of the South established as anyone in the State of Virginia but if there is any truth in men we need not longer contend."[70] Writing from the trenches near Petersburg, a man in the 38th Virginia told a similar tale but marveled that one of the four who left his company had been a man worth $200,000, a fact that became "the topic of conversation."[71]

In these desperate times, Lee abandoned most punishment, pleading with men to remain until spring. He continued the policy of furloughs, with quotas at four per 100 men, and liberally authorized absences based on family emergencies or merit. The government also offered bonus furloughs of thirty days to men who could secure 20,000 pounds of forage. There was one exception: soldiers living beyond North Carolina rarely could secure furloughs because officers feared they could not return.[72] Enough men remained in the army to make Grant's life difficult, but the final bleeding of the Army of Northern Virginia had begun.

Because of imperfect sources, it is difficult to perceive a pattern in desertions or to determine who the strongest supporters of the war were. Letters suggest that an officer cadre composed of slave owners and sons of either up-and-coming people or prominent families provided a core of support. Beyond this it is difficult to generalize, except that desertions of any degree inevitably represented farmers and laborers because these men composed the bulk of Virginia society and, thus, the military. As the comments above indicate, a sense of defeat had entered portions of the army, affecting even the best soldiers who might have hoped for Confederate independence. A North Carolina soldier in January 1865 heard talk of peace among the civilians around Petersburg and did not expect many in the army to fight beyond spring. A trooper in the 10th Virginia Cavalry noted about the same time: "If none deserted but cowards it would be diferent but some are deserting that had been good Soldiers ever since the war commenced."[73]

We also cannot judge those who remained as the most patriotic because they sometimes stayed more for pragmatic reasons than ideological ones. Because Virginia contained the Confederate capital and a major army, government agents and military personnel patrolled the countryside, increasing the likelihood of catching men on the run. Citizens joined this effort, chasing and holding small parties of deserters until enrollment officers came. Vigilantes in Campbell County and Albemarle rooted out pockets of deserters who preyed on farms, although some deserters remained out of reach in remote areas.[74] Thus the best chance deserters had to avoid capture lay in running to the enemy—not always an easy option for men who had endured so much for so long. Leaving one's comrades also might be risky. One North Carolinian reported to his wife that Confederate soldiers fired on colleagues who ran toward Union lines. Taking everything into account, this soldier rejected the pleas of his wife to come home and remained with his company.[75]

Signs of disaffection on the home front and within the army can mask the significant portion of the citizenry who still hoped for independence despite losing hope and confidence in their government. Virginia Confederates fell into three groupings: those with unflagging hopes for victory, those who lost heart and wished for a quick end, and those who saw bleak prospects ahead but were willing to keep the faith as long as Lee led the army. The proportions within each category cannot be accurately measured, but until the spring of 1865 a majority favored armed resistance. In January 1865, the public offered no dissent when the Congress and the president promoted Lee to general-in-chief of all the Confederate forces. The men in the ranks and the people at home were joined by a sense of common sacrifice that was almost populist in nature, fueled by their faith in a military figure who had built his career on overcoming long odds against him. It did not matter that the government proved inefficient or incompetent: emergency had molded its shape, and peace would bring new battles over its nature.

Consequently, it was typical to see seemingly contradictory feelings expressed in complaints to the government in these dark times, such as the petition from twenty-eight women in Harrisonburg. The petitioners from the war-torn Shenandoah Valley demanded the right to bear arms to protect their homes; they requested that the War Department sanction their raising of a regiment of women between the ages of 16 and 40. "We have been subjected to every conceivable outrage and suffering and this we believe is owing to the incompetency of the Confederate Army upon which we depend for defense." The petitioners added, "We propose to leave our hearthstones—to endure any sacrifice—any privation for the ultimate success of our Holy Cause." The offer was rejected, but the incident illustrates the protean nature of Confederate identity, which could reject the government—and the men in the army who failed to perform their masculine roles as protectors—while remaining loyal to the cause of independence.[76]

Another example more clearly indicates how problems with the government did not equate with a loss of hope in the Confederate cause. Late in the war, John B. Jones in the War Department expressed nothing but contempt for the administration that kept him employed as a clerk. He believed Davis was inept as a war-time commander and that the Conscription Bureau was nothing more than the corrupt pawn of the rich, handing out exemptions for kickbacks from speculators. He favored cleaning out the entire cabinet, but this frustration with government did not equal discouragement with the cause. During peace talks in the winter of 1865, he maintained that independence should remain the foundation of southern terms. He cheered when the Congress elevated the military leader to general-in-chief, but even that promotion did not go far enough. The clerk hoped that Lee could nudge Davis aside and run the country like a generalissimo. Jones presents quite a paradox: on one hand he criticized the Confederate government for excessive power that threatened individual liberties, yet he had no compunction against Lee's assuming the role of a military dictator. He underscores the trust the Confederate public placed in Lee, similar to the Revolutionary generation's confidence in handing power to General George Washington. Not everyone, of course, would have agreed with Jones—most prominently Lee himself. Yet the illustration reminds that it was possible to be discouraged by one's government, and mad at the rich, while still pulling for the Confederacy.[77]

To feed the spirits of soldiers and civilians in these dark times, Confederate Virginians resorted to a familiar device—public meetings, in which participants endorsed resolutions for continued prosecution of the war. Spurred by failed negotiations between Davis and Lincoln to halt hostilities, community leaders again attempted to rally the home front. The meetings began in Richmond, sparked by formation of a central committee to collect supplies for the army. The metaphor of the "Confederate Revival" provides an apt expression for this time of civic renewal.[78] Speakers sounded like preachers whipping congregations into fresh commitment to the cause, except that the fate of these sinners rested in the hands of an angry tyrant known as Lincoln. The combination of revival and revolutionary rhetoric sometimes sounded like Thomas Paine at a nineteenth-century camp meeting.

Take the example of William H. Harman, one of the larger slave owners in Augusta County. On February 27, he counseled Staunton residents to retain the trust of God, the heritage of liberty bequeathed by their Fathers, and the righteous anger of a people wronged. The nine resolutions passed recommitted people to the "watchfires of Liberty lighted in 1861," indicated that a united people could not lose, spurned talk of reconstruction as "but another name for submission to tyranny," and sanctioned the use of slaves in the army. The endorsement of slaves was portrayed as an act condoned by God to use all possible power to resist wicked oppression. Because of this meeting, sixty-five "gentlemen" contributed more than 100 barrels of flour, 8,000 pounds of meat, and $100,000 in government bonds. These were pillars of society such as M. G. Harman, Alexander H. H. Stuart, J. M. McCue, and Hugh W. Sheffey. Lynchburg followed suit with similar action by its leaders.[79] The meetings probably did not lift civilian spirits much, or for long. They could, however, have established an example of sacrifice that left these men trusted by the Confederate public when it came time to pick up the pieces in the postwar world.

Soldiers participated in their own version of this civic revival, although evidence suggests that officers sometimes manipulated the outcome. A soldier in the 38th Virginia Infantry from Pittsylvania County indicated that officers called the men together to vote on resolutions that professed the desire of the regiment to continue fighting. All except a half-dozen soldiers rejected the resolutions prepared by the officers, although the writer failed to clarify whether the soldiers rebelled against the sentiments of the document or against the procedure itself. Officers ignored the results and published the proceedings as if they had received endorsement. The men began to protest, but officers broke the movement by threatening to file charges of mutiny. Fearing the matter would stimulate desertions, commanders of the 38th Virginia subsequently opened the men's mail to check for further signs of rebellion.[80]

As winter turned to spring, most people knew the war was lost but could not abandon all hope as long as any semblance of Lee's army held the field. The Danville Road remained the one lone artery for food from the deeper South, meaning that the enemy had slowly squeezed shut the provision lifeline for the state. Other than public officials, no white men were left who could significantly increase the army. Hopes for the future now rested on adding slaves to the military. Grant's men kept stretching Lee's defenses outside of Petersburg. After the war, John Baldwin remembered about this period that everyone looked for the fall of the Confederacy and believed it had to come "& yet if any one dared to utter his thoughts he was set upon & cuffed without mercy."[81] He did not exaggerate. When news reached Charlottesville that Richmond had fallen to the enemy, a crowd at the courthouse listened as Randolph Tucker, Professor Minor, and other community leaders encouraged resistance against subjugation by Yankees. The audience exploded in applause, although not everyone shared the enthusiasm. A few men who spoke of reunion were seized, and officials had to restrain the crowd from harming them. Sarah Strickler Fife retained hope that the fallen capital meant nothing if the resourceful Lee could work more miracles. Sitting in her room as the Confederate cause melted away with the army, she still envisioned a future of further resistance against the United States as she wrote: "I fear the war has just begun."[82]

6

The Problem of Confederate Identity

The war feeling around here is like a burning bush with a wet blanket wrapped around it. Looked at from the outside, the fire seems quenched. But just peep under the blanket and there it is, all alive, and eating, eating in.
—Unidentified Virginian,
Summer 1865

Shortly after the Union army occupied Richmond and the Army of Northern Virginia surrendered, the curious rushed into the state to learn more about these puzzling Confederates and their feelings regarding reunification. Northerners had many questions, especially whether their former enemies would accept their fate and pledge loyalty to the restored Union. Of the freedpeople's position few had doubts: a majority of them eagerly welcomed the Union occupation force and showed ample enthusiasm for supporting the Republican Party. But it was uncertain whether Confederates would cooperate with or resist the conquerors—perhaps through guerrilla warfare or by joining with the French in Mexico to launch another war against the United States. In the immediate aftermath of Lee's surrender, northerners hoped that the Confederacy would go gently into its night, but few took for granted that defeat had quelled the rebellion completely as they carefully probed for signs of resistance.

Visitors touring Virginia immediately after the war found little cause for alarm. The Confederate populace was bone weary of fighting. Reviving a shattered economy commanded attention in this often-bewildering time of social and political turmoil. Soldiers said that they had given their best, had been beaten, and must get

134

on with life. In Richmond, the Radical press crowed about the Unionist sentiment, especially among the freedpeople, and enjoyed noting the hostility that poor whites expressed about, as Whitelaw Reid called the planters, "their late rebel masters." White laborers were also angry with the Confederate government for burning much of Richmond. Reports located rebel sentiment only among the F.F.V.'s, or the First Families of Virginia as the elites of the state were called. Observers consistently indicated that the most ardent were prosperous women who openly snubbed Union officers.[1] It seemed possible that poor whites might align with African Americans, or at least repudiate the planters responsible for the tragic conditions the South now faced. Even with the soldiers who had fought for the South, social intercourse with northern visitors proved more cordial than expected, disrupted only occasionally by a bitter outburst.

As they had from the beginning of the war, however, northerners overestimated the pro-Union sentiment as they confused acquiescence with loyalty. The war had resolved secession, signified a new supremacy of nation over state, and ended slavery. Few white Virginians would go any further as they tried to reconstruct the social relations they had known before the war. Slaveholding women expressed some of the strongest attitudes in this regard. A month after the war ended, Sarah Strickler Fife of Albemarle County fumed over being forced to give up "our best beloved institution." She added: "I truly believe that African slavery is right. I love it & all the South loves it. It suits us, & I do not see how we can do without it."[2] Still, most white southerners accepted that slavery was gone and rationalized that the change would allow the section to join the march toward progress, eliminate the major contention between the two regions, or—in the view of disgruntled whites—punish the men who had held down white labor in favor of slave labor. Neither rich nor poor whites believed that the freedpeople should vote or achieve social equality. Nor did white workers whom Republicans hoped to attract to the party of free labor welcome competition for jobs from the black workers flooding towns across the state. As naive as it sounds today, Confederate Virginians expected that except for the items noted above they could restore the world they had known without interference from the federal government in "southern affairs." Attempts to regulate race relations, punish rebels, or control elections betrayed in their opinion the spirit of the surrender terms at Appomattox and Lincoln's plan for wartime reconstruction. Former Confederates expected Virginia to be left alone as long as the people accepted defeat and took no further acts against the government.[3]

Immediate priorities for the Union military in the postwar world concerned restoring order to chaos and ensuring that Virginians did not starve. The war ended with civilians scrambling for food and not much changed with the surrender. The conflict had wasted Virginia's economy, causing an estimated $457 million in losses, including slaves.[4] As visitors traveled the state they described an area of destruction shaped like a crescent, beginning in the lower Shenandoah Valley, extending eastward across northern Virginia, and bending southward along the Tidewater. Chimneys stood like tired sentinels guarding barren land. Near Manassas most homes had been abandoned. A traveler heading along the James River toward Richmond noticed patches of corn outside many places, but the crop was stunted and late, planted hastily by returning soldiers with few implements. Beyond damage to structures and fields, the most notable change to the land was the absence of wood. Armies had burned fence rails on farms and cleared forests near their camps. Wood was needed not only for rebuilding but also to ensure a harvest: to protect crops, farmers needed to erect new rails because unfenced land was considered open to use by grazing livestock, hunters, and travelers no matter the damage caused. Not surprisingly, when the Southern Claims Commission began to reimburse loyalists for wartime losses from the Union army, wood figured prominently on lists of claims.[5]

Cities and towns within this crescent of destruction fared little better. Although population centers offered greater security from the enemy (and from one's own soldiers for that matter), the invaders had left many in ruins. In Fredericksburg, holes in the walls of buildings reminded an observer of the shelling that the town had endured in December 1862. Few homes had been rebuilt by the summer of 1865. Richmond had caused some of its own problems via the Burnt District, or the charred remains of Confederate stores and private shops in the city torched during the government's evacuation. The city was overcrowded with refugees, migrating African Americans, and the Union army. Recovery would be difficult because of scarce resources and no money. After all, once the Union army controlled an area the rich immediately became poor unless they held specie or U.S. currency instead of worthless Confederate notes and bonds. If the countryside was hard pressed for crops, then the cities and towns stared at potential disaster.[6]

Throughout the state, federal military authorities disbanded civil government and assumed control. Once soldiers had limited pillaging and protected property from further destruction, officers concentrated on relief efforts for the hungry—provided that the participants took the oath of loyalty. Northerners took special delight in noting that most of the people who sought these rations were former Confederates, not the freedpeople. Some explained this phenomenon by saying that that the freedpeople either had the wherewithal to make it on their own or entertained no expectations of support from the government. Neither answer completely satisfies, although both might be partly true. Used to living on the margin, the freedpeople had developed social networks of mutual assistance that likely helped in this difficult transition, yet several years later the situation reversed itself as many were forced to seek rations from the Freedmen's Bureau. The white men accepting food immediately after the surrender apparently were recently freed prisoners of war, but white women were by far the dominant presence at the commissary. Judging by the silks that mingled with calico they came from all ranks of society. They swallowed both food and pride by claiming that the defeated deserved this help. "You ought to do something for us," one woman told the U.S. agents who supplied rations, "for you've took away our niggers."[7]

Despite these gloomy circumstances, there was reason to hope that better days lay ahead. Portions of the state had escaped relatively unscathed. Just 40 miles west of Richmond, Amelia County had bright expectations for oats. Farmers there harvested wheat by June and were delighted that the crop came in about normal. No tobacco had been planted because of the risk of its being overrun by the Union army during the time when the seeds would have been sowed. Indian corn was behind for the same reason, but if labor and other resources held, enough food should come in to hold off starvation. Southampton seemed in similar shape, suggesting that the counties along the North Carolina border might rebound fairly quickly in food production. Helping the process were benevolent efforts on the part of the American Union Commission, a northern-born society that provided utensils, seeds, and other necessities for putting in a crop.[8]

As for industry and commerce, there was nowhere to go but up. Merchants in Richmond's Burnt District quickly began rebuilding. Though business returned, it took years to achieve anything like the prewar economy. Important to any improvement was the transportation system. The Union had destroyed rail lines around the state's periphery, and the Confederate army had done the same for some of the interior as Lee's men burned bridges and rail lines along the southern tier to retard pursuit after evacuating the city. The U.S. military started the process of repairing what soldiers on both sides had damaged. More ironically, as the Union army demobilized it left behind horses and mules that civilians in some areas could use to put in a crop.[9]

Despite this help, the occupying troops annoyed the public by forcing people to display allegiance to the United States while hiding reminders of the Confederacy. First had come the loyalty oaths for acquiring rations. Authorities extended the same oaths as a requirement for conducting business, for securing wedding licenses, and for restoring the right to vote and hold public office. There was a concurrent battle over national symbols. By early May, U.S. flags flew over strategic portions of the sidewalk, forcing people to pass under them. Some refused, expressing their resentment of the occupation by stepping into the street or crossing to another side. Perhaps they felt the same as A. Judson Crane, a former Unionist in Richmond whom Lincoln had appointed as District Attorney in 1861: "I wept four years ago when I saw the old flag hauled down," he told a northern newspaperman, "and I tell you the truth, I wept a great deal harder the other day when I saw it go up again."[10] Of course, the government prohibited showing the Confederate flag and the military arrested anyone who flew the colors, threatening to try perpetrators for treason.

Finally, Federal authorities cracked down on wearing rebel gray. A few of months after the surrender soldiers continued to wear uniforms. Officials ordered this to end but modified the edict when people complained that the uniform was the only clothing available to some veterans. Anyone wearing the gray had to remove badges of rank or buttons with military insignia, covering the latter with cloth if no plain buttons could be had. Seeing Confederate officers "strut" in their uniforms angered Thomas Morris Chester, an African American correspondent for a Philadelphia newspaper. He refused to accept the excuses about having no other suits and preferred to see men forced to don items discarded by Union soldiers discharged from the army. This struck him as justice because "they did not hesitate to strip our wounded and dead."[11] Federal authorities did not seriously consider such a step, but Union soldiers eagerly enforced the decree about buttons, summarily stripping the contraband when spotted on the wearer. Confederates countered by draping buttons in black crape and wearing black armbands on their sleeves, which signified mourning for both family members and the Confederacy.

Despite these minor conflicts, by early June the confidence of former Confederates had grown. Life crept back to a pace. Although intrusive, the Union military seemed more interested in protecting property than creating a revolution in the social structure of the South. Loyalty oaths and the disfranchisement of rich people and certain Confederate officials had irked, but the annoyance declined as pardons were easily won through brokers who ran paperwork to Washington and back for a fee. It also helped that the military was interested in restoring order in the most expedient way, even if that meant using former Confederates. Authorities in Richmond, for instance, installed former Mayor Joseph Mayo as the most viable option for keeping the peace. Mayo quickly instituted a police force and required passports to restrict travel of freedpeople, jailing those who could furnish no evidence of an employer. Here the goals of former Confederates meshed with the U.S. military. Black labor remained a crucial ingredient for postwar recovery and preservation of the southern hierarchy. The defeated hoped to keep the freedpeople on plantations and farms and the victors wanted to ease the burden of relief.[12]

The people hurt by such arrangements were Union loyalists: the freedpeople, a segment of white southerners, and transplanted northerners. Southern Unionists were particularly upset by the leniency shown to former Confederates, blaming the policy for helping put political power in the wrong hands. Rebel sentiment appeared strong even in such unlikely places as Charlestown, deep within loyalist West Virginia. A Unionist complained about this situation: "The war feeling here is like a burning bush with a wet blanket wrapped around it. Looked at from the outside, the fire seems quenched. But just peep under the blanket and there it is, all alive, and eating, eating in." He wanted stronger support for Unionists, claiming "every act of conciliation shown the Rebels is just letting in so much air to feed the fire."[13]

Confederate Virginians were sending the message that while they accepted defeat they neither repudiated nor apologized for their actions. How much they retained ties to Confederate and antebellum times was reflected in the battles over labor and the first elections in the state. Left without supervision, planters would have instituted near slavery, binding workers through peonage or apprenticeship enforced by county courts. The Freedmen's Bureau stepped in to encourage contracts to clarify relationships. The agreements typically demanded twelve-month tenures, committing African Americans to certain planters. Although resembling slavery, this departed from old ways by releasing the owner (now manager) from responsibilities for care and substituting institutions—especially the law—for planters as the regulator of behavior on farms. Paternalism remained part of the planter psyche but it now bowed to legal formalism. Problems with these arrangements surfaced as the freedpeople walked away from work situations that had grown too repressive or in which employers refused to pay. The Freedmen's Bureau at first supervised disputes but could not do so forever. Once civil authority returned for good, it would matter more than ever who occupied the minor judiciary that policed these violations.[14]

The elections to determine who sat in these public offices were a disaster for the federal government and the freedpeople. Shaping the tone of the return of civil authority was Francis H. Pierpont. He had been instrumental during the war in cleaving western Virginia from the Old Dominion, running a "restored" government of Virginia from Union-controlled Alexandria, and amending the state's constitution. Assuming control as governor by late May, he scheduled community elections beginning in July; state and congressional balloting for October. Pierpont refused to exclude former Confederates from the polls at a time when the freedpeople had no voting rights because he believed it unwise to establish a government based on only one-tenth of the eligible voters. The electorate thanked the governor for this leniency by choosing people who had served either before or during the war. Southampton's local elections wore the Whiggish look held in 1864. Richmond chose six Confederate veterans, and most of the councilmen and alderman were familiar faces. Voting in Augusta County went about the same. John B. Baldwin was chosen as a representative to the General Assembly, where he became Speaker of the House, and Alexander H. H. Stuart won election to the U.S. Congress. This alarmed a northern public and southern Unionists who wanted at least some sign of apology among the populace; instead, it appeared that former Confederates had positioned themselves once again to challenge authority.[15]

Part of this resurgent Confederate identity may have resulted from the way the war ended with no cataclysmic defeat of the Army of Northern Virginia. Union Colonel Charles Wainwright mused about this at Appomattox as news of the surrender came. A battle such as Gettysburg, he believed, would have been a more poetic end. "As it is," he noted, "the rebellion has been worn out rather than suppressed."[16] Yet this cannot be the only factor in the electorate's choosing incumbents. The situation raises questions about the reasons for southern defeat, especially claims that internal divisions ruptured the South as either the poor or middling farmers—and sometimes both—quit fighting a rich man's war.[17] Voters returned to public office the very political leaders they supposedly blamed for the plight of their families and the South. Instead of selecting new people, they fell in line behind familiar men when filling public offices three months after the surrender.

It cannot be stated precisely who voted in these elections, yet the broader context indicates some support existed among middling groups for these Confederate political leaders. Also, an occasional piece of evidence emerges to suggest that some of the working class identified with the struggle for independence. While touring Richmond, a northerner came upon a resident who vehemently criticized the Confederate government. His own daughter had been injured in an explosion at an ammunition factory during the war. When the father showed the scars to a northern visitor, the daughter admitted the seriousness of the accident, then surprised the observer with: "'But I didn't mind it,' she added, 'for it was in a good cause.'"[18] We could dismiss this as a peculiarity. But it might be useful to take this anecdote at face value—as well as the other evidence of people clinging to their Confederate past—and try to understand how this loyalty had been constructed during the war.

The conflict nudged Virginia into the Confederacy in a way that enhanced, rather than eliminated, local and state identities. In making this argument, I borrow from David M. Potter who offered what still seems the most sensible analysis of southern identity. He claimed that national identities do not dominate but mesh local interests with the broader goals. People are complicated creatures who can easily contain a hierarchy of loyalties, some of them seemingly contradictory. But it is the way that local blends with national that matters most. Thus people may not fight for the nation but for the community or neighborhood. When local goals fall into line with national purpose, the combination creates a powerful motivating force.[19]

By the time secession came, white Virginians had gained an increasing awareness of themselves as part of a region that differed from the North materially and spiritually. Conflict with northerners over the expansion of slavery had given birth to the "Virginia southerner." Lincoln's proclamation for militia against the Deep South had transformed that identity into the Virginia Confederate by providing the final proof that the Yankee attempted to ignore the Constitution, abolish slavery, instigate servile insurrection, and create a colonial economy through the force of a consolidated government hostile to southern interests. However, once they joined the Confederacy the people had to redefine themselves.

Some, of course, did not participate in the Confederacy but chose to retain their Union loyalties. Western Virginians broke from the rest of the state and, in doing so, unintentionally provided a release valve for deserters, Dunkards, and other disaffected persons.[20] Not all Unionists left immediately. Some endured economic and social harassment from neighbors rather than leave home. Many remained until at least 1862, when it became apparent they would have to go into the army because of conscription. Some members of pietist sects, such as Mennonites, tried to remain neutral or at least stay out of the military. However, suspected Unionists faced increasing persecution as war continued and, as Sheridan's men withdrew from the Valley in 1864, a number of conscientious objectors in the Shenandoah region packed their belongings and moved to safer places.[21] Virginia's location on the frontier of the nation gave Unionists, when they found conditions too intolerable, a place to go rather than having to find sanctuary within the state. This means that Virginia had a somewhat different experience from Alabama, Georgia, and North Carolina whose states harbored pockets of disaffected civilians who could not leave the Confederacy as easily as the people in the Old Dominion. A stronger core of Confederate support probably existed within Virginia from the beginning because of this quirk of geography.

Meanwhile, those joining the Confederacy had to come up with a reason for leaving the Union. They quickly adopted the ideology, as James McPherson has demonstrated for soldiers, of resisting subjugation from a government intent on denying southerners their liberties. The list of liberties to protect varied according to the person but included the right to own slaves, pursue one's own economic choices, live without fear of insurrection caused by northern extremists, use the territories in any way an individual saw fit, and maintain the voice of southerners in national politics.[22] Within weeks of war's outbreak, the Lincoln government handed ideologues fresh fodder when it moved to keep Maryland in the Union and control dissent in general. The suspension of habeas corpus and military arrests that characterized this period raised eyebrows of Virginians who considered Maryland a sister state that would have come into the Confederate fold if allowed. Reading about this and general political activity in the North, William Blackford of Lynchburg abandoned his Unionist proclivities. He was especially repulsed by arbitrary arrests, the destruction of newspaper presses by mobs, and suspension of habeas corpus. The activities seemed to him evidence that the Lincoln government had never intended to preserve the Constitution. "Now we may well ask what is wanting to complete the enslavement of the people," he pondered, adding, "Was there any thing worse than this state of things in the despotism of Louis 15?" He believed the infusion of foreigners had corrupted "the spirit of saxon liberty"; otherwise it was incomprehensible how the spirit of 1776 had died within the section.[23]

While Virginians at first focused on the preservation of liberty, Saxon purity, and the heritage of the Revolution, they increasingly incorporated protection of homes and vengeance as a reason for fighting and a difference between themselves and northerners. As early as 1861 newspapers condemned the Union army for waging war on civilians, but this became a more prominent component of Virginia-Confederate identity as the Union army stepped across the Potomac and the Shenandoah in the spring of 1862. Depredations against civilian property increased under Major General John Pope's brief tenure, and when the Union military shelled Fredericksburg before the battle of December 1862 it allowed Virginians to identify themselves and their Confederate colleagues as different from these barbarians and vandals who refused to recognize the rights of noncombatants. The actions of Union soldiers against civilians proved the lack of respect that the North held for property. That they preyed on helpless women, "stole" slaves, shelled churches, and desecrated family Bibles provoked bitter recrimination. "No victory of the war has ever done me so much good," one Virginia soldier noted about the destruction of Fredericksburg in December of 1862. "I *hate* them worse than ever in the first place, and then their destruction of poor old Fredericksburg! It seems to me that I dont do anything from morning to night but hate them worse & worse."[24]

Violations of women, whether symbolically or physically, sparked the strongest reactions over treatment of civilians. Accounts of the enemy invariably mentioned how Union soldiers entered women's rooms and pawed through wardrobes and, as they did during an orgy of destruction at Fredericksburg, sometimes paraded in the streets in women's clothing. Confederates expected their women to be protected as noncombatants and any actions against them—no matter how well deserved—provoked outcries that sometimes seemed out of proportion with the offense. When Major General Benjamin Butler governed Union-occupied Louisiana, Confederate women taunted Federal soldiers and dumped chamber pots on them as they passed in the streets. Butler ended this nuisance by claiming that anyone continuing in this behavior would be considered ladies of the night and treated accordingly. The Confederate public branded Butler a "beast" for his order.[25] Most of the incidents against white women involved intimidation and threats rather than physical assault; however, on one occasion a woman told her husband that a friend returning from Memphis had encountered ten Yankees who stripped a woman naked on the street and violated her. The Virginian wrote her husband in the army, "Shoot them, dear husband, every chance you get. Hold no conference with them. They are devil furies who thirst for your blood and who will revenge themselves upon your helpless wife and children. It is God's will and wish for you to destroy them. You are his instrument and it is your Christian duty."[26]

Confederates used this behavior by northern soldiers to expand on antebellum images of southerners as more respectful toward property and women, less concerned with material goods, and more religious—in sum, more civilized. This required overlooking occasions when Union soldiers protected civilian property, the atrocities by Confederate guerrillas in Missouri and Kansas, and the speculation that went on at home. Although tainted, the characterizations functioned as motivations for fighting and as a means of identifying oneself in contrast to one's enemy. One woman who professed herself as becoming a warmer southerner believed that northerners had colder, more mathematical minds that lent themselves naturally to despotic ways of thinking. She also equated exorbitant prices in the Confederacy as examples of Yankee behavior among southerners.[27] Virginians at times accused the Yankees of causing the war because of the profit mentality, not just to dominate the South economically but to boost prices and capitalize on contracts created by wartime demand. Conversely, Confederates hoped the Yankees would quit pursuing the war if it emptied northern purses: Virginians joined their comrades in watching the fluctuations in the price of gold as a barometer of northern commitment to the conflict.

So far we have mentioned little about slavery, but the peculiar institution existed as part of the Confederate mentality in subtle ways. It became a symbol of a way of life that celebrated liberty for white people rather than preservation of an institution for a limited number of the wealthy. In the early going, slavery appeared in public discourse as a basis for fighting, sometimes quite unabashedly. Vice President Alexander Stephens's speech in which he stated that the Confederacy rested on a cornerstone of slavery offers the most frequently cited example, but even in Virginia newspapers readers could find statements that protection of slavery provided a central cause for secession. For instance, a Lynchburg editor in 1861 proclaimed: "We do not deny that slavery is the cause, or furnished the occasion for this war." As the war continued, these frank admissions declined in favor of goals that included a broader public. William C. Rives, for instance, asserted in 1863 that the war had become one for "national" independence.[28] Slavery then served as a metaphor for what would happen if the Union won. A despotic government would enslave all white men and women. Midway through the conflict, with emancipation a war aim of the Union, public discourse raised the color bar, indicating that one of the outcomes would be a leveling of the races. When juxtaposed with gender conventions, the images portrayed the dire consequences of what could result and, whether apocryphal or not, accurately foreshadowed the battles for public space in the Reconstruction period.

The war applied another layer to Virginia-Confederate identity. From late 1863 on, as shortages in provisions worsened, the cause assumed a heightened awareness that self-sacrifice would grace Virginia Confederates in their attempt at independence and link them with their Revolutionary ancestors. Some observed that a soft life had fostered complacency over freedom and that the current generation had to endure hardships to protect this precious commodity for the future.[29] Comparison with the struggles against the British undergirded this line of reasoning, especially the similarity of the two generals upon whom rested the chances for success, Washington and Lee. The two were related through Lee's marriage to Mary Custis and the general embodied most of the attributes compatible with the self-conceptualization of the South: that of a Christian gentleman who fought like a warrior yet with restraint against civilians. His biggest attribute undoubtedly was his success against various Union generals, which maintained hope in independence. And as Virginians lost faith in their government late in the war, they looked increasingly to this army as the bearer of their identity.

The evolution of this cause uniquely suited Virginians in meshing local with Confederate concerns. Although it is doubtful that the common folk accepted unequivocally the thought outlined above—and probably added their own meaning to liberty and independence—the state's circumstances blended interests with ideology more evenly than most of the states in rebellion. By fighting for homes, Virginia Confederates also fought for the nation. All witnessed devastation of property or disruption of life by the enemy without distinguishing among planters, farmers, or the poor. When ideologues talked about the lack of respect for property, the concept rested on a hard material base that incorporated the interests of slave owners in human chattel and of middling and poor farmers who lost fence rails and subsistence. The army also broadened the horizon of interests beyond that of community. Sons, husbands, brothers, and cousins in the military carried the concerns of loved ones to other sections of the state and the Confederacy. In none of the cases above did the public have to relinquish state or local identities in favor of national ones. Civilians elevated their own communities in praising the Army of Northern Virginia and celebrated Virginia pride by marking the achievements of Lee, one of the state's foremost citizens.

The Confederate government itself wore something of a familiar look. The southern Piedmont could be proud of Thomas Bocock who served as Speaker of the House in the Congress. The two most influential secretaries of war, George Wythe Randolph and James Seddon, were prominent Virginians. They dominated the office from 1862 through early 1865, guiding the institution and enforcement of conscription, impressment, and exemptions. Political leaders from other states, especially North Carolina, periodically complained that too much patronage went the Old Dominion's way. The seminal study of southern conscription similarly concluded that the Upper South contained the least political friction because of experienced and practical leaders and an enemy army that "was always near and formidable." The government existed as something familiar, "not a mysterious something beyond the horizon that could be conjured by the imagination into the proportions of a monster, obsessed with a passion to consume the rights of the States and the people." Because of the proliferation of Virginians in the bureaucracy, citizens of the Old Dominion at least had the comfort of dealing with the devils they knew.[30]

Yet a political culture that celebrated the independence of its electorate guaranteed that Virginians would protest the more irritating actions of their devils. Ideology and familiar faces in government carried empty stomachs only so far. Discontent built to dangerous levels by the spring and summer of 1863, yet it remained in check for a few reasons. One was the wartime context in which civilians accepted a certain amount of hardship as necessary, providing that victory appeared possible and that all segments of the public sacrificed equally for the cause. While some questioned whether their government had become as despotic as the North, the majority rationalized that the strong measures by the Confederacy intended to preserve liberty, not deny it, and were instituted to control speculation and extortion. When favoritism continued and shortages escalated, discord manifested itself in the bread riot of 1863 and absenteeism from the army. Officials no longer could ignore the problem of class-based legislation as momentum built to eliminate certain privileges, especially substitution. In some respects, disaffection helped prolong the war by providing nationalist leaders with the support to exact greater sacrifices from the wealthy. These leaders might have pressed for an end to substitution anyway as the best recourse in a desperate time, yet it seems questionable that they would have expended political capital on provisions for the needy—with corresponding increases in their own tax burden—had the public not demanded this attention. Whatever the motivation, Old-line Whigs and secession Democrats who championed nationalist measures responded to the people who complained that the war had become a poor man's fight. Planters, slave-owning professionals, and small-scale farmers in the western region found kindred souls among large planters such as Thomas Jefferson Randolph and William C. Rives in the tobacco belt. Town-based professionals such as Charles Button in Lynchburg also tired of the farmers who withheld crops while townspeople suffered.

This jointure of large eastern planters with elements from west of the Blue Ridge echoed the relationship that had promoted reform in antebellum Virginia, such as the passage of a new constitution in 1830.[31] In the 1850s this alliance had given smaller farmers living west of the Blue Ridge increasing political clout. Beginning with elections after the constitution of 1851 expanded suffrage, governors either hailed from west of the Blue Ridge or courted the support of this section for the votes to win. Planters encountered problems having their way in the General Assembly. Eastern planters could not overturn fence laws that would end the open grazing valued by owners of smaller farms. More important, when Virginia attempted to enact Constitutional changes during the war to tighten restrictions on suffrage, they failed to pass. Similar provisions succeeded in Georgia.[32] In wartime Virginia, where western farmers proved essential for supplying grain, leaders had to recognize the desires of smaller farmers and artisans who nonetheless continued to express concerns through old channels of political habit led by a slaveholding elite.

When viewing the war from the local perspective, the political leadership appears more competent than studies have suggested—or at least more responsive to concerns within the Old Dominion. The merits of Jefferson Davis versus Abraham Lincoln have consumed historical inquiry at the expense of understanding the middle range of the Confederacy's politicians who performed double or triple duties as community, state, and national representatives.[33] Persons such as Baldwin continued to fulfill antebellum political obligations. Other former Whigs experienced at least a minor resurgence midway through the conflict, indicating that they had not lost public trust and that war had failed to sever relations or techniques for forging consensus built over decades. From January 1864 until the surrender at Appomattox, Virginians in the General Assembly and the Congress took the lead in promoting the passage of measures that would provide more aid for the needy and exact more sacrifice from the rich. These leaders also visited the home front to articulate the causes for fighting (as well as the dangers of capitulation) and commit the prosperous to public resolutions pledging a certain level of support for the war.

How the public interpreted these gestures remains difficult to say with certainty. Sources remain biased toward the wealthy and more prosperous people when it comes to measuring motivations for supporting the fight. The public complained to the government about inequities but, with the exception of the South's love affair with Robert E. Lee, few wrote letters of praise about leaders or analyzed the impact of public policy. Poor women, for instance, never mentioned whether the efforts to feed them or allow the purchase of provisions at government prices answered discontent or caused them to think their voices were being heard, at least locally if not nationally. After local efforts were stepped up to combat hunger, and national legislation seemed to exact a higher measure of effort from planters, the most visible forms of public anger diminished. Crime still continued in cities, which in part reflected concerns about food.

However, no more bread riots occurred and desertion came under better control in Virginia, at least momentarily, before growing again over the bleak winter of 1864–1865. We also know that the public considered buying food at government prices and direct aid to the needy increasingly desirable and complained when mismanagement or enemy raids disrupted the distribution. Overall, the efforts to mitigate hardships did not resolve the problems adequately. Critics complained that the measures came too late, involved too much government power, or failed to provide enough control. Yet did these measures help the public see a greater enemy in the Union army than in their own officials? I suspect so, although the evidence remains circumstantial and by no means displaces the hostility and sense of betrayal within the common people against the Davis government that had caused so much sacrifice for increasingly little gain.[34]

Something kept the Confederate army, filled primarily with nonplanters, intact long enough to push the Union war effort to the utmost and give it a chance to win well into the summer of 1864. Compulsion by Confederate provost marshals could explain partly why 8,000 of 12,000 deserters were returned to the army, yet force cannot account for all of this dynamic or how Virginia mobilized between 77 and 93 percent of its eligible white males. The proclivity of citizens to disobey authority and encourage absenteeism from the army no matter the penalty has been well documented. It may be, as Reid Mitchell's study of soldiers suggests, that a greater degree of national spirit, built by a common bond of military experience, existed within the ranks but it would have been impossible to sustain without support from the civilian population.[35] This is not to say that the cause filled the hearts of everyone and that a loss of will had no bearing on defeat. Nationalism likely remained flawed or at least not what we think of today. Most men preferred to fight for their neighborhoods and resisted efforts to send them to other regions. When it appeared Richmond might fall, an Albemarle County woman blurted out her concern first for "my own brave Virginia! my own loved, long-suffering Virginia."[36] Identification with nation never supplanted, if indeed it ever does, local concerns for white persons in the Confederacy, but it achieved impressive results and continued to live after the war even with some common folk, like the working woman in Richmond who had been injured in the explosion of an ammunition factory. However imperfect was Confederate identity—and the evidence indicates that it was in the process of forming and would face internal debates about its content and meaning even if the South had won—it was good enough to win deep into 1864.

After the fall of Atlanta, the destruction of the Shenandoah Valley, and the election of Lincoln, the Confederacy began to fall apart in Virginia. The constant struggle to provide enough men and food reaped a bitter harvest as the chance of success dwindled. By the winter of 1864–1865 weariness had set in and the public lost confidence in the Confederate apparatus. Identity had transferred to the army, but even that could not sustain the public forever. Once the soldiers surrendered at Appomattox, only a minority of Virginians could fathom continuing armed resistance.

Some have asserted that the lack of guerrilla warfare proves that nationalism was insufficient and, thus, a cause of defeat.[37] This seems a stretch for Virginia. Slavery—or the desire to hold onto a black labor force—made such a proposition risky at best, but even in the nonslaveholding areas, guerrilla war demanded unpalatable choices. Partisan warfare by rangers under John S. Mosby had visited areas already and threatened to get out of hand when both sides began reprisal hangings of prisoners. Raids on Union supply lines also invariably sparked further destruction to the property of Confederate loyalists. No military leader worth his salt favored what was called black flag warfare and Lee spoke out decidedly against it. To conduct this activity in a way that would lead to independence, rather than degenerate into brigandage, required new leaders to coordinate the effort. In any event, guerrilla activity would draw warfare into portions of the South previously untouched and force partisans to take food from a citizenry trying to fill depleted larders. Returning to the United States offered a more sensible course. Confederate Virginians expected most of life, including political participation, to resume its normal course without social revolution or punitive campaigns. If the Old Dominion's experience is any indication, it appears that a persistent enemy, whose military campaigns strained resources to the breaking point, eroded the will to fight in all but the hardiest souls.

When the conquerors threatened to support revolutionary change in Virginia and the rest of the South, it awakened Confederate identity by posing a new enemy in a slightly different context that helped return incumbents to postwar political offices. Without better voting records we cannot know if all portions of society participated in the elections. It may also be true that the voting merely reflected a return to antebellum habits, continuing a trend begun in Virginia with the midterm elections of 1863. But it also may be true that the populace was not unhappy with the rich or that all political leaders were percieved as being corrupt and inept. Instead, the electorate may have seen in their postwar leaders the Virginians who had tried to mitigate suffering during the bleakest times of scarcity or who had remained the most consistent in the failed attempt at independence. Constancy of purpose under pressure offered attractive political credentials to Confederate Virginians trying to limit change in their lives.

Whatever the case, northern officials greeted evidence of continued Confederate identity with increasing alarm. July 4 had passed unobserved by much of the white community who did not want to celebrate the birthday of the Union that had conquered them, while African Americans turned out in full force to commemorate their independence, imparting a new meaning to an old national holiday. Political power kept passing into the hands of the former enemies of the United States. When Virginia's General Assembly reconstituted in December, the legislators repealed the act recognizing West Virginia and enacted vagrancy laws and other repressive measures to recreate a facsimile of slavery through which to pin labor down. Legislators also asked for repeal of the test oath for loyalty and wanted Jefferson Davis released from prison. Some wanted Robert E. Lee installed as governor, which he politely but firmly declined.[38]

By January 1866, Radicals in Congress had seen enough of this activity and convened the Joint Committee on Reconstruction to determine the extent of resistance and whether it raised concerns of renewed fighting. Major General Alfred Terry, who supervised military affairs in Virginia, painted a bleak picture for Unionists and the freedpeople, as both groups faced social and economic pressures. Courts presided over by former Confederates, he testified, denied rights to both and failed to adjudicate either civil or criminal cases fairly. The Confederate population in general tried to ignore the military and Unionist elements. Asked what motivated these people, Terry told the committee: "In the first place, having failed to maintain the separate nationality which they asserted, they desire to keep themselves a separate people, and to prevent, by any means in their power, our becoming a homogeneous nation; second, the desire to make treason honorable and loyalty infamous, and to secure, as far as they may be able, political power."[39] Terry may have overstated the case but a disturbing amount of Confederate sentiment remained in the state—enough at least to make the northern public nervous that it might lose the peace.

Virginia-Confederate identity had changed dramatically between 1861 and 1865. It was born in reaction to Lincoln's proclamation as the final event in a series of conflicts that had defined the South in antagonism to the North. It had broadened beyond the interests of slaveholders to describe a liberty-loving country protecting itself from the coercion of a consolidated government. It was further deepened in Virginia as the antithesis of the Yankee barbarian bent on destroying property, threatening women, desecrating churches, and raising the Negro over white men and women. Even these powerful components did not capture everyone's loyalties as privations and favoritism created divisiveness within the public and libertarians and nationalists debated the proper relationship of individual to government—in effect, the meaning of nationalism. Those who could not quite accept the Davis government looked to the army as the bearer of Confederate identity and wished either that the war would end or that honest politicians or a military dictator named Lee would lead the people to the promised land of independence. Now, in the postwar world, the memory of Confederate sacrifice would become important for creating new political bonds, raising fresh problems of how to incorporate wartime dissidents, the freedpeople, and postwar traitors known as "scalawags." The federal government also faced a dilemma in that the freedpeople willingly supported national reunion while the white majority did not. Could former Confederates be made to abandon their loyalties and accept a new national identity along with their former slaves? Or must a compromise be struck by crafting a memory of war that celebrated the common sacrifice of both sections, minus their black residents? The creation of new identities would accomplish more than providing the content of ceremonies, monuments, and history books that give future generations meaning through their past—the process would also provide ways of representing and validating power within a newly forming nation.

Notes

Introduction

1. Escott, *After Secession;* Owens and Cooke, eds., *The Old South in the Crucible of War;* Beringer and others, *Why the South Lost the Civil War;* Hahn, *The Roots of Southern Populism;* Durrill, *War of Another Kind.*

2. Informing this work is the assumption that nationalism is a socially constructed, psychological identity in which different groups of people imagine themselves as linked in a community. Benedict Anderson has developed this concept in *Imagined Communities.* For other works, see Hobsbawm and Ranger, eds., *The Invention of Tradition;* Hobsbawm, *Nations and Nationalism Since 1780;* Faust, *The Creation of Confederate Nationalism;* Potter, "The Historian's Use of Nationalism and Vice Versa" in *The South and the Sectional Conflict,* 34–83.

3. Thompson, "Patricians and Plebs," in *Customs in Common: Studies in Traditional Popular Culture,* 16–96; Moore, *Injustice.*

4. Bensell, *Yankee Leviathan,* 165–66; Escott, "The Cry of the Sufferers," in *Civil War History* 23, 228–40; Wallenstein, *From Slave South to New South,* 110–20.

5. Bensell, for instance, has noted that the greatest support for centralization of the Confederate government came from the Upper South. See his *Yankee Leviathan,* 235.

6. Rable, *The Confederate Republic;* Luraghi, *The Rise and Fall of the Plantation South,* 78–9.

7. Carmichael, "The Last Generation" and his *Lee's Young Artillerist,* 1–6; Rable, *Civil Wars;* Faust, *Mothers of Invention.*

8. Unidentified to James A. Seddon, February 5, 1863, Letters Received, Confederate Secretary of War, RG 109, microcopy M437, roll 80, file no. A31, National Archives, Washington, D.C.

Chapter 1

1. Cyrus H. Cline, Sr., "Description of Old Home, Mother, Father, and Sisters," unpub. ms., Fredericksburg-Spotsylvania National Military Park (FSNMP).

2. Richmond *Daily Examiner,* April 16, 1861, quoted in Cappon, *Virginia Newspapers,* 17 [quote]; Crofts, *Reluctant Confederates,* 314–5, 332–52. For expression of liberty, see John B. Minor to Mary B. Blackford, April 16, 1861, Blackford Family Papers, box 6, folder 79, Southern Historical Association, Wilson Library, University of North Carolina, Chapel Hill [hereafter cited as SHC]; Lynchburg *Virginian,* April 16, 1861; Sarah Strickler Fife Diary, November 13, 1861, Alderman Library, University of Virginia, Charlottesville [hereafter cited as UVa]. For liberty as central to antebellum debate, see Watson, *Liberty and Power;* Thornton III, *Politics and Power in a Slave Society.*

3. J. D. Imboden to John McCue, December 3, 1860, McCue Family Papers, box 4, UVa.

4. McPherson, *Battle Cry of Freedom,* 255; Golden, "The Secession Crisis in Virginia," 4, 21–2; Potter, *The Impending Crisis,* 505–6; Nevins, *The Emergence of Lincoln: Prologue to Civil War,* 2:469; Craven, *The Coming of the Civil War,* 434.

5. Genovese, "Yeomen Farmers in a Slaveholders' Democracy," 331–42; J. William Harris, "The Organization of Work on a Yeoman Slaveholder's Farm," *Agricultural History,* 64 (Winter 1990), 39–52; Kenzer, *Kinship and Neighborhood,* 9–25.

6. Fox-Genovese and Genovese, *The Fruits of Merchant Capital,* 52–3; Craven, *Soil Exhaustion as a Factor in the Agricultural History of Virginia and Maryland,* 122–61; Gray, *History of Agriculture in the Southern U.S.,* 2:663–7, 758, 762–9, 909–13.

7. *Seventh Census of the United States, 1850,* 1:278; and *Eighth Census of the United States, 1860,* 2:159; Shanks, *The Secession Movement in Virginia,* 12; Noe, *Southwest Virginia's Railraod,* 37–9.

8. Gray, *History of Agriculture in the Southern U.S.,* 2:816–20, 881; Reid, "Slave Agriculture and Staple Crops in the Virginia Piedmont," esp. Table 2.1, p. 72. Figures on wheat versus tobacco farming based on "Mr. William Irby's report, 1860, to the Nottoway Club," in *Southern Planter,* 21 (June 1861), 323–5.

9. Stauffenberg, "Albemarle County," 15, 21–4, 27, 41 [quote].

10. *The* (Abingdon, Va.) *Democrat,* January 16, 1858.

11. Shanks, *The Secession Movement,* 11–2; Stauffenberg, "Albemarle County," 43.

12. R. H. Early to Brother, December 1, 1855, and R. H. Early to Papa, January 12, 1856, Jubal A. Early Papers, LC.

13. Fields, "The Agricultural Population of Virginia," 149–50, 144.

14. Bruce, *Virginia Iron Manufacture in the Slave Era*, 305; Tripp, "Restive Days," 26–8; Genovese, "Yeomen Farmers." Duty on slave patrols lasted three months, with selections made by magistrates on county courts. Henrico County, for example, drafted for this service in May 1861 a merchant, shopkeeper, blacksmith, gauger at the custom house, auctioneer, slave trader, bookbinder, paper hanger, furniture dealer, grocer, and a few farmers. See Bailey, *Henrico Home Front*, 6–9.

15. Dew, *Ironmaker to the Confederacy*, 24–6; Freehling, *Drift Toward Dissolution*, 243–4; Bruce, *Virginia Iron Manufacture*, 234–7.

16. Starobin, *Industrial Slavery*, 211–3 [quote]; Rachleff, *Black Labor in Richmond*, 4–5. For an alternative view see Genovese, *Political Economy of Slavery*, 232–5.

17. *Eighth Census of the United States, 1860*, 4:243, 2:155; Manuscript Census Returns, 1860, Albemarle and Augusta County, Free Population and Slave Schedules, microcopy, NA; Horst, *Mennonites in the Confederacy*, 15–6; Siegel, *The Roots of Southern Distinctiveness*, 86–91; Freehling, *The Road to Disunion*, 164–6.

18. Freehling, *Drift Toward Dissolution*, 234–5; Shanks, *The Secession Movement in Virginia*, 12.

19. Manuscript Census Returns, 1860, Augusta County, Free and Slave Schedules, microcopy, NA. Orville Vernon Burton has cautioned against relying too much on the bound census books for this kind of work. See his *In My Father's House Are Many Mansions*, 44.

20. For the pervasiveness of slave owning throughout the South, see Olsen, "Historians and the Extent of Slave Ownership in the Southern United States," 105. The census divided Augusta into three districts: Staunton/District 1, First District, and North Sub-Division. The records on hiring were more meticulous for the first two areas but nearly incomprehensible for the third. For Staunton and the First District, 347 of 3,412 slaves (10.2 percent) were involved in hiring transactions. See Manuscript Census Returns, 1860, Augusta County, Slave Schedules, NA. For other information on hiring, see Bruce, *Virginia Iron Manufacture*, 273; Morgan, *Emancipation in Virginia's Tobacco Belt*, 57–76; Dew, *Ironmaker to the Confederacy*, 26–7, and his *Bonds of Iron;* Goldfield, *Urban Growth in the Age of Sectionalism*, 130–8; Starobin, *Industrial Slavery in the Old South*, 128–37; Bancroft, *Slave-Trading in the Old South*, 147–8. Bancroft estimated the total number of hired slaves in the 1850s at 15,000, which amounted to only 3 percent of the state's 490,000 slaves. The reliability of this estimate is unknown because Bancroft supplied no documentation. Perhaps the best indication of the prevalence of slave hiring lies in the new business that formed to handle these transactions. Bancroft discovered through city directories that Rich-

mond in 1860 boasted at least 18 people who called themselves slave agents. See Ibid.

21. Bean, "The Ruffner Pamphlet of 1847," 260–82; Maddex, *Virginia Conservatives*, 15; Freehling, *Drift Toward Dissolution*, 231–4; Ambler, *Sectionalism in Virginia*, 283, 297–9.

22. Simpson, *A Good Southerner*, 203, 214–5.

23. Shanks, *The Secession Movement in Virginia*, 209–12, 272 (n.199); Freehling, *Drift Toward Dissolution*, 235–41; McFarland, "Extension of Democracy," 33; Ambler, *Sectionalism in Virginia*, 268. For the taxation sentiments among northwesterners, see Reese, ed., *Proceedings of the Virginia State Convention of 1861*, 2:6–25.

24. Crofts, *Reluctant Confederates*, 159–60; Robert Johnson quoted in Shanks, *The Secession Movement in Virginia*, 208.

25. Shanks, *The Secession Movement in Virginia*, 211–3; Curry, *A House Divided*, 6–8, 53.

26. Steven Hahn's study of the Georgia Upcountry concluded: "In a social order that conferred status upon the ability to command the allegiances of lesser men, intracounty rivalries often reflected competition among members of the elite and their followers for influence." See Hahn, *Roots of Southern Populism*, 94–5. On political culture, see McCurry, *Masters of Small Worlds*, 239–76; Cecil-Fronsman, *Common Whites*, 31–66; Ford, *Origins of Southern Radicalism*, 108–33, 303–5; Harris, *Plain Folk and Gentry in a Slave Society*, 110–9; Escott, *Many Excellent People*, 22–3; Thornton, *Politics and Power in a Slave Society*, 155–60; Thomas, *Confederate Nation*, 8–14.

27. Shade, *Democratizing the Old Dominion*, 11, 28–30, 91–2, 154–5; Crofts, *Old Southampton*, 186–92 and his *Reluctant Confederates*, 47–8; Richey, "The Virginia State Convention of 1861," 26–7; Kenzer, *Kinship and Neighborhood*, 56; McFarland, "Extension of Democracy," 17–9.

28. Sarah Payne to Cousin Mary, November 7, 1870, Sarah Pannill Payne Letters, UVa.

29. Freehling, *Drift Toward Dissolution*, 235–41; Ambler, *Sectionalism in Virginia*, 261–4; McFarland, "Extension of Democracy," 8–10.

30. Jubal A. Early, "To the Voters of the County of Franklin," July 20, 1850, Jubal A. Early Papers, Scrapbook, LC; Genovese, *The Slaveholders' Dilemma*; Wish, *George Fitzhugh*, 192, 220–2, 224.

31. Maddex, *Virginia Conservatives*, 11–2; McFarland, "Extension of Democracy," 15–7, 21–5, 38–40; Freehling, *Road to Disunion*, 513–5.

32. For examples, see Waddell, *Annals of Augusta County*, 454–5; Unidentified to son, March 6, 1861, Beal-Davis Papers, subseries 1.1, box 2, folder 29, SHC; Reese, *Proceedings of the Virginia State Convention of 1861*, 1:585–6, 630–2, 633–5, 655–9.

33. Citizens of Augusta County to the Governor, June 21, 1860, Executive Papers, box 415, Library of Virginia, Richmond [hereafter cited as LV].

34. Ford, *Origins of Southern Radicalism*, 50–1, 84; Hahn, *Roots of Southern Populism*, 107. On republicanism, see Shalhope, "Toward a Republican Synthesis," 49–80; Wilentz, "On Class and Politics in Jacksonian America," 45–63. For how slavery influenced notions of freedom, see Morgan, *American Slavery, American Freedom*.

35. "Virginia Illustrated," *Harper's New Monthly Magazine*, XI (August 1855), 289–90; Wyatt-Brown, *Southern Honor*, 327–61.

36. Shanks, *The Secession Movement in Virginia*, 79–82; Staunton *Vindicator*, March 9, 1860; Matthews, *Religion in the Old South*, 160–2; Escott, *Many Excellent People*, 27; Crofts, *Old Southampton*, 186.

37. "Address to the Farmers of Virginia" quoted in Olmsted, *The Cotton Kingdom*, 587–90; Gray, *Agriculture in the Southern U.S.*, 2:929; "Virginia State Agricultural Society," *Southern Planter*, XX (January 1860), 41–8.

38. *Southern Planter*, 19 (March 1859), 131–2, 146–8, and Eaton, *The Mind of the Old South*, 32.

39. "On the Importance of Elevating Mechanics and Artizans to a Social Equality with Other Professions," in *Southern Planter*, 21 (April 1861), 222–4.

40. Scarborough, ed., *The Diary of Edmund Ruffin*, 1:285–6. For the impact of the home market on southern industry, see Genovese, *Political Economy of Slavery*, 23–6.

41. Link, *A Hard Country and a Lonely Place*, 6–7; Simpson, *A Good Southerner*, 151–4.

42. Staunton *Vindicator*, March 16, 1860.

43. *Sourthern Planter*, 16 (June 1856), 189.

44. *Sourthern Planter*, 18 (August 1858), 467–72 and (March 1858), 168–75.

45. Scarborough, ed., *The Diary of Edmund Ruffin*, 1:8–13; *Southern Planter 16* (September 1856), 280.

46. *Southern Planter*, 20 (January 1860), 41–8.

47. Wish, *George Fitzhugh*, 32–53; Genovese, *World the Slaveholders Made*, 212; Faust, *The Ideology of Slavery*, 18–20, 127–9, 272–4; "Communication," *Southern Planter*, 16 (July 1856), 195.

48. "Celebration at Jamestown," *Southern Literary Messenger*, 24 (June 1857), 434–66; "Report of the Mount Vernon Association," Ibid., (July 1857), 69–70.

49. Governor's Communication Relative to Purchase of Sections in Hollywood Cemetery, Doc. no. 50, Virginia House Documents, microfilm, roll 19, LV; Waddell, *Annals of Augusta County*, 420.

50. Shanks, *The Secession Movement in Virginia*, 66; "The Edinburgh Review on the Political Crisis in the U.S.," *Southern Literary Messenger*, 24 (January 1857), 22–32; Robert Beale Davis to Wilbur, October 16, 1856, Beale-Davis Papers, subseries 1.1, box 1, SHC.

51. Staunton *Vindicator*, January 6, 1860.

52. J. Early to Jubal, May 15, 1860, Early Papers, LC. For the importance of militia units, see McCurry, *Masters of Small Worlds*, 265–71.

53. Dumond, *The Secession Movement*, 124–9.

54. Staunton *Vindicator*, November 23, 1860; Golden, "The Secession Crisis in Virginia," 164 [quote]. Citizens of Loudoun County expressed similar notions in a public meeting. See Poland, "Loudoun County During the Civil War," 14.

55. Rubin, "Between Union and Chaos," 406; Reese, *Proceedings of the Virginia State Convention*, 1:366–7 [quote].

56. Dumond, *The Secession Movement*, 215; Crofts, *Reluctant Confederates*, 336–8; Morgan, *Emancipation in Virginia's Tobacco Belt*, 85–6; Bensell, *Yankee Leviathan*, 91–3; Bowman, "Conditional Unionism and Slavery in Virginia," 34.

57. Sarah Fife Diary, November 13, 1861, UVa.

58. Staunton *Vindicator*, May 17, 1861.

Chapter 2

1. Jones, *Rebel War Clerk's Diary*, 1:49–50; R. O. Davidson to Jefferson Davis, May 2, 1861, Letters Received, Confederate Secretary of War Papers, Record Group 109, microfilm, roll 2, file no. 862-1861, National Archives, Washington. [Herafter cited LRCSW.]

2. Military-age males based on *O.R.*, ser. IV, vol. 3:103.

3. Olivia Alexander Page to Edwin R. Page, July 17, 1861, Randolph Family Papers, acc. no. 8937, box 1, UVa [quote]. For persecution of Unionists, see M. L. Roadcap to John B. McGuffin, June 3, 1861, McGuffin Family Papers, UVa, and William Pannill to Francis H. Pierpont, January 6, 1866, Executive Papers, LV; Hunnicutt, *The Conspiracy Unveiled*, 270–1, 291.

4. Lynchburg *Virginian*, May 15, 1861; T. Lloyd Benson, "The Plain Folk of Orange: Land, Work, and Society on the Eve of the Civil War," in Ayers and Willis, eds., *The Edge of the South*, 71. This trend matches enlistments for North Carolina charted by Martin Crawford in "Confederate Volunteering and Enlistment in Ashe County, North Carolina," 29–50.

5. Staunton *Vindicator*, June 21, 1861.

6. "Hurrah for Sambo," Lynchburg *Virginian*, April 25, 1861. Free black men volunteered to aid the Confederacy for a number of reasons. Some volunteered from patriotism, others out of hope for better treatment, and still more from community pressure or fear of impressment. See Boulden, "Lynchburg, Virginia: A City of War," 35; McPherson, *The Negro's Civil War*, 23–5; Jordan, *Black Confederates and Afro-Yankees*, 216–7.

7. H. L. Clay to Dear General, May 4, 1861, LRCSW, roll 2; Johnston, *Narrative of Military Operations*, 60.

8. Ran Sifer to Miss Maggie [E. Williams], September 8, 1861, Marguerite Williams Papers, SHC; G. W. Latham to G. W. Bagby, Octo-

ber 23, 1861, Bagby Papers, VHS. Also see Mitchell, *Civil War Soldiers*, 56–9.

9. J. R. Woltz to Jeff Davis, April 17, 1861, LRCSW.

10. A. G. Balley and others, January 4, 1862, LRCSW, roll 23, file no. 9947.

11. Lucy Wood Butler Diary, May 24, 1861, UVa.

12. William Blackford Diary, April 20, 1861, Blackford Family Papers, box 2, vol. 5, UVa. For offers to donate slaves, see J. Ralls Abell to John Letcher, April 20, 1861, and George C. Gilmer to Gov. John Letcher, April 21, 1861, Executive Papers, LV.

13. Goff, *Confederate Supply*, 49–50; *O.R.*, ser. IV, 1:959.

14. R. W. Gibbes, Inspector of Hospitals for Virginia to L. P. Walker, [July, 1861], LRCSW, roll 6, file no. 2837; Waddell, *Annals of Augusta County*, 459–60; Jordan, *Charlottesville and the University of Virginia in the Civil War*, 45–6; Boulden, "Lynchburg, Virginia: A City of War," 36.

15. Lynchburg *Virginian*, August 28, 1861 and September 28, 1861; Liz McCue to John McCue, November 14, 1861, and F. G. Peters to John McCue, July 26, 1861 [quote], McCue Family Papers, box 4, UVa.

16. A. Monroe to Colonel Charles Blue, December 4, 1861, LRCSW, roll 18, file no. 8374 [quote]; R. T. Hubard to Colonel Edmund W. Hubard, April 25, 1861, Hubard Family Papers, box 16, folder 178, SHC.

17. Lynchburg *Virginian*, April 4, 1862 and August 29, 1861.

18. Lynchburg *Virginian*, April 4, 1862.

19. Lynchburg *Virginian*, November 12, 13, 14, 19, 22, 1862. The committee established McDaniel & Irby, commission merchants, as the agents for salt.

20. See, for instance, Campbell County Court, Order Book 28, pp. 291, 297, and Augusta County Court, Order Book 59, pp. 202–3, both in LV; Manarin, *Richmond at War*, 198; Lonn, *Salt as a Factor in the Confederacy*, 110.

21. Alexander H. H. Stuart to Dear Sir, July 20, 1861, LRCSW, roll 5, file no. 2527.

22. *O.R.*, ser. I, vol. 5:817–9, 820–1 [quote] 826; Wright Gatewood to Jefferson Davis, August 12, 1861, John T. Harris to Governor Letcher, August 13, 1861, and J. Marshall McCue to Colonel Walker, August 18, 1861, all in LRCSW, roll 7, file nos. 3161, 3172, and 3420.

23. Thomas Bragg to Honorable J. P. Benjamin, November 25, 1861, LRCSW, roll 16, file no. 7873; Major R. L. T. Beale to Honorable J. P. Benjamin, November 24, 1861, LRCSW, roll 17, file no. 7964; Scarborough, ed., *Diary of Edmund Ruffin*, 2:40; Ira Berlin and others, *Freedom: A Documentary History of Emancipation*, ser. 1, 1:782–3.

24. *O.R.*, ser. I, vol. 9:49.

25. Robert C. Mcluer to Governor Letcher, October 4, 1861, LRCSW, roll 11, file no. 6301.

26. R. C. Seldon to Secretary of War, November 6, 1861, LRCSW, roll

16, no. 7379; Jed Hotchkiss to Sara, January 2, 1862, Hotchkiss Papers, LC, reel 4, frame 383.

27. Poland, "Loudoun County During the Civil War," 29; Jordan, *Black Confederates*, 211; Sutherland, *Seasons of War*, 69–70; Berlin and others, *Freedom*, 1:760 [quote].

28. Superintendent J. F. Pendleton to John Letcher, December 3, 1861, LRCSW, roll 17, no. 8084; B. G. Brown to Brother, December 14, 1861, Brown Family Papers, UVa, acc. no. 3513.

29. J. H. Hunter to Hon. R. M. T. Hunter, November 22, 1861, LRCSW, roll 16, file no. 7758–1861.

30. *O.R.*, ser. IV, vol. 1:963.

31. For a similar observation of North Carolina, see Kenzer, *Kinship and Neighborhood*, 17–28.

32. Schlotterbeck, "Plantation and Farm," 214, 218–21, and his "'Social Economy' of an Upper South Community," in *Class, Conflict, and Consensus: Antebellum Southern Community Studies*, eds. Burton and McMath, 3–28; Harris, "The Organization of Work on a Yeoman Slaveholder's Farm," 39–52; Fields, "Agricultural Population of Virginia," 163.

33. Schlotterbeck, "Plantation and Farm," 240–4; Olmsted, *The Cotton Kingdom*, 529; Waddell, *Annals of Augusta County*, 430–1.

34. Cecil-Fronsman, *Common Whites*, 211–2.

35. Lynchburg *Virginian*, September 28, 1861; Sutherland, *Seasons of War*, 89.

36. McFarland Diary, October 21 and 23, 1861, Francis McFarland Papers, reel I, Part IV, vol. 12, UVa; *O.R.*, ser. II, vol. 2:1368–70, and IV, vol. 1:586–93; Lynchburg *Virginian*, October 2 and 12, 1861; Jones, *A Rebel War Clerk's Diary*, 1:82–3.

37. Randolph's statement attached to M. L. Anderson to Governor Letcher, March 20, 1862, LRCSW, roll 29, file no. A95-1862.

38. Martha Sublett & Thomas Sublett, January 18, 1862, Thomas F. Kelley Papers, Special Collections Library, Duke University, Durham, N.C. [hereafter cited as Duke]; Lynchburg *Virginian*, February 25, 27, 28 and March 5, 1862.

39. Radley, *Rebel Watchdog*, 15; John Taylor to Colonel A. T. Bledsoe, March 4 and 6, 1862, LRCSW, roll 74, file nos. T37, T44; Morris, "Confederate Lynchburg, 1861–1865," 57–8; Chesson, *Richmond After the War*, 31. Pay for the eleven members of Lynchburg's night watch ranged from $52.50 to $38.75 per person. See the Lynchburg *Virginian*, March 4, 1862.

40. J. T. Hubard to Uncle, February 21, 1862, box 16, folder 181, Hubard Family Papers, SHC.

41. *O.R.*, ser. IV, 1:923–5, 924 [quote], 1114; Richmond *Dispatch*, February 10 and 12, 1862.

42. *Acts of the General Assembly, 1861–1862*, 47–9; Lynchburg *Virginian*, February 25, 1862.

43. *O.R.*, ser. I, vol. 12, pt. 3:835, and ser. IV, vol. 1:1009–10; Jed Hotchkiss to Wife, March 18, 1862, Hotchkiss Papers, LC, roll 4, frame 385; Socrates Maupin Faculty Notes, February 21 and 24, 1862, UVa.

44. W. T. Early to Honorable John Letcher, March 12, 1862; Langhorne & Scott to Honorable John Letcher, February 24, 1862; and T. D. Jennings to Governor Letcher, March 11, 1862, all in Executive Papers, LV.

45. Waddell, *Annals of Augusta County*, 466; Horst, *Mennonites in the Confederacy*, 52–61.

46. *O.R.*, I, vol. 12, pt. 3:835.

47. *Acts of the General Assembly, 1861–1862*, 50–1.

48. Mrs. M. B. Clopton to General Randolph, March 22, 1862, LRCSW, roll 37, file no. B181; Watkins Kearns Diary, April 2–3, 1862, VHS; Horst, *Mennonites in the Confederacy*, 63–4; Lynchburg *Virginian*, April 17, 1862; Casler, *Four Years in the Stonewall Brigade*, 70; Chambers, *Stonewall Jackson*, 1:438; Jed. Hotchkiss to wife, April 14, 1862, Hotchkiss Papers, microfilm, roll 4, frame 399, LC.

49. Pollard, *Southern History of the War*, 1:364–5.

50. Moore, *Conscription and Conflict*, 18. For disaffection in the Tidewater, see Scarborough, ed., *Diary of Edmund Ruffin*, 2:186–9.

51. William Blackford Diary, April 17, 1861, Box 2, v. 5, UVa.

52. Martha Sublett & Thomas Sublett to [indecipherable], January 18, 1862, Thomas F. Kelley Papers, Duke; Lynchburg *Virginian*, March 17, 1862, and John Letcher to the Senate and House of Delegates, March 25, 1862, in *O.R.*, ser. IV, vol. 1:1021–2; Hill Carter to John Letcher, February 3, 1862, LRCSW, roll 25, no. 10502.

53. *O.R.*, ser. I, vol. 12, pt. 3:832–3; *Journal of the Congress of the Confederate States*, 2:106.

54. Unidentified to Frances Peyton Atkinson, Mary McGuire, Eleanor Augusta Stuart, February 21, 1862, Stuart Family Papers, VHS.

55. *O.R.*, ser. IV, vol. 1:988.

Chapter 3

1. Pollard, *Southern History of the War*, 1:373; Message of the Governor, May 5, 1862, in *Virginia House Documents, Annual Reports, 1861–1862*, Doc. 4, microfilm 1063, LV, reel 19, p. iii; Boney, *John Letcher*, 162–3. Although not as stridently as opponents in Georgia, Governor Letcher collided with President Davis over one instance when the Confederate government wanted to conscript students from the Virginia Military Institute. Both sides cooperated in bringing a test case quickly before the Supreme Court of Appeals in Virginia. See William H. Richardson to Secretary of War, October 11, 1862, LRCSW, roll 69, file no. R567, and *O.R.*, ser. IV, vol. 2:123–4.

2. For resistance, see Tatum, *Disloyalty in the Confederacy*, 155–65;

Wiley, *The Road to Appomattox*, 56–7; and B. G. Brown to father and mother, January 22, 1863, Brown Family Papers, UVa, acc. no. 3513. For the relatively mild reaction of Virginians to conscription, see Moore, *Conscription and Conflict*, 297–8. For draft unrest in the North, consult McPherson, *Battle Cry of Freedom*, 608–11; Iver Bernstein, *The New York City Draft Riots*.

3. *O.R.*, ser. IV, vol. 1:1081–82; *Journal of the Congress of the Confederate States*, 2:204, 260, 270, 282, 289; Escott, *After Secession*, 70–1; for pacifist reaction, see Horst, *Mennonites in the Confederacy*, 77–8; for a physician denied Confederate exemption, see Thomas K. Durborow to the Hon. Secretary of War, May 3, 1862, LRCSW, roll 43, file no. D214.

4. Campbell County Court, Order Book 28, pp. 340, 347, LV; James H. Binford to Captain J. A. Coke, April 5, 1863, Circulars, Letters, etc., Conscript Office, 1863–1864, RG 109, entry 23, NA.

5. Lynchburg *Virginian*, September 20, 1862. For petitions that show the local boards functioning to push men into the service, see W. T. Early to Hon. Jno. Letcher, March 12, 1862, Executive Papers, March–April 1862, folder March 5–6, and R. H. Glass to Dear Sir, March 12, 1862, Executive Papers, March–April 1862, folder March 11–12, LV. For the comment about Wytheville, see John B. Floyd to John Letcher, June 29, 1862, *House Documents*, Doc. No. 45, microfilm 1063, LV, reel 20, pp. 82–3.

6. Acts of Congress, Orders, Circulars Concerning Conscription, NA, RG 109, ch. 1, vol. 258½, pp. 4–6; Moore, *Conscription and Conflict*, 67–8.

7. Abner Anderson to Mr. Sutherlin, April 28, 1862, William T. Sutherlin Papers, box 2, folder 17, SHC [emphasis the writer's].

8. Morris, "Confederate Lynchburg," 59.

9. Lynchburg *Virginian*, November 5 and November 14, 1862; Joseph Norris to Geo. W. Randolph, October 1, 1862, LRCSW, roll 64, file no. N167; *O.R.*, ser. IV, vol. 2:171.

10. E. V. Garber to William B. Keyser, May 28, 1862, LRCSW, roll 72, file no. S894; Driver, *52nd Virginia Infantry*, 28.

11. Beringer and others, *Why The South Lost*, 266, 435, 439; Escott, *After Secession*, 125–8. For observations that some deserted because of family hardship, see Mitchell, *Civil War Soldiers*, 170–1; Wiley, *Johnny Reb*, 135–9; Lonn, *Desertion During the Civil War*, 16–9.

12. This analysis owes a debt to the muster rolls from selected units in the H. E. Howard Series of Virginia regimentals and Ruffner, "Civil War Desertion from a Black Belt Regiment," in *The Edge of the South*, 79–108.

13. Lonn, *Desertion During the Civil War*, 90, 231–2. Two factors contributed to the increase in desertion among units from the southwest in 1863. Union soldiers conducted cavalry incursions into the area in late December and threatened again in early 1863. Militia groups in the area under John B. Floyd also were being transferred from state to Confederate service. See John R. Woods to Micajah Woods, February 24, 1863, Woods Papers, box 1, UVa.

14. Ruffner, "Civil War Desertion," 95.

15. Escott, *After Secession*, 100–3.

16. Lynchburg *Virginian*, January 30, 1862; Turner, *Letters of Spears and Pettit*, 1:60.

17. Lonn, *Desertion During the Civil War*, 15.

18. Addison B. Roler Diary, July 13 and August 18, 1861, VHS; Wm. W. Minor to Father, October 3, 1861, Minor-Carr-Terrill Papers, UVa.

19. J. A. Sutherland to Sister & Cousins, August 8, 1861, James A. Sutherland Papers, Duke.

20. Lonn, *Desertion During the Civil War*, 17; DeLeon, *Four Years in Rebel Capitals*, 140–1.

21. *O.R.*, ser. I, vol. 5:1045.

22. Casler, *Four Years in the Stonewall Brigade*, 49–50; G. E. Crist to Cousin, March 18, 1862, McGuffin Family Papers, UVa, acc. no. M1314.

23. J. G. H. to Callie Anthony, February 5, 1862, Anthony Family Correspondence, UVa., acc. no. 8374; John B. Baldwin to Hon. J. P. Benjamin, January 22 and February 15, 1862, LRCSW, roll 31, file no. B35; *O.R.*, ser. IV, vol 1:898–901.

24. Elias Davis to Mrs. G. A. Davis, October 14, 1862, Elias Davis Papers, folder 1, SHC.

25. Micajah Woods to John R. Woods, March 5, 1863, Woods Papers, UVa, acc. no. 10279; Early, *A Memoir of the Last Year of the War*, 127–8.

26. Deglar, *The Other South*, 175; Current, *Lincoln's Loyalists*, 215–6, 218.

27. *O.R.*, ser. I, vol. 11, pt. 3:614–5.

28. C. L. Proffit to William and Mary Proffit, February 26, 1863, Proffit Family Letters, folder 2, SHC; Casler, *Four Years in the Stonewall Brigade*, 114–5; Alexander, *Fighting for the Confederacy*, 191–3.

29. Sarah Strickler Fife Diary, April 27, 1862, UVa; Blackford, *Letters from Lee's Army*, 39–40; McDonald, *Reminiscences of the War and Refugee Life*, 37.

30. Hd. Qrs. Ewell's Division, September 29th, 1862, Early Papers, The New York Historical Society.

31. *Charleston Daily Courier*, February 5, 1863.

32. Fleet and Fuller, *Green Mount*, 199.

33. For works emphasizing the community's influence on desertion, see Hallock, "Role of the Community in Civil War Desertion," 123–4; Reid, "A Mob of Stragglers and Cowards," 64–77; and Bearman, "Desertion as Localism: Army Unit Solidarity and Group Norms in the U.S. Civil War," 321–42.

34. Staunton *Spectator*, January 6, 1863 and Staunton *Vindicator*, February 20 and May 29, 1863; Lynchburg *Virginian*, June 19, 1862; Asbury Myers quoted in Driver, *52nd Virginia*, 137.

35. John Taylor to Col. A. T. Bledsoe, May 23, 1862, and John Taylor to Genl. Randolph, June 28, 1862, LRCSW, roll 74, file nos. T205, T280; Brig.

Genl. W. C. Whiting to Gen. R. E. Lee, June 14, 1862, LRCSW, roll 77, file no. W490; William H. Crank to Hon. Geo. W. Randolph, August 12, 1862, LRCSW, roll 39, file no. C896.

36. Cooper's orders in Lynchburg *Virginian*, July 1, 1862; John Avis to Hon. George W. Randolph, Staunton, Virginia, July 25, 1862, LRCSW, roll 30, file no. A297; Morris, "Confederate Lynchburg," 57–8.

37. Directive of James H. Binford, February 11, 1863, and James H. Binford to Captain J. A. Coke, April 5, 1863, both in Circulars, Letters, Etc., Conscript Office, 1863–1864, RG 109, entry 23, NA.

38. Lynchburg *Virginian*, August 29, 1862.

39. Lynchburg *Virginian*, January 9, 1863.

40. Jno. B. Baldwin to James A. Seddon, December 12, 1862, LRCSW, roll 81, file no. B10-1863; Lynchburg *Virginian*, August 26 and 27, 1862; Bensell, *Yankee Leviathan*, 143; *Acts of the General Assembly of Virginia, 1862–1863*, 106–8. For complaints about liquor, see J. Shannon to Sir, May 5, 1863, LRCSW, roll 111, file no. S338; Capt. Wm. B. Mallory to Hon. Geo W. Randolph, July 24, 1862, LRCSW, roll 61, file no. M999.

41. Tripp, "Restive Days," 146–7; Lynchburg *Virginian*, January 20, 1863; Staunton *Vindicator*, April 3, 1863.

42. Lynchburg *Virginian*, August 7, September 3, December 1, 1862; March 5 and 21, 1863.

43. Staunton *Vindicator*, March 6, 1863; Lynchburg *Virginian*, March 3 and April 1, 1863. For prices on farm supplies, see Lynchburg *Virginian*, September 14, 1863.

44. J. Marshall McCue to Hon. George W. Randolph, July 26, 1862, LRCSW, roll 61, file no. M1020.

45. Elizabeth D. White to Governor, June 24, 1862, Executive Papers, LV; Augusta County Court, Order Book 59, p. 75, LV.

46. Kean, *Inside the Confederate Government*, 40; Fleet and Fuller, *Green Mount*, 207.

47. Lynchburg *Virginian*, October 15, November 17 and 27, 1862. Impressment act in *SHSP*, 49:12–6.

48. *Acts of the General Assembly of the State of Virginia, 1863–1864*, 123–4.

49. Branscome, "Impressment in the State of Virginia," 28–9; *SHSP*, 47:126–8. For disparity in prices of early impressment in Virginia, see Register of Claims, 1861–1863, Confederate Quartermaster General, RG 109, Chapter V., vol. 43, pp. 14, 17, NA.

50. *SHSP*, 48:252–6.

51. Alexander and Beringer, *Anatomy of the Confederate Congress*, 139–65; *SHSP*, 48:112–3, 204–7, 213–4, 240–7, 280–2; Branscome, "Impressment in Virginia," 20–3; Yearns, *The Confederate Congress*, 116–20; *O.R.*, ser. 4, vol. 2:469–72.

52. John Landstreet to wife, March 22, 1863, Landstreet Letters, VHS.

53. Chesson, "Harlots or Heroines?" 131–75.

54. Wise to Father, March 21, 1863, Peter Wise and Frank W. Letters,

Duke; George Woodville Latham to Lucy Parke (Chamberlayne) Bagby, March 15, 1863, Bagby Family Papers, VHS [Lynchburg quote].

55. John B. Minor to William M. Blackford, March 27, 1863, Blackford Papers, box 6, folder 84, SHC; Lynchburg *Virginian*, March 19, 26, 1863; Lancelot Minor Farm Journal, 1863, Records of Antebellum Southern Plantations, ser. E, pt. 1, reel 36, frames 693–4.

56. Chesson, *Richmond After the War*, 40–4, and his "Harlots or Heroines?" 131–75; Pryor, *Reminiscences of Peace and War*, 237–9; Jones, *Rebel War Clerk's Diary*, 1:284–6; Thomas, *Confederate Nation*, 202–5; Rable, *Civil Wars*, 108–10.

57. Scarborough, ed., *Diary of Edmund Ruffin*, 2:612–4, 621; Crabtree and Patton, *Edmonston Diary*, 380. For drayman strike, see Tripp, "Restive Days," 145. Peace impulse in John R. Woods to Micajah, February 25, 1863, Woods Papers, box 1, UVa; Lynchburg *Virginian*, March 9, 1863.

58. Augusta County, for instance, set aside $1 per week for each spouse and 50 cents per week for each child of needy soldiers. See minutes of November 24, 1862, Augusta County Court, Order Book 59, p. 75, LV.

59. For small notes, see Augusta County Court, December 27, 1862, Order Book 59, p. 104, LV, and *Acts of the General Assembly, 1863*, 3.

60. Manarin, *Richmond at War*, 320–2. On public relief in general, see Bremner, *The Public Good*, 74–8; Escott, "'The Cry of the Sufferers,'" 231–2; Ramsdell, *Behind the Lines*, 40, 62–8; Zornow, "Aid for Indigent Families of Soldiers in Virginia," 454–8.

61. McGuire, *Diary of a Southern Refugee*, 252–5.

62. Gorgas, *Journals of Josiah Gorgas*, ed. Wiggins, 59–60; Cleary Diary, May 23, 1863, p. 33, VHS.

63. Moore, *Injustice*, 146.

64. Blair, ed., *A Politician Goes to War*, Geary letters, 40–1.

65. Sarah Strickler Fife Diary, March 16, 1862, UVa; William Selwyn Ball, "Reminiscences of an Old Rebel," typescript [c.1929], VHS. Wm. M. Blackford Dairy, April 20, 1862, volume 6, Box 2, UVa.

66. Jed Hotchkiss to Wife, May 26, 1862, Hotchkiss Papers, LC, reel 4, frame 425; Wm. M. Blackford Diary, April 20, 1862, volume 6, Box 2, UVa.

67. Maury, *Betty Herndon Maury Diary*, 52, 55. Other comments concerning fleeing slaves on 60, 66, 71; Hunnicutt, *Conspiracy Unveiled*. 354–5, 379; Patrick, *Inside Lincoln's Army*, 114–5.

68. Lynchburg *Virginian*, July 22, August 9, and 11, 1862; James M. Harris to Thomas H. Ellis, August 4, 1862, LRCSW, roll 46, file no. E137.

69. Slave prices in Lynchburg *Virginian*, October 27, 1862 and January 30, 1863; Jed Hotchkiss to Wife, March 21, 1862, Hotchkiss Papers, roll 4, frame 386, LC; Richmond *Enquirer*, October 21, 1862.

70. Grimsley, "Conciliation and Its Failure," 317–35. For a similar interpretation, see McPherson, *Battle Cry of Freedom*, 501–2.

71. J. C. Richey to J. R. Tucker, August 7, 1862, LRCSW, roll 69, file no. R490.

72. *O.R.*, vol. 12, pt. 2:50–2; A. S. Dandridge to Father, August 5, 1862, Bedinger-Dandridge Family Papers, box 4, Duke; John A. Wiant to Dear Brother, September 12, [1862], Brown Family Papers, UVa; Buck, *Sad Earth, Sweet Heaven*, 121. For vengeance as a motivator, see McPherson, *What They Fought For*, 18–25.

73. Blair, "Barbarians at Fredericksburg's Gate," in *Decision on the Rappahannock*, ed. Gary W. Gallagher, 142–70.

74. *O.R.*, vol. 51, pt. 2:665–6; Morris, "Confederate Lynchburg," pp. 62–3; Manarin, *Richmond at War*, 275; Massey, *Refugee Life in the Confederacy*, 252–3; Richmond *Daily Dispatch*, January 1, 1863; *Richmond Enquirer*, January 2, 1863.

75. *Southern Confederacy* (Atlanta, Ga.), December 27, 1862; *Daily Lynchburg Virginian*, December 20, 1862; *Richmond Enquirer*, December 23, 1862; *Richmond Whig*, December 22, 1862; *Augusta (Ga.) Chronicle & Sentinel*, January 10, 1863; Jackson, *The Southern Women and the Second American Revolution*, 49–50; Richmond *Dispatch*, December 16, 1862; Lynchburg *Virginian*, April 2, 1863.

Chapter 4

1. *SHSP*, 50:150–1; Moore, *Conscription and Conflict*, 44–5. For a similar interpretation—and chapter title—concerning changes in Georgia's wartime financial policy, see Wallenstein, *From Slave South to New South*, 110–20.

2. Escott, "'The Cry of the Sufferers,'" 232, 234, 238. Richard Franklin Bensell also claims that price controls in 1864 were "in all probability, an even more effective means of redistributing income from the owners of plantations to indigent families" than the 1862 tax provisions. See his *Yankee Leviathan*, 166. Not all agree. For the opinion that the Confederacy never ventured into public relief, see Coulter, *Confederate States of America*, 424.

3. Thomas C. Elder to Wife, May 8, 1863, Thomas Claybrook Elder Papers, VHS; Richmond *Daily Dispatch*, May 8, 1863.

4. *SHSP*, 49:66–8, 80–3, 145–6, 152–4; *O.R.*, ser. IV, 3:355.

5. *SHSP*, 49:152; Acts of Congress, Orders, Circulars Relating to Conscription, RG 109, ch. 1, vol. 258$^{1}/_{2}$, pp. 15–6, NA: Coulter, *Confederate States of America*, 319–20; Moore, *Conscription and Conflict*, 73–4; Yearns, *Confederate Congress*, 80–1.

6. Moore, *Conscription and Conflict*, 74–5; *O.R.*, ser. IV, 2:558–9, 573, 728–9.

7. Yearns, *Confederate Congress*, 81; John Woods to Son, May 14, 1863, Woods Papers, UVa; James H. Binford to Sir, May 28, 1863, Circulars, Letters, Orders Relating to the Conscript Office at Richmond, 1863–1864, RG 109, entry 23, NA.

8. John B. Minor to James A. Seddon, May 29, 1863, LRCSW, roll 103, file no. M433 [emphasis the writer's].

9. Yearns, *Confederate Congress*, 49–54; Boney, *John Letcher of Virginia*, 192–3; Maddex, *Virginia Conservatives*, 25. For Virginia's delegation to Congress see, *O.R.*, ser. 4, 3:1187, 1189, 1191, and Alexander and Beringer, *Anatomy of the Confederate Congress*, 354–89.

10. Alexander and Beringer, *Anatomy of the Confederate Congress*, 103; Rable, *The Confederate Republic*, 218–9, 226–35; Yearns, *Confederate Congress*, 53.

11. Richmond *Daily Dispatch*, May 30, June 1, 1863, and Staunton *Vindicator*, June 12, 1863.

12. Robert E. Lee to Col. L. B. Northrup, January 8, 1863, in *O.R.*, ser. I, vol. 51, (2):667; Goff, *Confederate Supply*, 88.

13. Fremantle, *Three Months in the Southern States*, 223. Also see Williams, *From the Cannon's Mouth*, 213–4.

14. *O.R.*, ser. 4, 2:302, 334–5.

15. *O.R.*, ser. I, vol. 27, (3) 845–6; Goff, *Confederate Supply*, 167; Wm. H. Payton to Governor, April 9, 1864, LRCSW, roll 138, file no. P104.

16. Trowbridge, *The Desolate South*, 67.

17. For other examples of barter, see Cornelius Dabney Diary, January 19, 1863, folder 2, SHC; editor of the Lexington *Gazette* in Driver, *Lexington and Rockbridge County in the Civil War*, 47.

18. Dowdey and Manarin, *The Wartime Papers of R. E. Lee*, 508; Nolan, *Lee Considered*, 90–6.

19. Kean, *Inside the Confederate Government*, 80–1 [emphasis the writer's].

20. J. C. Shields to District Enrollment Officers, July 17, 1863, in Circulars, Letters, Orders Regarding the Conscript Office at Richmond, 1863–1864, RG 109, Entry 23, NA; Acts of Congress, Orders, Circulars Relating to Conscription, RG 109, ch. 1, vol. 258½, NA.

21. Jones, *Rebel War Clerk's Diary*, 2:15; Captain T. W. Hutter to J. L. Smith, August 22, 1863, and Captain E. McCormick to Captain J. L. Smith, Lynchburg, August 22, 1863, both in Letters Received, Quartermaster General's Bureau, RG 109, microcopy 469, roll 6, file no. H228, NA. [Hereafter cited as QGB.]

22. J. W. Hampton and J. H. Robinson to Captain O. F. Weiseger, July 12, 1863, roll 5, file no. H282, QGB; Jones, *Rebel War Clerk's Diary*, 2:140; Rable, *Civil Wars*, 131–3.

23. Statistical Reports of Conscripts in Virginia, RG 109, ch. 1, vol. 250, NA; Gorgas, *Journals of Josiah Gorgas*, Wiggens, ed., 79. The statistics for men reporting to the camps of instruction understate the actual numbers who reported. An accurate assessment cannot be determined because, as always, the draft accounted for only a portion of the men who went into the army. When facing conscription, most men bypassed camps of instruction to enter the ranks directly as they could choose the unit in which they served.

This frustrated conscripton officers who preferred to keep better track of the men and direct them to units in need, but no one could stop the practice.

24. Captain Frank M. Imboden Diary, July 10, 13, 31, 1863, UVa, acc. no. 2983a; Sarah Strickler Fife Diary, July 30, 1863, UVa.

25. Casler, *Four Years in the Stonewall Brigade*, 183–4; *O.R.*, ser. I, vol. 32, (1) 608.

26. Elias Davis to Mrs. G. A. Davis, August 14, 1863, Elias Davis Papers, folder 2, SHC.

27. Jones, *Rebel War Clerk's Diary*, 2:3–4; Provost Marshal General's Report in House Executive Documents, First Session, 39th Congress, no. 1, vol. IV, pt. 1, pp. 139–41. For desertion among North Carolinians, see Bardolph, "Inconstant Rebels," 163–89, and his "Confederate Dilemma," 61–86 and 179–210; Sutherland, *Seasons of War,* 268.

28. *O.R.*, ser. IV, 2:687.

29. Lynchburg *Virginian*, August 20, 1863.

30. R. E. Lee to Jefferson Davis, July 27, 1862, *O.R.*, 27, pt. 3:1040–1; R. E. Lee to Jefferson Davis, August 17, 1863, in Dowdey and Manarin, *Wartime Papers of R. E. Lee*, 591; General Orders No. 84 establishing the furloughs may be found in Richmond *Daily Dispatch*, August 20, 1863; Elias Davis to Mrs. G. A. Davis, November 17, 1863, and Elias Davis to Mrs. G. A. Davis, January 4, 1864, Elias Davis Papers, folder 2, SHC.

31. William Beverly Pettit to Bell, April 10, 1864, in Turner, *Letters of Speairs and Pettit*, 2:19; John N. Pearce to Miss Lizzie Brown, December 21, 1863, Brooke-Stoddard Papers, UVa; W. Brown to Papa, [c. 1864], Brown Family Papers, UVa, acc. no. 3513.

32. R. E. Lee to Jefferson Davis, August 8, 1863, and R. E. Lee to Jefferson Davis, August 17, 1863, in Dowdey and Manarin, *Wartime Papers of R. E. Lee*, 589, 591; *O.R.*, ser. I, vol. 29, (2) 806–7. For Davis's leniency, see Davis, *Jefferson Davis*, 531. For deserters near Scottsville in lower Albemarle County, see Staunton *Vindicator,* September 11, 1863.

33. Casler, *Four Years in the Stonewall Brigade*, 188–90; C. J. Winston to Uncle, February 7, 1864, Winston-Clark Papers, VHS; Lynchburg *Virginian*, March 22, 1864.

34. Lynchburg *Virginian*, September 24 and 14, 1863.

35. Richmond *Daily Dispatch*, September 10, 30, 1863; Lynchburg *Virginian*, September 19, 1863; Staunton *Vindicator,* September 11, 1863; Richmond *Daily Enquirer,* October 24, 1863; King, *Louis T. Wigfall*, 183–4; Branscome, "Impressment in the State of Virginia," 101–2. Augusta, Monroe, and Campbell counties endorsed similar measures. *Richmond Whig*, October 2 and 17, 1863.

36. Prices in Lynchburg *Virginian*, September 7, 1863; December 21, 1863; and March 4, 1864.

37. Cornelius Dabney Diary, October 2, 1863, folder 2, SHC.

38. Staunton *Vindicator*, July 3, 1863.

39. Lynchburg *Virginian*, April 22, July 31, August 1, 1863; Staunton *Vindicator*, September 11, November 6, 1863. For Charlottesville, see Moore, *Albemarle: Jefferson's County*, 202. Henrico County Court followed this trend, increasing its commitment for relief of soldiers from $4,000 in March 1863 to $50,000 by November, funding this effort with 6 percent bonds with interest payable every six months. Bailey, *Henrico Home Front*, 114, 162.

40. *Acts of the General Assembly, 1863*, 20–4; Campbell County Court, December 1863, Order Book 28, p. 404, and September Term, 1864, Order Book 29, p. 41, LV. For a while, refugees caused problems in the administration of these programs. They sometimes received double rations or pay—from the community they had fled from and also from the community where they currently lived. It took a while for counties and the state to sort this out, eventually deciding that the area in which people currently resided held the responsibility for care. See Augusta County Court, March 28, 1864, Order Book 59, p. 318, LV and *Acts of the General Assembly, 1863–1864*, 48.

41. Rice, *The Life of Jonathan M. Bennett*, 138–40; *Acts of the General Assembly, 1863–1864*, 3, 24–5.

42. Lynchburg *Virginian*, November 30, December 4, 15, 1863, and April 17, 1875; Robert R. Prentis to James Seddon, May 16, 1864, LRCSW, file no. P144.

43. Manarin, *Richmond at War*, 320–1, 348, 356, 371, 382–5, 387, 389, 408, 410; Thomas, *Confederate State of Richmond*, 146.

44. Lynchburg *Virginian*, August 3, 15, 1863.

45. E. D. Christian to James A. Seddon, March 30, 1864, LRCSW, roll 123, file no. C317; Robert R. Prentis to James Seddon, May 16, 1864, LRCSW, file no. P144. For a similar assessment, see Thomas, *Confederate State of Richmond*, 147.

46. Lucy W. Otey and Mrs. John W. Speed to Honorable G. W. Randolph, October 17, 1862, LRCSW, roll 67, file no. 0105; Martha Haisloss to Jefferson Davis, April 17, 1864, LRCSW, roll 129, file no. H268.

47. Jones, *Rebel War Clerk's Diary*, 2:61.

48. Kean, *Inside the Confederate Goverment*, 116 [emphasis his]. For seizing goods of farmers on the way to market, see Jones, *Rebel War Clerk's Diary*, 2:101.

49. Lynchburg *Virginian*, September 23, 1863; Richmond *Daily Dispatch*, September 24, 25, 1863; Jones, *Rebel War Clerk's Diary*, 2:67–8; 76–7.

50. Richmond *Daily Dispatch*, October 12, 1863; Thomas, *Confederate State of Richmond*, 148–9.

51. Lynchburg *Virginian*, September 23, 1863.

52 Richmond *Daily Dispatch*, October 12, 1863.

53. *Richmond Whig*, October 6, 7, 9, 13, 24, 1863; Richmond *Enquirer*, October 6, 1863; Richmond *Daily Dispatch*, October 22, 23, 1863.

54. Richmond *Daily Dispatch*, October 23, 1863; Thomas, *Confederate State of Richmond*, 149; Kean, *Inside The Confederate Government*, 107.

55. Lynchburg *Virginian*, October 22, 1863.

56. Inaugural Address of the Governor of Virginia, January 6, 1864, in Virginia House Documents, M1068, reel 20, Doc. no. 18, pp. 8–10, LV.

57. *Richmond Whig*, October 6, 1863; Jones, *Rebel War Clerk's Diary*, 2:66.

58. Morris, "Confederate Lynchburg," 81–2, 84; Lynchburg *Virginian*, February 9, 15, 1864.

59. James H. Binford to Capt. J. A. Coke, November 16, 1863, and James H. Binford to Capt. J. A. Coke, November 19, 1863, Circulars, Letters, Orders Concerning the Conscript Office, 1863–1864, RG 109, entry 23, NA; Staunton *Vindicator*, November 27, 1863.

60. See "4th Call for Slaves to Work on Public Defenses in Virginia," in Executive Papers, March–June 1863, folder March 14–31, LV.

61. Unidentified to the Secretary of War, February 5, 1863, LRCSW, roll 80, file no. A31; James H. Binford to District Enrolling Officers, September 16, 1863, in Circulars, Letters, Orders Concerning the Conscript Office, 1863–1864, RG 109, entry 23, NA.

62. Jones, *Rebel War Clerk's Diary*, 2:30–1.

63. *Richmond Whig*, November 13, 1863.

64. *Journal of the Congress of the Confederate States*, 3:446–7; *O.R.*, ser. IV, 2:1024–49.

65. Elias Davis to Mrs. G. A. Davis, December 10, 1863, Elias Davis Papers, folder 2, SHC; Lynchburg *Virginian*, December 21, 1863, January 2, 1864; Pollard, *Southern History*, 2:189–91; *O.R.*, ser. IV, 2:1041; *SHSP*, 50:26, 39–40, 51–2, 65, 105–6, 115–7, 119–21, 127–34, 150–8; James H. Binford to District Enrolling Officers, Circular No. 7, January 16, 1864, Enrollment Officer Records, Rockingham County, VHS; Jones, *Rebel War Clerk's Diary*, 2:121–2, 126.

66. Lynchburg *Virginian*, January 2, 4, 27, 28, February 2, 1864; *O.R.*, ser. IV, 3:12.

67. Reports of November 1, 1863, February 12, and March 7, 1864, in Statistical Reports of Conscripts in Virginia, RG 109, ch. 1, vol. 250, NA.

68. *O.R.*, ser. IV, 3:97.

69. Ball, *Financial Failure*, 187–9.

70. *O.R.*, ser. IV, 3:208; Staunton *Vindicator*, March 4, 1864; Lynchburg *Virginian*, March 19, 1864; Yearns, *Confederate Congress*, 205, 207–8.

71. Scarborough, ed., *The Diary of Edmund Ruffin*, 3:340–1; Morris, "Confederate Lynchburg," 75; William M. Blackford Diary, February 18, 1864, box 2, vol. 8, UVa, acc. no. 4763; W. J. Kinchelor to Annie, February 21, 1864, John W. Daniel Papers, box 2, UVa, acc. no. 158.

72. *O.R.*, ser. IV, 3:178–81; Bensell, *Yankee Leviathan*, 130–1, 135–9. Summaries of the military, currency, and tax bills in Lynchburg *Virginian*, February 19, 1864.

73. Staunton *Vindicator,* February 5, 26, 1864; Slave Schedules, Augusta County, 1860, NA; John B. Baldwin to Secretary of War, March 3, 1864, and John B. Baldwin to Secretary of War, March 23, 1864, LRCSW, roll 120, file nos. B304 and B307.

74. Monthly Report for September 1864, Enrolling Department of Virginia, Inspection Reports, Adjutant and Inspector General's Office, RG 109, microcopy M935, roll 2, file no. A20, NA [Hereafter cited as AIGO]; see circular from the Bureau of Conscription in Lynchburg *Virginian,* April 14, 1864. Some discrepancy exists in counting these details and exemptions. Another report in the Inspector General papers places the numbers considerably lower for Virginia. A. J. Hays reported for the period from February 17 to August, 17, 1864, that 105 agriculturists and overseers had been exempted and another 232 persons detailed for this work, or a total of 337. I have chosen to go with the higher numbers to present the worst possible scenario. See A. J. Hays to Colonel Jno. B. Sale, August 30, 1864, AIGO, roll 7, file no. H40.

75. Mrs. John P. Michie to J. A. Seddon, March 26, 1864, LRCSW, M215, roll 135, file no. M215, and W. A. Staples to Hon. J. A. Seddon, August 7, 1864, LRCSW, roll 11, file no. S259.

76. Martha Haisloss to Hon. Jefferson Davis, April 17, 1864, LRCSW, roll 129, file no. H268.

77. Pollard, *Southern History of the War,* 2:190–1.

78. Jones, *Rebel War Clerk's Diary,* 2:82.

79. *O.R.,* ser. I, vol. 33, p. 186; Frank G. Ruffin to William M. Randolph, December 26, 1863, Preston-Radford Papers, box 3, UVa acc. no. 6353.

Chapter 5

1. Cyrus H. Cline, Sr., "Description of Old Home, Mother, Father and Sisters," Fredericksburg-Spotsylvania National Military Park; Horst, *Mennonites in the Confederacy,* 100–3; *O.R.,* ser. I, vol. 43, pt. 1, 30.

2. Louisa A. Minor Diary, March 5, 1864, UVa [emphasis hers]; *O.R.,* ser. I, 33:162–8.

3. Duke, "Reminiscences," 193–4, Duke Family Papers, vol. 1, box 1, UVa; Lynchburg *Virginian,* September 22, 1864; McDonald, *War Diary and Reminiscences,* 238.

4. Jones, *Rebel War Clerk's Diary,* 2:64, 79; Sarah Strickler Fife Diary, January 27 and December 19, 1864, UVa.

5. Rawleigh William Downman to Mary Alice Downman, January 16, 1864, Downman Family Papers, VHS; Thomas Davis Ranson to Frances Peyton Atkinson, June 2, 1864, Stuart Family Papers, VHS. In the Engineer's Bureau, a man had received from a friend in the army a "capital cheerful & inspiring letter speaking in hopeful strains & describing Genl L's

blows on Grant as most telling." See Alfred L. Rives to Sadie, May 23, 1864, Rives Papers, VHS.

6. Wiley, *Reminiscences of Big I*, 52–3; *O.R.*, ser. IV, 3:379; Goff, *Confederate Supply*, 199; Jed. Hotchkiss to My Own Dear One, April 21, 1864, Hotchkiss Papers, reel 4, frame 569, LC.

7. W. J. Kinchelor to Annie, January 23, 1864, John W. Daniel Papers, box 2, UVa acc. no. 158. For a supporting view that the Confederacy had resolved some of its supply problems to the army during the Overland Campaign, see Woodworth, *Davis & Lee at War*, 270.

8. William H. Peyton to Governor, May 19, 1864, Executive Papers, folder May 1864, LV.

9. Jed. Hotchkiss to Sara, June 19, 1864, Hotchkiss Papers, LC, reel 4, frame 584; Morris, "Confederate Lynchburg," 84; Staunton *Vindicator*, May 13, 1864; Scarborough, ed., *Diary of Edmund Ruffin*, 3:497–8.

10. Goff, *Confederate Supply*, 214; Staunton *Vindicator*, April 29, 1864.

11. George W. Lay to Office of Inspector General of Conscription, July 22, 1864, AIGO, roll 3, file no. 6-c. For the problems caused by poor impressment agents, see Ramsdell, *Behind the Lines in the Southern Confederacy*, 117.

12. Dabney & Somers to Lt. Col. A. H. Gold, April 13, 1864, LRQGD, roll 8, file no. H126. In this case, the department ordered the horses returned to the foundry.

13. J. H. Smith to J. A. Seddon, March 31, 1864, LRQMGD, roll 9, file no. S341; James G. Paxton to James A. Seddon, February 29, 1864, LRCSW, roll 137, file no. P176; E. Murray to Colonel, February 23, 1865, Inspection Reports, AIGO, M935, roll 9, file no. M-48, NA.

14. G. N. Musgrave to Sir, March 11, 1864, LRQMGD, roll 9, file no. M203; assessors' statements in Lynchburg *Virginian*, August 22, 1864.

15. William H. Langhorne to Major J. G. Paxton, March 31, 1864, LRQMGD, roll 8, file no. D304.

16. V. M. Epps to unidentified, April 6, 1864, LRQMGD, roll 8, file no. D304; Statement of James E. Haskins, March 28, 1864, LRQGD, roll 8, file no. E67.

17. George Rable has provided the clearest articulation of the divisions within leaders. See his *Confederate Republic*, 157–8. The temptation exists to adopt Raimondo Luraghi's concept of political class to describe this group, for they functioned as something of a conscience for their peers, considered problems on the highest possible political level, and advocated the short-term economic sacrifices necessary for long-term success. However, this concept imparts to these planters a coherence of outlook, unity of purpose, and nobility that rarely existed. See, Luraghi, *Rise and Fall of the Plantation South*, 78–9.

18. Scarborough, ed., *Diary of Edmund Ruffin*, 3:498–9; *O.R.*, ser. IV, 3:389–92.

19. Lynchburg *Virginian*, July 18, 15, 1864; Blackford, *Letters from Lee's Army*, 268.

20. *The Daily Chronicle* (Charlottesville, Va.), July 19, 1864, in LRCSW, roll 124, file no. C424.

21. Lynchburg *Virginian*, July 25, 1864; Staunton *Vindicator*, July 29, 1864.

22. Bailey, *Henrico Home Front*, 196–8.

23. Staunton *Vindicator*, July 29, 1864; *O.R.*, ser. 4, 3:492.

24. Lynchburg *Virginian*, February 18, 1865; Pollard, *Southern History of the War*, 2:457. For debates on commissary and quartermaster fraud, see *SHSP*, 52:69–74, 122–3, 343–5.

25. Rawleigh William Downman to Mary Alice, January 1, 1865, Downman Family Papers, VHS [emphasis Downman's].

26. Blackford, *Letters from Lee's Army*, 268.

27. William B. Harrison to E. W. Hubard, August 21, 1864, Hubard Family Papers, box 17, folder 189, SHC.

28. W. A. Staples to Hon. J. A. Seddon, August 7, 1864, LRCSW, roll 11, file no. S259.

29. Lynchburg *Virginian*, August 15, 1864; Morris, "Confederate Lynchburg," 120; List of Civil Employees in the Employ of Major H. M. Bell, Quartermaster at Staunton, August 9, 1864, LRQMGD, roll 10, file no. B529.

30. Lynchburg *Virginian*, November 12, 1864; *SHSP*, 51:289–90, 351–2, 411–2.

31. Thomas Y. Peyton to Col. R. H. Chilton, November 5, 1864, AIGO, roll 10, file no. P19; E. Murray to Col. R. H. Chilton, February 23, 1865, AIGO, roll 9, file no. M48. For others who claim that currency problems lay behind Confederate defeat, see Ball, *Financial Failure*, 1–2; Ramsdell, *Behind the Lines*, 85.

32. Circular from J. A. Early, Head Quarters, Valley District, February 12, 1864, LRCSW, roll 12, file no. 21; John Hart to Secretary of War, August 6, 1864, LRCSW, roll 130, file no. H410.

33. Lynchburg *Virginian*, September 3, 19, 26 [quote], 1864.

34. Augusta County Court session of October 24, 1864, Order Book 59, pp. 386–9, LV.

35. Colt, *Defend the Valley*, 356–7.

36. Pollard, *Southern History of the War*, 2:481; Goff, *Confederate Supply*, 224–5, 234; Ramsdell, ed., *Laws of the Confederate Congress*, 152.

37. Berlin, *Freedom*, ser. 1., vol. 1:767–78.

38. Brewer, *The Confederate Negro*, 13–4; Register of Free Negroes Enrolled and Detailed, May 1864–January 1865, Bureau of Conscription, Virginia, RG 109, ch. 1, vol. 241, NA.

39. E. Murray to Colonel, February 23, 1865, inspection reports, AIGO, roll 9, file no. M48; Detailed Men and Employees at CSA Ordnance Depot,

Lynchburg, Inspection Reports, AIGO, roll 4, file no. C61; Captain R. Turk to Office of Chief Inspector for Transportation, August 26, 1864, LRQGD, roll 11, file no. T182. These last two citations contain information on daily wages. The ordnance depot in Lynchburg paid skilled workers roughly $8 per day while the daily rates in the Quartermaster Depot at Staunton were only about half that amount, ranging from $3 to $5. Because all of these men were detailed workers, the wages were considered extra-duty pay—money on top of the basic monthly allowance for soldiers. For discussion of quartermaster use of black people, see Brewer, *Confederate Negro*, 26–9.

40. Report of Inspection of Iron Works &c. at Wytheville, Va., November 14, 1864, in Extracts from Inspection Reports, RG 109, ch. 1, vol. 26, p. 2, NA.

41. Fellow Citizens to Governor William Smith, Madison Court House, November 2, 1864, Executive Papers, folder, 1864-October, LV. For slave owners in Campbell County, see Lynchburg *Virginian*, October 26, 1864; Flournoy and others, eds., *Calendar of Virginia State Papers* 11:259; Morgan, *Emancipation in Virginia's Tobacco Belt*, 102–3.

42. Augusta County Court, Order Book 59, December 13, 24, 31, 1862, pp. 87–8, 100, 105; Campbell County Court, Order Book 28, October 1862, pp. 312, 314–6; Albemarle County Court, Minute Book 1859–1862, November 1862, pp. 426–7, 439–44, all in LV. Requisitions for slaves in Virginia were issued October and November 1862, March and August 1863, January and December 1864, and March 1865. See Brewer, *Confederate Negro*, 140–52.

43. Augusta County Court, Order Book 59, October 16, 21, 27, 29, and November 28, 1863, pp. 249–50, 260–1, 264, 274–5; Campbell County Court, Order Book 28, October 22, 31, 1863, pp. 393–4; *Message of the Governor, January 7, 1863* (Richmond: William F. Ritchie, 1863), xviii–xix, in Virginia House Documents, Doc. no. 1, M1063, reel 19, all in LV.

44. Brewer, *Confederate Negro*, 15; Jordan, *Black Confederates*, 266–7; *Inaugural Address of the Governor, January 1, 1864*, Doc. no. 19, table 1 in House Documents, M1063, reel 20, LV. After the war, the Freedmen's Bureau estimated that around Norfolk, Portsmouth, Fortress Monroe, and Yorktown roughly 70,000 slaves congregated who had been freed during the war. See *Norfolk Virginian*, January 1, 1866.

45. Ash, *When the Yankees Came*, 76–107.

46. Thomas Y. Peyton to Colonel R. H. Chilton, November 5, 1864, Inspection Reports, AIGO, roll 10, file no. P23; A. S. Cunningham to R. H. Chilton, February 26, 1865, Inspection Reports, AIGO, roll 4, file no. C61.

47. Bailey, *Henrico Home Front*, 93–9; 172–8; 222–6. Further details about slave impressment in Brewer, *Confederate Negro*, 140–52; *O.R.*, ser. 4, 2:426–30, and 3:851–3; Branscome, "Impressment in Virginia," 89–90, 91–2, 96.

48. Flournoy and others, eds., *Calendar of State Papers*, 11:259–61; Statement of Auditor of Number of Slaves for Service, March 25, 1865, and John D. Alexander to Colonel Munford, March 23, 1865 [quotation], both in Executive Papers, folder 1865-March 16–31, LV. [Emphasis in original.]

49. Campbell County Court, Order Book 28, February 8 and 17, 1864, pp. 419–20, LV.

50. R. T. Hubard to Brother [Colonel E. W. Hubard], November 4, 1864, Hubard Family Papers, box 17, folder 190, SHC.

51. M. G. Harman to President Jefferson Davis, January 12, 1865, LRCSW, roll 148, file no. H38; Scarborough, ed., *Diary of Edmund Ruffin*, 3:711–2.

52. B. H. Anthony to Cally, February 20, 1865, Anthony Family, UVa; Durden, *The Gray and the Black*, 225–67; Scarborough, ed., *Diary of Edmund Ruffin*, 3:624, 711–2, 748–9, 754, 784, 794.

53. *O.R.*, ser. IV, 3:1161–2.

54. *O.R.*, ser. IV, 3:354–64 [quote on p. 354].

55. Ibid., p. 356.

56. Lynchburg *Virginian*, May 25, 1864.

57. James F. Brown to Governor, March 2, 1864, and B. F. McVeigh to William Smith, March 26, 1864, both in Executive Papers, folder 1864-March, LV; John M. Speed to William Smith, June 5, 1864, Executive Papers, folder 1864-June, LV.

58. Lynchburg *Virginian*, July 13, 1864; *O.R.*, ser. IV, 3:912.

59. Details for Agriculture and Other Necessities, Monthly Return for September 1864, AIGO, roll 2, file no. A20.

60. *O.R.*, ser. IV, 3:906–12. For a less complimentary view about Smith's efforts, see Jones, *Rebel War Clerk's Diary*, 2:332.

61. *O.R.*, ser. IV, 3:712–3, 715.

62. J. C. Shields to Captain R. H. Catlett, November 1, 1864, RG 109, ch. 1, vol. 250, NA; Staunton *Vindicator*, October 21, 1864.

63. Lynchburg *Virginian*, October 13, 14, 17, 1864; Morris, "Confederate Lynchburg," 121; Jed. Hotchkiss to wife, November 5, 1864, JHP, roll 4, frame 622, LC.

64. Thomas Y. Peyton to Colonel R. H. Chilton, November 11, 1864, AIGO, roll 11, file no. P25; Thomas Y. Peyton to Col. R. H. Chilton, October 29, 1864, AIGO, roll 10, file no. P21.

65. Thomas Y. Peyton to Colonel R. H. Chilton, November 5, 1864, AIGO, roll 10, file no. P-23; Manda to Jinnie E. S., December 5, 1864, James A. Sutherland Papers, Duke.

66. Rable, *Confederate Republic*, 282; Alexander H. H. Stuart to William J. Rush, January 13, 1865, Steele Family Papers, box 1, UVa, acc. no. 10616.

67. *SHSP*, 52:142–4, 185–7, 192–6, 208–11; *O.R.*, ser. IV, 3:1176–7.

68. Lynchburg *Virginian*, December 16, 1864.

69. Jones, *Rebel War Clerk's Diary*, 2:367.

70. Jim to William J. Griggs [winter 1864–1865], Griggs Family Papers, VHS.

71. James M. Norman to William T. Sutherlin, January 14, 1865, William T. Sutherlin Papers, box 3, folder 20, SHC.

72. E. C. Barnes to Mother, January 12, 1865, Barnes Family Papers, UVa.; C. J. Winston to Uncle, January 22, 1865, Winston-Clark Papers, VHS.

73. Keever, *Keever Civil War Letters*, 44; [unidentified] to Dear Sister, January 30, 1865, Elizabeth Hairston Papers, subseries 1.2, folder 6, SHC.

74. George W. Dabney Diary, January 13, 1865, Cheswell Dabney Papers, UVa acc. no. 3315; Lynchburg *Virginian*, July 16, 1864, January 19 and February 6, 1865.

75. A. C. Keever to wife and children, February 25, 1865, and March 5, 1865 in Keever, *Keever Civil War Letters*, 48–9.

76. Quoted in Shultz, "Women at the Front," 271; Jones, *Rebel War Clerk's Diary*, 2:347.

77. Jones, *Rebel War Clerk's Diary*, 2:349, 364–5, 368, 372, 403–4, 406.

78. Durden, *The Gray and the Black*, 187–203.

79. Staunton *Vindicator*, March 24 and 31, 1865; Lynchburg *Virginian*, February 11, 12, March 2, 1865. Also see, Hotchkiss, *Make Me a Map of the Valley*, 258.

80. James M. Norman to William T. Sutherlin, January 26, 1865, Sutherlin Papers, box 3, folder 20, SHC. For an example of such resolutions, see Lynchburg *Virginian*, February 8, 1865.

81. John B. Baldwin to Alexander H. H. Stuart, n.d., Stuart Family Papers, section 2, VHS.

82. Sarah Strickler Fife Diary, April 3, 1865, pp. 48–9, UVa.

Chapter 6

1. Chester, *Black Civil War Correspondent*, 289–90, 292, 301–2, 308; Reid, *A Radical View*, 2:201 [quote].

2. Sarah Strickler Fife Diary, May 15, 1865, UVa, p. 56. For reactions of southern women to the war, see Faust, *Mothers of Invention*.

3. Waddel, *Annals of Augusta County*, 515; on the southern mood, see *Report of the Joint Committee on Reconstruction*, 2:45–6; Lowe, *Republicans and Reconstruction in Virginia*, 35–6.

4. Maddex, *Virginia Conservatives*, 36; Morgan, *Emancipation in Virginia's Tobacco Belt*, 129.

5. Lowe, *Republicans and Reconstruction in Virginia*, 27–9; Trowbridge, *The Desolate South*, 52, 57–8; Dennett, *South as It Is*, 7.

6. For descriptions of Richmond, see Chester, *Black Civil War Correspondent*, 291–4; Chesson, *Richmond After the War*, 57–9; and Pollard, *Southern*

History of the War, 2:492–4. For Fredericksburg, see Trowbridge, *The Desolate South,* 84–5, and Blair, "Barbarians at Fredericksburg's Gate," in Gallagher, ed., *Decision on the Rappahannock,* 113–41.

7. Chesson, *Richmond After the War,* 72–4, 94–5; Chester, *Black Civil War Correspondent,* 315–6; Peter Rachleff, *Black Labor in Richmond, 1865–1890* (Urbana and Chicago: University of Illinois Press), 13–33; Trowbridge, *The Desolate South,* 78–80, 92–4 [quote].

8. Dennett, *South as It Is,* 13, 25; Trowbridge, *The Desolate South,* 94–5; Crofts, *Old Southampton,* 219.

9. Morgan, *Emancipation in Virginia's Tobacco Belt,* 129–30; Dennett, *South at It Is,* 69.

10. Reid, *A Radical View,* 2:203–4.

11. Chester, *Black Civil War Correspondent,* 320–1.

12. Rachleff, *Black Labor in Richmond,* 35–7; Chesson, *Richmond After the War,* 90–1; Statement of Albert Brooks, [June 1865], Records of the Assistant Commissioner for the State of Virginia, Bureau of Freedmen, Refugees, and Abandoned Lands, 1865–69, Record Group 105, National Archives, Washington, D.C. (microfilm), roll 59.

13. Trowbridge, *The Desolate South,* 41.

14. Morgan, *Emancipation in Virginia's Tobacco Belt,* 138–9.

15. Lowe, *Republicans and Reconstruction in Virginia,* 32–5, 41–4; Crofts, *Old Southampton,* 225–6, 333; Chesson, *Richmond After the War,* 92–3. For a similar occurrence in Augusta County, see Waddell, *Annals of Augusta County,* 513–4.

16. Wainwright, *A Diary of Battle,* 520–1.

17. For a portion of the burgeoning literature that attributes defeat to internal conflicts, see Escott, *After Secession;* Hahn, *Roots of Southern Populism;* Owens and. Cooke, eds., *The Old South in the Crucible of War;* Harris, *Plain Folk and Gentry in a Slave Society;* Beringer and others, *Why the South Lost the Civil War;* Faust, *The Creation of Confederate Nationalism;* Durrill, *War of Another Kind;* Marten, *Texas Divided;* Tatum, *Disloyalty in the Confederacy.* Recently, historians have contended that the South lost the war less because of internal conflicts than a combination of factors that included the impact of the Union army. See, for instance, Boritt, ed., *Why the Confederacy Lost,* esp. 17–42; McPherson, *Battle Cry of Freedom;* Gallagher, *The Confederate War.*

18. Trowbridge, *The Desolate South,* 91–2.

19. Potter, "The Historian's Use of Nationalism," in *The South and the Sectional Conflict,* 34–83.

20. One of the strongest Unionist areas was Martinsburg, which became part of West Virginia. Confederates consistently rated it as Unionist and abolitionist, specially because of the influence of railroad workers for the Baltimore & Ohio line there. See J. B. Magruder to Papa, December 4, 1862, Magruder Papers, Duke; Blackford, *Letters from Lee's Army,* 130.

21. Horst, *Mennonites in the Confederacy,* 103–9.

22. McPherson, *What They Fought For,* 9–13.

23. William Blackford Diary, May 8 and August 29, 1861 [quotes], v. 5, box 2, UVa.

24. B. Lewis Blackford to Father, December 23, 1862, Blackford Papers, box 6, folder 83, SHC. For a sampling of similar reactions to general Union actions against property and civilians, see *Richmond Enquirer,* June 27, 1861; Sarah Strickler Fife Diary, January 9, 1865, UVa; *Message of the Governor . . ., January 7, 1863* (Richmond: Wm. F. Ritchie, 1863), House Executive Documents, doc. No. 1, reel 19, vi–vii, LV.

25. Mrs. Rev. Luther Emerson, Memorandum of Events, July 2, 1862, Emerson Papers, UVa.

26. Bell to husband, October 1, 1863, in Turner, *Letters of Speairs and Pettit,* 1:155.

27. Mary B. R. to Mary Harter, April 23, 1862, Duke Family Papers, UVa.

28. Lynchburg *Virginian,* September 4, 1861, October 6, 1864; William C. Rives, August 24, 1863, ms. of letter printed in Lynchburg *Virginian,* September 1, 1863, Rives Papers, VHS. When a newspaper in southwestern Virginia resumed publication after the war, its editor characterized the fight that had recently ended as "a struggle for nationality and independence." See *The* (Abingdon, Va.) *Virginian,* December 8, 1865.

29. Thomas F. Kelley to Cousin, August 30, 1864, T. F. Kelley Papers, Duke.

30. Moore, *Conscription and Conflict,* 297–8.

31. Freehling, *Drift Toward Dissolution,* 77–8.

32. Maddex, *The Virginia Conservatives,* 23; Rable, *The Confederate Republic,* 39–40; J. B. Magruder to unidentified, March 29, 1862, Magruder Papers, Duke. For Georgia, see Johnson, *Toward a Patriarchal Republic.*

33. Potter, "Jefferson Davis and the Political Factors in Confederate Defeat," in Donald, *Why the North Won the Civil War,* 91–114; Escott, *After Secession.*

34. Trowbridge, *The Desolate South,* 90.

35. Mitchell, *Civil War Soldiers,* 168.

36. Sarah Strickler Fife Diary, April 3, 1865, UVa.

37. Beringer and others, *Why the South Lost,* 436–42; Kerby, "Why the Confederacy Lost," 344–5; for a contrary view, see Gallagher, *The Confederate War,* 120–1, 123–7, 140–4; Frederickson, *Why the Confederacy Did Not Fight a Guerrilla War.*

38. Maddex, *Virginia Conservatives,* 39; Lowe, *Republicans and Reconstruction in Virginia,* 45–7.

39. *Report of the Joint Committee on Reconstruction,* 2:144.

Bibliography

Primary Sources

Manuscripts

Alderman Library, University of Virginia, Charlottesville
  Anthony Family Papers
  Barbour Family Papers
  Barnes Family Papers
  Blackford Diaries (Launcelot M. and William M.)
  Blackford Family Papers
  Thomas S. Bocock Papers
  Brooke-Stoddard Family Papers
  Brown Family Papers
  Salley N. Burnley Papers
  Lucy Wood Butler Diary
  Fannie B. Tompkins Childress Papers
  Clark Family Papers
  George W. Dabney Diary
  John W. Daniel Papers
  Davis Family Papers
  Duke Family Papers
  R. T. W. Duke Papers
  Emerson Family Papers
  Sarah Strickler Fife Diary

Z. Lee Gilmer Diary
J. Risque Hutter Diary
Captain Frank Imboden Diary
John D. Imboden Papers
King Family Papers
McCue Family Papers
Francis MacFarland Papers
McGuffin Family Papers
Socrates Maupin Faculty Notes
Louisa H. A. Minor Diary
Sarah Pannill Payne Letters
Lt. Charles Richard Phelps Papers
Preston-Radford Papers
Randolph Family Papers
Rives Family Letters
Lydia Laundes Maury Skeels Papers
Steele Family Papers
Alexander H. H. Stuart Papers
Terrel Family Papers
Micajah Woods Papers
Fredericksburg-Spotsylvania National Military Park
Cyrus Cline, Sr., "Description of Old Home"
Virginia Historical Society, Richmond
Aylett Family Papers
Bagby Family Papers
Baldwin Family Papers
William Selwyn Ball Reminiscences
Barbour Family Papers
Brown Family Papers
Carrington Family Papers
Chamberlayne Family Papers
Dearing Family Papers
Downman Family Papers
Mary Washington (Cabell) Early Diary
Thomas Claybrook Elder Papers
Benjamin Lyons Farinholt Diary, 1862
Gilmer Family Papers
Griggs Family Papers
Hugh Blair Grigsby Papers
Achilles Whitlocke Hoge Diary
Holladay Family Papers
Watkins Kearns Diary
John Landstreet Letters
McCue-Robertson Family Papers

Aquila Johnson Peyton Diary
Preston Family Papers
Rives Family Papers
Rockingham County, Enrollment Officer Records
Addison B. Roler Diary
Alexander H. H. Stuart Papers
Stuart Family Papers
Williams Family Papers
Septimus Ligon Williams Papers
Winston-Clark Papers
Southern Historical Collection of the Manuscripts Department, University
    of North Carolina, Chapel Hill, North Carolina
Beal and Davis Family Papers
Blackford Family Papers
Thomas Bragg Diary
Cornelius Dabney Diary
Elias Davis Papers
Elizabeth Seawell Hairston Papers
Hubard Family Papers
Fannie Page Hume Diary
Proffit Family
William Thomas Sutherlin Papers
Nicholas Philip Trist Papers
Tucker Family Papers
Marguerite Williams Papers
Anita (Dwyer) Withers Diary
Special Collections Library, Duke University, Durham, North Carolina
Bedinger-Dandridge Family Papers
Confederate States of America, Executive Department Papers, Conscrip-
    tion Department, Richmond
George William Bagby Papers
Charles Brown Papers
John B. Danforth Papers
Thomas F. Kelley Papers
John Bowie Magruder Papers
William McCutcheon Papers
William A. Pace Papers
James A. Sutherland Papers
Library of Congress
Jubal A. Early Papers
Jedediah Hotchkiss Papers
National Archives
Manuscript Census Returns, Population and Slave Schedules 1860, Albe-
    marle, Augusta, and Campbell Counties

RG 109, Confederate Archives
Acts of Congress, Orders, and Circulars Relating to Conscription, ch. I, vol. 258 $^1/_2$
Adjutant and Inspector General's Office, Inspection Reports
Agricultural Exemption Book, ch. I, vol. 235, Circulars, Letters, and Orders Concerning the Conscript Office at Richmond, 1863–1864, entry 23
Extracts from Inspection Reports ch. I, vol. 26
Free Negroes Enrolled and Assigned, ch. I, vol. 235
Instructions to Officers and Agents Receiving Tax in Kind, 1863, ch. V, vol. 199 $^1/_2$
Letters Received, Confederate Quartermaster General
Letters Received, Confederate Secretary of War
Letters Sent by Conscript Inspector for Virginia, 1864–1865, ch. I, v. 239
Record of Exemptions November 1862–October 1863, ch. I, vol. 251
Register of Officers and Employees in Enrolling Department in Virginia, 1862–1865, ch. I, vol. 257
Statistical Reports on Conscripts in Va., September 1862–February 1865, ch. 1, v. 250
Tax Returns, Assessor and Collectors, entry 63, box 54
RG 216, Southern Claims Commission Records
Augusta and Campbell Counties
Library of Virginia, Richmond
RG 3, Office of the Governor, Executive Papers
Letters Received, Governor John Letcher
Letters Received, Governor William Smith
RG 11, District Courts
Minute Books: Campbell, Augusta, Albemarle Counties
Virginia House Documents

Printed Sources

Government Records

Berlin, Ira, Barbara Jeanne Fields, Thavolia Glymph, Joseph P. Reidy, and Leslie S. Rowland, eds. *Freedom: A Documentary History of Emancipation, 1861–1867, Selected from the Holdings of the National Archives of the United States, Destruction of Slavery*, ser. 1, vol. 1. Cambridge: Cambridge University Press, 1985.

Bailey, James H. *Henrico Home Front: A Picture of Life in Henrico County, Virginia, from May 1861 through April 1865*. Richmond: Whittet & Shepperson, 1963.

Flournoy, H. W., William P. Palmer, S. MacRae, and R. Colston, eds. *Calendar of Virginia State Papers and Other Manuscripts from January 1, 1836 to April 15, 1869; Preserved in the Capitol at Richmond*. 11 vols. Richmond: 1875–1893.

House Executive Documents, 1st Session, 39th Congress, no. 1, vol. IV, series no. 1251.

Joint Committee on Reconstruction. *Report of the Committee on Reconstruction*, 1st Session, 39th Congress. 2 vols. Washington: Government Printing Office, 1866.

Journal of the Congress of the Confederate States of America. 7 vols. Washington: Government Printing Office, 1904–1905.

Manarin, Louis H., ed. *Richmond at War: The Minutes of the City Council, 1861–1865*. Chapel Hill: University of North Carolina Press, 1966.

Ramsdell, Charles W., ed. *Laws and Joint Resolutions of the Last Session of the Confederate Congress (November 7, 1864–March 18, 1864) Together with the Secret Acts of Previous Congresses*. Durham, N.C.: Duke University Press, 1941.

Reese, George H., ed. *Proceedings of the Virginia State Convention of 1861*. 4 vols. Richmond: Virginia State Library, 1965.

U.S. Bureau of the Census. *Seventh Census of the United States, 1850*. 4 vols. Washington: Government Printing Office, 1855.

U.S. Bureau of the Census. *Eighth Census of the United States, 1860*. 4 vols. Washington: Government Printing Office, 1865.

U.S. War Department. *The War of the Rebellion: A Compilation of the Official Records of the Union and Confederate Armies*. 128 vols. Washington: Government Printing Office, 1880-1901.

Virginia General Assembly. *Acts of the General Assembly of the State of Virginia, Passed in 1861–2*. Richmond: William F. Ritchie, 1862.

———. *Acts of the General Assembly of the State of Virginia, Passed at Called Session, 1862*. Richmond: William F. Ritchie, 1862.

———. *Acts of the General Assembly of the State of Virginia, Passed at Adjourned Session, 1863*. Richmond: William F. Ritchie, 1863.

———. *Acts of the General Assembly of the State of Virginia, Passed at Called Session, 1863*. Richmond: William F. Ritchie, 1863.

———. *Acts of the General Assembly of the State of Virginia, Passed at Session of 1863–4*. Richmond: William F. Ritchie, 1864.

Periodicals

Charlottesville *Daily Chronicle*
DeBow's Review
Harper's New Monthly Magazine
Lynchburg *Virginian*
Richmond *Daily Dispatch*

Richmond *Daily Enquirer*
Richmond *Daily Examiner*
Richmond *Examiner*
Richmond *Whig*
Southern Literary Messenger
Southern Planter
Staunton *Vindicator*
The (Abingdon, Va.) *Democrat*

Diaries, Letters, Journals, and Memoirs

Alexander, Edward Porter. *Fighting for the Confederacy: The Personal Reminiscences of General Edward Porter Alexander.* Ed. Gary W. Gallagher. Chapel Hill: University of North Carolina Press, 1989.

Allan, Elizabeth Randolph Preston. *The Life and Letters of Margaret Junkin Preston.* New York: Houghton Mifflin Co., 1903.

Bacott, Ada. *A Confederate Nurse: The Diary of Ada W. Bacott, 1860–1863.* Ed. Jean V. Berlin. Columbia, S.C.: University of South Carolina Press, 1994.

Beale, Jane Howison. *The Journal of Jane Howison Beale of Fredericksburg, Virginia: 1850–1862.* Fredericksburg: Historic Fredericksburg Foundation, 1979.

Blackford, L. Minor. *Mine Eyes Have Seen the Glory: The Story of a Virginia Lady, Mary Berkeley Minor Blackford, 1802–1896.* Cambridge: Harvard University Press, 1954.

Blackford, Mrs. Susan Leigh. *Letters from Lee's Army: Or, Memoirs of Life in and out of the Army in Virginia During the War Between the States.* Ed. Charles Minor Blackford III. New York: Charles Scribner's Sons, 1947.

Blackiston, Henry C. *Refugees in Richmond: Civil War Letters of a Virginia Family.* Princeton: Princeton University Press, 1989.

Blair, William A., ed. *A Politician Goes to War: The Civil War Letters of John White Geary.* With an introduction by Bell Irvin Wiley. University Park, Penn.: Pennsylvania State University Press, 1995.

Buck, Lucy Rebecca. *Sad Earth, Sweet Heaven: The Diary of Lucy Rebecca Buck.* Ed. William P. Buck. Birmingham, Ala.: The Cornerstone, 1973.

Casler, John O. *Four Years in the Stonewall Brigade.* 1893. Reprint, Dayton, Ohio: Morningside Books, 1982.

Chamberlayne, Ham. *Ham Chamberlayne—Virginian: Letters and Papers of an Artillery Officer in the War for Southern Independence, 1861–1865.* Richmond: Dietz Printing Company, 1932.

Chester, Thomas Morris. *Thomas Morris Chester, Black Civil War Correspondent: His Dispatches from the Virginia Home Front.* Ed. R. J. M. Blackett. Baton Rouge: Louisiana State University Press, 1989.

Colt, Margaretta Barton. *Defend the Valley: A Shenandoah Family in the Civil War*. New York: Orion Books, 1994.

Crabtree, Beth Gilbert, and James W. Patton, eds. *"Journal of a Secesh Lady": The Diary of Catherine Ann Devereaux Edmondston, 1860–1865*. Raleigh, N.C.: Division of Archives and History, 1979.

DeLeon, Thomas Cooper. *Four Years in Rebel Capitals: An Inside View of Life in the Southern Confederacy from Birth to Death*. 1890. Reprint. New York: Time-Life Books, Inc., 1983.

Dennett, John Richard. *The South As It Is: 1865–1866*. Ed. Henry M. Christman. New York: Viking Press, 1965.

Dowdey, Clifford, and Louis H. Manarin, eds. *The Wartime Papers of R. E. Lee*. New York: Bramhall House, 1961.

Early, Jubal A. *A Memoir of the Last Year of the War for Independence of the Confederate States of America*. Toronto: Lovell & Gibson, 1866.

Fleet, Betsy, and John D. P. Fuller. *Green Mount: A Virginia Plantation Family during the Civil War: Being the Journal of Benjamin Robert Fleet and Letters of His Family*. Charlottesville: University Press of Virginia, 1977.

Fremantle, Arthur James Lyon. *Three Months in the Southern States: April–June, 1863*. Lincoln: University of Nebraska Press, 1991.

Gache, Louis-Hoppolyte. *A Frenchman, a Chaplain, a Rebel: The War Letters of Louis-Hippolyte Gache*. Chicago: Loyola University Press, 1981.

Gorgas, Josiah. *The Journals of Josiah Gorgas, 1857–1878*. Ed. Sarah Woolfolk Wiggins. With a foreword by Frank E. Vandiver. Tuscaloosa: University of Alabama Press, 1995.

Hotchkiss, Jedediah. *Make Me A Map of the Valley: The Civil War Journal of Stonewall Jackson's Topographer*. Ed. Archie P. McDonald. Dallas: Southern Methodist University Press, 1973.

Hunnicutt, James V. *The Conspiracy Unveiled: The South Sacrificed; or, the Horrors of Secession*. Philadelphia: J. B. Lippincott, 1863.

Jackson, H. W. R. *The Southern Women and the Second American Revolution: Their Trials, &c., Yankee Barbarities Illustrated*. Atlanta: Intelligencer Steam-Power Press, 1863.

Johnston, Joseph E. *Narrative of Military Operations: Directed, during the Late War Between the States, by Joseph E. Johnston*. Bloomington: Indiana University Press, 1959.

Jones, J. William, and others, eds. *Southern Historical Society Papers*. 52 vols. plus 2 vol. index. 1876–1959. Reprint. Millwood, N.Y.: Kraus Reprint Company, 1980.

Jones, John B. *A Rebel War Clerk's Diary at the Confederate States Capital*. 2 vols. Philadelphia: J. B. Lippincott, 1866.

Kean, R. G. H. *Inside the Confederate Government: The Diary of Robert Garlick Hill Kean, Head of the Bureau of War*. Ed. Edward Younger. New York: Oxford University Press, 1957.

Keever, Elsie, ed. *Keever Civil War Letters*. Lincolnton, N.C.: Elsie Keever, 1988.

Manarin, Louis H., and Clifford Dowdey, eds. *The Wartime Papers of R. E. Lee*. New York: Bramhall House, 1961.

Maury, Betty Herndon. *The Civil War Diary of Betty Herndon Maury*. Ed. Robert A. Hodge. Fredericksburg, Virginia: n.p., 1985.

McDonald, Cornelia M. *A Diary with Reminiscences of the War and Refugee Life in the Shenandoah Valley*. Nashville: Cullom and Ghertner, 1934.

McGuire, Judith W. *Diary of a Southern Refugee During the War, by a Lady of Virginia*. 1867. Reprint. Lincoln: University of Nebraska Press, 1995.

Olmsted, Frederick Law. *The Cotton Kingdom: A Traveller's Observations on Cotton and Slavery in the American Slave States*. Ed. Arthur M. Schlesinger. New York: Alfred A. Knopf, 1953.

Patrick, Marsena R. *Inside Lincoln's Army: The Diary of General Marsena Rudolph Patrick, Provost Marshal General, Army of the Potomac*. Ed. David S. Sparks. New York: Thomas Yoseloff, 1964.

Pollard, Edward A. *Southern History of the War*. 2 vols. in one. New York: Fairfax Press, 1977.

Pryor, Sara Agnes. *Reminiscences of Peace and War*. New York: Macmillan, 1904.

Putnam, Sallie B. *Richmond During the War: Four Years of Personal Observation*. 1867. Reprint. Lincoln: University of Nebraska Press, 1996.

Reid, Whitelaw. *A Radical View: The 'Agate' Dispatches of Whitelaw Reid, 1861–1865*. Ed. James G. Smart. Memphis: Memphis State University Press.

Scarborough, William K., ed. *The Diary of Edmund Ruffin*. 3 vols. Baton Rouge: Louisiana State University, 1972–1989.

Trowbridge, John T. *The Desolate South, 1865–1866: A Picture of the Battlefields and of the Devastated Confederacy*. Ed. Gordon Carroll. Boston: Little, Brown, and Company, 1956.

Turner, Charles W., ed. *Civil War Letters of Arabella Speairs and William Beverly Pettit of Fluvanna County, Virginia: March 1862–March 1865*. 2 vols. Roanoke, Va.: Virginia Lithography & Graphics Company, 1989.

———. *My Dear Emma: War Letters of Col. James K. Edmondson, 1861–1865*. Verona, Va.: McClure Printing Company, 1978.

Waddell, Joseph A. *Annals of Augusta County, Virginia*. 2d ed. Harrisonburg, Va.: C. J. Carrier Company, 1986.

Wiley, Bell Irvin, ed. *Reminiscences of Big I: By William Nathaniel Wood, Second Lieutenant in Lee's Army*. 1956. Reprint. Wilmington, N.C.: Broadfoot Publishing Company, 1987.

———. *A Southern Woman's Story: Life in Confederate Richmond*, by Phoebe Yates Pember. Jackson, Tenn.: McCowat-Mercer Press, 1959.

Williams, Alpheus S. *From The Cannon's Mouth: The Civil War Letters of Gen-*

eral Alpheus S. Williams. Ed. with intro. by Milo M. Quaife. Detroit: Wayne State University Press, 1959.

Secondary Works

Books

Alexander, Thomas B., and Richard Beringer. *The Anatomy of the Confederate Congress: A Study of the Influences of Member Characteristics on Legislative Voting Behavior.* Nashville, Tenn.: Vanderbilt University Press, 1972.

Ambler, Charles H. *Sectionalism in Virginia from 1776 to 1861.* 1910. Reprint. New York: Russell & Russell, 1964.

Anderson, Benedict. *Imagined Communities: Reflections on the Origins and Spread of Nationalism.* London: Verso, 1983.

Ash, Stephen V. *Middle Tennessee Society Transformed, 1860–1870: War and Peace in the Upper South.* Baton Rouge: Louisiana State University, 1988.

———. *When the Yankees Came: Conflict & Chaos in the Occupied South, 1861–1865.* Chapel Hill: University of North Carolina Press, 1995.

Ayers, Edward L., and John C. Willis, eds. *The Edge of the South: Life in Nineteenth-Century Virginia.* Charlottesville: University of Virginia Press, 1991.

Ball, Douglas B. *Financial Failure and Confederate Defeat.* Urbana: University of Illinois Press, 1991.

Bancroft, Frederick. *Slave-Trading in the Old South.* Baltimore: J. H. Furst Company, 1931.

Bensell, Richard Franklin. *Yankee Leviathan: The Origins of State Authority in America, 1859–1877.* Cambridge: Cambridge University Press, 1990.

Beringer, Richard E., Herman Hattaway, Archer Jones, and William N. Still, Jr. *Why the South Lost the Civil War.* Athens: University of Georgia Press, 1986.

Bernstein, Iver. *The New York City Draft Riots: Their Significance and Politics in the Age of the Civil War.* New York: Oxford University Press, 1990.

Boney, F. N. *John Letcher of Virginia: The Story of Virginia's Civil War Governor.* Tuscaloosa: University of Alabama Press, 1966.

Borritt, Gabor S., ed. *Why the Confederacy Lost.* New York: Oxford University Press, 1992.

Bremner, Robert H. *The Public Good: Philanthropy and Welfare in the Civil War Era.* New York: Alfred A. Knopf, 1980.

Brewer, James H. *The Confederate Negro: Virginia's Craftsmen and Military Laborers, 1861–1865.* Durham, N.C.: Duke University Press, 1969.

Bruce, Kathleen. *Virginia Iron Manufacture in the Slave Era.* New York: The Century Company, 1930.

Burton, Orville Vernon. *In My Father's House Are Many Mansions: Family and Community in Edgefield, South Carolina.* The Fred W. Morrison Series in Southern Studies. Chapel Hill: University of North Carolina Press, 1985.

Burton, Orville Vernon and Robert McMath, eds. *Class, Conflict, and Consensus: Antebellum Southern Community Studies.* Westport, Conn.: Greenwood Press, 1982.

Cappon, Lester J. *Virginia Newspapers, 1821–1935.* New York: D. Appleton-Century Company, 1936.

Carmichael, Peter S. *Lee's Young Artillerist: William R. J. Pegram.* Charlottesville: University of Virginia Press, 1995.

Cecil-Fronsman, Bill. *Common Whites: Class and Culture in Antebellum North Carolina.* Lexington: University Press of Kentucky, 1992.

Chambers, Lenoir. *Stonewall Jackson.* 2 vols. 1959. Reprint. Wilmington, N.C.: Broadfoot Publishing Company, 1988.

Chesson, Michael B. *Richmond After the War, 1865–1890.* Richmond: Virginia State Library, 1981.

Coulter, E. Merton. *The Confederate States of America, 1861–1865.* Baton Rouge: Louisiana State University, 1950.

Craven, Avery O. *The Coming of the Civil War.* 1942; 2d ed. Chicago: University of Chicago Press, 1957.

———. *Soil Exhaustion As a Factor in the Agricultural History of Virginia and Maryland, 1606–1860.* 1926. Reprint. Gloucester, Mass.: Peter Smith Publishing Company, 1965.

Crofts, Daniel W. *Old Southampton: Politics and Society in a Virginia County, 1834–1869.* Charlottesville: University Press of Virginia, 1992.

———. *Reluctant Confederates: Upper South Unionists in the Secession Crisis.* Chapel Hill: University of North Carolina Press, 1989.

Current, Richard Nelson. *Lincoln's Loyalists: Union Soldiers from the Confederacy.* Boston: Northeastern University Press, 1992.

Curry, Richard Orr. *A House Divided: A Study of Statehood Politics and the Copperhead Movement in West Virginia.* Pittsburgh: University of Pittsburgh Press, 1964.

Davis, William C. *Jefferson Davis: The Man and His Hour.* New York: Harper Collins, 1992.

Deglar, Carl N. *The Other South: Southern Dissenters in the Nineteenth Century.* New York: Harper & Row, 1974.

Dew, Charles B. *Bonds of Iron: Master and Slave at Buffalo Forge.* New York: Norton, 1994.

———. *Ironmaker to the Confederacy: Joseph R. Anderson and the Tredegar Iron Works.* 1966. Reprint. Wilmington, N.C.: Broadfoot Publishing Company, 1987.

Donald, David, ed. *Why the North Won the Civil War.* Baton Rouge: Louisiana State University Press, 1960.

Driver, Robert J., Jr. *52nd Virginia Infantry.* Lynchburg, Virginia: H. E. Howard, 1986.

———. *Lexington and Rockbridge County in the Civil War.* Lynchburg, Virginia: H. E. Howard, 1989.

Du Bois, W. E. B. *Black Reconstruction in America, 1860–1880.* New York: Atheneum, 1992.

Dumond, Dwight L. *The Secession Movement, 1860–1861.* New York: MacMillan, 1931.

Durden, Robert F. *The Gray and the Black: The Confederate Debate on Emancipation.* Baton Rouge: Louisiana State University Press, 1972.

Durrill, Wayne K. *War of Another Kind: A Southern Community in the Great Rebellion.* New York: Oxford University Press, 1990.

Eaton, Clement. *A History of the Southern Confederacy.* New York: MacMillan, 1954.

———. *The Mind of the Old South.* 1964. Rev. ed. Baton Rouge: Louisiana State University, 1967.

Escott, Paul D. *After Secession: Jefferson Davis and the Failure of Confederate Nationalism.* Baton Rouge: Louisiana State University, 1978.

———. *Many Excellent People: Power and Privilege in North Carolina, 1850–1900.* Chapel Hill: University of North Carolina Press, 1985.

Faust, Drew Gilpin. *The Creation of Confederate Nationalism: Ideology and Identity in the Civil War South.* Baton Rouge: Louisiana State University Press, 1988.

———. *The Ideology of Slavery: Proslavery Thought in the Antebellum South, 1830–1860.* Baton Rouge: Louisiana State University Press, 1981.

———. *Mothers of Invention: Women of the Slaveholding South in the American Civil War.* The Fred W. Morrison Series in Southern Studies. Chapel Hill: University of North Carolina Press, 1996.

Ferguson, Ernest B. *Ashes of Glory: Richmond at War.* New York: Alfred A. Knopf, 1996.

Ford, Lacy K., Jr. *Origins of Southern Radicalism: The South Carolina Upcountry, 1800–1860.* New York: Oxford University Press, 1988.

Fox- Genovese, Elizabeth and Eugene D. Genovese. *The Fruits of Merchant Capital: Slavery and Bourgeois Property in the Rise and Expansion of Capitalism.* New York: Oxford University Press, 1983.

Frederickson, George M. *The Black Image in the White Mind: The Debate on Afro-American Character and Destiny.* New York: Harper & Row, 1971.

———. *Why the Confederacy Did not Fight a Guerrilla War After the Fall of Richmond: A Comparative View.* 35th Annual Fortenbaugh Memorial Lecture. Gettysburg: Gettysburg College, 1996.

Freehling, Alison Goodyear. *Drift Toward Dissolution: The Virginia Slavery Debate of 1831–1832.* Baton Rouge: Louisiana State University Press, 1982.

Freehling, William W. *The Road to Disunion: Secessionists at Bay, 1776–1854*. New York: Oxford University Press, 1990.

Gallagher, Gary W. *The Confederate War: Popular Will, Nationalism, and Strategy*. Cambridge: Harvard University Press, 1997.

Gallagher, Gary W., ed. *Decision on the Rappahannock: Causes and Consequences of the Fredericksburg Campaign*. Chapel Hill: University of North Carolina Press, 1995.

Genovese, Eugene D. *The Political Economy of Slavery: Studies in the Economy and Society of the Slave South*. New York: Pantheon Books, 1965.

————. *Roll, Jordan, Roll: The World the Slaves Made*. New York: Pantheon Books, 1974.

————. *The Slaveholders' Dilemma: Freedom and Progress in Southern Conservative Thought, 1820–1860*. Columbia: University of South Carolina Press, 1992.

————. *The World the Slaveholders Made: Two Essays in Interpretation*. 1969. new ed. Middletown, Conn.: Wesleyan University Press, 1988.

Goff, Richard. *Confederate Supply*. Durham, N.C.: Duke University Press, 1969.

Goldfield, David R. *Urban Growth in the Age of Sectionalism: Virginia, 1847–1861*. Baton Rouge: Louisiana State University, 1977.

Gray, Lewis Cecil. *History of Agriculture in the Southern United States*. 2 vols. Washington: Carnegie Institution, 1933.

Grimsley, Mark. *The Hard Hand of War: Union Military Policy Toward Southern Civilians, 1861–1865*. Cambridge: Cambridge University Press, 1995.

Hahn, Steven. *The Roots of Southern Populism: Yeoman Farmers and the Transformation of the Georgia Upcountry, 1850–1890*. New York: Oxford University Press, 1983.

Harris, J. William. *Plain Folk and Gentry in a Slave Society: White Liberty and Black Slavery in Augusta's Hinterlands*. Middletown, Conn.: Wesleyan University Press, 1985.

Hill, Louise B. *State Socialism in the Confederate States of America*. Charlottesville: Historical Publishing, 1936.

Hobsbawm, E. J. *Nations & Nationalism Since 1780: Programme, Myth, Reality*. Cambridge: Cambridge University Press, 1990.

Hobsbawm, Eric, and Terance Ranger, eds. *The Invention of Tradition*. Cambridge: Cambridge University Press, 1983.

Horst, Samuel. *Mennonites in the Confederacy: A Study of Civil War Pacifism*. Scottdale, Penn.: Herald Press, 1967.

Jimerson, Randall C. *The Private Civil War: Popular Thought During the Sectional Conflict*. Baton Rouge: Louisiana State University Press, 1988.

Johnson, Michael. *Toward a Patriarchal Republic: The Secession of Georgia*. Baton Rouge: Louisiana State University Press, 1977.

Jordan, Ervin L., Jr. *Black Confederates and Afro-Yankees in Civil War Virginia*. Charlottesville: University Press of Virginia, 1995.

———. *Charlottesville and the University of Virginia in the Civil War.* Lynchburg, Virginia: H. E. Howard Publishing Company, 1988.

Kenzer, Robert C. *Kinship and Neighborhood in a Southern Community: Orange County, North Carolina, 1849–1881.* Knoxville: The University of Tennessee Press, 1987.

King, Alvy L. *Louis T. Wigfall: Southern Fire-Eater.* Baton Rouge: Louisiana State University Press, 1970.

Link, William A. *A Hard Country and a Lonely Place: Schooling, Society, and Reform in Rural Virginia, 1870–1920.* Chapel Hill: University of North Carolina Press, 1986.

Lonn, Ella. *Desertion During the Civil War.* New York: The Century Company, 1928.

———. *Salt As a Factor in the Confederacy.* Tuscaloosa: University of Alabama Press, 1965.

Lowe, Richard. *Republicans and Reconstruction in Virginia, 1856–1870.* Charlottesville: The University Press of Virginia, 1991.

Luraghi, Raimondo. *The Rise and Fall of the Plantation South.* New York: New Viewpoints, 1978.

Maddex, Jack P. *The Virginia Conservatives, 1867–1879: A Study in Reconstruction Politics.* Chapel Hill: University of North Carolina Press, 1970.

Marten, James. *Texas Divided: Loyalty and Dissent in the Lone Star State, 1856–1874.* Lexington: University of Kentucky Press, 1990.

Massey, Mary Elizabeth. *Refugee Life in the Confederacy.* Baton Rouge: Louisiana State University Press, 1964.

Matthews, Donald G. *Religion in the Old South.* Chicago: University of Chicago Press, 1977.

McCurry, Stephanie. *Masters of Small Worlds: Yeoman Households, Gender Relations, and the Political Culture of the Antebellum South Carolina Low Country.* New York: Oxford University Press, 1995.

McPherson, James M. *Battle Cry of Freedom: The Civil War Era.* New York: Oxford University Press, 1988.

———. *The Negro's Civil War: How American Negroes Felt and Acted during the War for the Union.* 1965. New ed. Urbana: University of Illinois Press, 1982.

———. *What They Fought For, 1861–1865.* Baton Rouge: Louisiana State University, 1994.

———. *For Cause & Conrades: Why Men Fought in the Civil War.* New York: Oxford University Press, 1997.

Mitchell, Reid. *Civil War Soldiers: Their Expectations and Experiences.* New York: Viking Press, 1988.

Mohr, Clarence. *On the Threshold of Freedom: Masters and Slaves in Civil War Georgia.* Athens: University of Georgia Press, 1986.

Moore, Albert B. *Conscription and Conflict in the Confederacy.* New York: Hillary House Publishers, 1963.

Moore, Barrington. *Injustice: The Social Bases of Obedience and Revolt*. White Plains, N.Y.: M. E. Sharpe, 1978.

Moore, James Tice. *Albemarle: Jefferson's County, 1727–1976*. Charlottesville: University Press of Virginia, 1976.

Morgan, Edmund. *American Slavery, American Freedom: The Ordeal of Colonial Virginia*. New York: W. W. Norton, 1975.

Morgan, Lynda J. *Emancipation in Virginia's Tobacco Belt, 1850–1870*. Athens: University of Georgia Press, 1992.

Munford, Beverly. *Virginia's Attitude Toward Slavery and Secession*. Richmond: L. H. Jenkins, 1909.

Nevins, Allan. *The Emergence of Lincoln: Prologue to Civil War, 1859–1861*. 2 vols. New York: Charles Scribner's Sons, 1950.

Nolan, Alan. *Lee Considered: General Robert E. Lee and Civil War History*. Chapel Hill: University of North Carolina Press, 1991.

Noe, Kenneth W. *Southwest Virginia's Railroad: Modernization and the Sectional Crisis*. Urbana: University of Illinois Press, 1994.

Owens, Harry P., and James J. Cooke, eds. *The Old South in the Crucible of War*. Jackson: University Press of Mississippi, 1983.

Peyton, J. Lewis. *History of Augusta County, Virginia*. Bridgewater, Virginia: C. J. Carrier, 1953.

Potter, David M. *The Impending Crisis, 1848–1861*. New York: Harper & Row, 1976.

———. *The South and the Sectional Conflict*. Baton Rouge: Louisiana State University Press, 1968.

Quarles, Benjamin. *The Negro in the Civil War*. Boston: Little, Brown, and Company, 1953.

Rable, George C. *Civil Wars: Women and the Crisis of Southern Nationalism*. Urbana: University of Illinois Press, 1989.

———. *The Confederate Republic: A Revolution Against Politics*. Chapel Hill: University of North Carolina Press, 1994.

Rachleff, Peter. *Black Labor in Richmond, 1865–1890*. Urbana: University of Illinois Press, 1989.

Radley, Kenneth. *Rebel Watchdog: The Confederate States Army Provost Guard*. Baton Rouge: Louisiana State University Press, 1989.

Ramsdell, Charles W. *Behind the Lines in the Southern Confederacy*. Baton Rouge: Louisiana State University Press, 1944.

Rice, Harvey Mitchell. *The Life of Jonathan M. Bennett: A Study of Virginia in Transition*. Chapel Hill: University of North Carolina Press, 1943.

Rudé, George. *The Crowd in History: A Study of Popular Disturbances in France and England, 1730–1848*. New York: Wiley, 1964.

Shackelford, George Green. *George Wythe Randolph and the Confederate Elite*. Athens: University of Georgia Press, 1988.

Shade, William G. *Democratizing the Old Dominion: Virginia and the Second*

Party System, 1824–1861. Charlottesville and London: The University Press of Virginia, 1996.

Shanks, Henry T. *The Secession Movement in Virginia, 1847–1861*. Richmond: Garrett & Massie, 1934.

Shifflett, Crandall A. *Patronage and Poverty in the Tobacco South: Louisa County, Virginia, 1860–1900*. Knoxville: University of Tennessee Press, 1982.

Siegel, Frederick F. *The Roots of Southern Distinctiveness: Tobacco and Society in Danville, Virginia, 1780–1865*. Chapel Hill: University of North Carolina Press, 1987.

Simpson, Craig M. *A Good Southerner: The Life of Henry A. Wise of Virginia*. Chapel Hill: The University of North Carolina Press, 1985.

Starobin, Robert S. *Industrial Slavery in the Old South*. New York: Oxford University Press, 1970.

Sutherland, David E. *Seasons of War: The Ordeal of a Confederate Community, 1861–1865*. New York: The Free Press, 1995.

Tatum, Georgia Lee. *Disloyalty in the Confederacy*. Chapel Hill: University of North Carolina Press, 1934.

Thomas, Emory M. *The Confederate Nation, 1861–1865*. New York: Harper & Row, 1979.

———. *The Confederate State of Richmond: a Biography of the Capital*. Austin: University of Texas Press, 1971.

Thompson, E. P. *Customs in Common: Studies in Traditional Popular Culture*. New York: The New Press, 1993.

Thornton, J. Mills, III. *Politics and Power in a Slave Society: Alabama, 1800–1860*. Baton Rouge: Louisiana State University Press, 1978.

Wallace, Lee A., Jr. *5th Virginia Infantry*. Lynchburg, Virginia: H. E. Howard, Inc., 1988.

Wallenstein, Peter. *From Slave South to New South: Public Policy in Nineteenth-Century Georgia*. Chapel Hill: University of North Carolina Press, 1987.

Watson, Harry L. *Liberty and Power: The Politics of Jacksonian America*. New York: Noonday Press, 1990.

Wiley, Bell Irvin. *Johnny Reb: The Common Soldier of the Confederacy*. Baton Rouge: Louisiana State University Press, 1943.

———. *The Road to Appomattox*. Memphis, Tennessee: Memphis State College Press, 1956.

———. *Southern Negroes, 1861–1865*. Baton Rouge: Louisiana State University Press, 1965.

Wish, Harvey N. *George Fitzhugh: Propagandist of the Old South*. 1934. Reprint. Gloucester, Mass.: Peter Smith Publishing Company, 1962.

Woodworth, Steven E. *Davis & Lee at War*. Lawrence: University of Kansas Press, 1995.

Wyatt-Brown, Bertram. *Southern Honor: Ethics & Behavior in the Old South*. New York: Oxford University Press, 1982.

Yearns, Wilfred Buck. *The Confederate Congress*. Athens: University of Georgia Press, 1960.

Articles

Alexander, Thomas B. "Persistent Whiggery in the Confederate South, 1861–1867." *Journal of Southern History* 27 (August 1961): 305–29.

Ash, Stephen V. "White Virginians Under Federal Occupation, 1861–1865." *Virginia Magazine of History and Biography* 98 (April 1990): 169–92.

Bardolph, Richard. "Confederate Dilemma: North Carolina Troops and the Deserter Problem." Parts 1 and 2. *North Carolina Historical Review* 46 (January 1989): 61–86 and (April 1989): 179–210.

———. "Inconstant Rebels." *North Carolina Historical Review* 41 (Spring 1964): 163–89.

Bean, William G. "The Ruffner Pamphlet of 1847: An Antislavery Aspect of Virginia Sectionalism." *Virginia Magazine of History and Biography* 61 (July 1953): 260–82.

Bearman, Peter S. "Desertion as Localism: Army Unit Solidarity and Group Norms in the U.S. Civil War." *Social Forces* 70 (1991): 321–42.

Bowman, Shearer Davis. "Conditional Unionism and Slavery in Virginia, 1860–1861: The Case of Dr. Richard Eppes." *Virginia Magazine of History and Biography* 96 (January 1988): 31–54.

Chesson, Michael B. "Harlots or Heroines? A Look at the Richmond Bread Riot." *Virginia Magazine of History and Biography* 92 (April 1984): 131–75.

Coddington, E. B. "Soldiers' Relief in the Seaboard States of the Southern Confederacy." *Mississippi Valley Historical Review* 37 (1950): 17–38.

Crawford, Martin. "Confederate Volunteering and Enlistment in Ashe County, North Carolina, 1861-1862." *Civil War History* 37 (March 1991): 29–50.

Escott, Paul D. " 'The Cry of the Sufferers': The Problem of Welfare in the Confederacy." *Civil War History* 23 (1977): 228–40.

Faust, Drew Gilpin. "Altars of Sacrifice: Confederate Women and Narratives of War." *Journal of American History* 76 (March 1990): 1200–28.

Gallagher, Gary W. "Home Front and Battlefield: Some Recent Literature Relating to Virginia and the Confederacy." *Virginia Magazine of History and Biography* 98 (April 1990): 135–68.

Genovese, Eugene D. "Yeoman Farmers in a Slaveholders' Democracy." *Agricultural History* 49 (April 1975): 331–42.

Grimsley, Mark. "Conciliation and Its Failure, 1861–1862." *Civil War History* 39 (December 1993): 317–35.

Hallock, Judith Lee. "Role of the Community in Civil War Desertion." *Civil War History* 29 (1983): 123–34.

Harris, J. William. "The Organization of Work on a Yeoman Slaveholder's Farm." *Agricultural History* 64 (Winter 1990): 39–52.

Kerby, Robert L. "Why the Confederacy Lost." *The Review of Politics* 35 (July 1973): 344–5.

Luraghi, Raimondo. "The Civil War and the Modernization of American Society: Social Structure and Industrial Revolution in the Old South before and during the Civil War." *Civil War History* 18 (September 1972): 230–50.

Noe, Kenneth. "Red String Scare: Civil War Southwest Virginia and the Heroes of America." *North Carolina Historical Review* 69 (July 1992): 301–22.

Olsen, Otto. "Historians and the Extent of Slave Ownership in the Southern United States." *Civil War History* 18 (June 1972): 101–16.

Reid, Brian Holden. "A Mob of Stragglers and Cowards." *Journal of Strategic Studies* 8 (1985): 64–77.

Rubin, Anne Sarah. "Between Union and Chaos: The Political Life of John Janney." *Virginia Magazine of History and Biography* 102 (July 1994): 381–416.

Shalhope, Robert E. "Republicanism and Early American Historiography." *William and Mary Quarterly* 39 (April 1982): 334–56.

———. "Toward a Republican Synthesis." *William and Mary Quarterly* 29 (January 1972): 49–80.

Sutherland, Daniel E. "Introduction to War: The Civilians of Culpeper County, Virginia." *Civil War History* 37 (June 1991): 120–37.

Wilentz, Sean. "On Class and Politics in Jacksonian America." *Reviews in American History* 10 (December 1982): 45–63.

Zornow, William Frank. "Aid for Indigent Families of Soldiers in Virginia, 1861–1865." *Virginia Magazine of History and Biography* 66 (1958): 454–58.

Theses and Dissertations

Bouldin, Mary Jane. "Lynchburg, Virginia: A City of War." Master's thesis, East Carolina University, 1976.

Branscome, James. "Impressment in the State of Virginia During the Civil War." Master's thesis, Wake Forest University, 1976.

Carmichael, Peter S. "The Last Generation: Sons of Virginia Slaveholders and the Creation of a Confederate Identity, 1850–1865." Ph.D. diss., Pennsylvania State University, 1996.

Fields, Emmett B. "The Agricultural Population of Virginia, 1850–1860." Ph.D. diss., Vanderbilt University, 1953.

Golden, Alan Lawrence. "The Secession Crisis in Virginia: A Critical Study of Argument." Ph.D. diss., Ohio State University, 1990.

Jones, Newton Bond. "Charlottesville and Albemarle County, 1819–1860." Ph.D. diss., University of Virginia, 1950.

Krug, Donna Rebecca Dondes. "The Folks Back Home: The Confederate Home Front during the Civil War." Ph.D. diss., University of California, Irvine, 1990.

McFarland, George M. "The Extension of Democracy in Virginia, 1850–1895." Ph.D. diss., Princeton University, 1934.

Morris, George Graham. "Confederate Lynchburg, 1861–1865." Master's thesis, Virginia Polytechnic Institute and State University, 1977.

Phillips, Edward H. "The Lower Shenandoah Valley during the Civil War: The Impact of War upon the Civilian Population and upon Civil Institutions." Ph.D. diss., University of North Carolina, 1958.

Poland, Charles Preston, Jr. "Loudoun County during the Civil War: A Study of a Border County in a Border State." Master's thesis, American University, 1961.

Reid, James Irvin. "Slave Agriculture and Staple Crops in the Virginia Piedmont." Ph.D. diss., University of Rochester, 1986.

Richey, Thomas Webster. "The Virginia State Convention of 1861 and Virginia Secession." Ph.D. diss., University of Georgia, 1990.

Schlotterbeck, John T. "Plantation and Farm: Social and Economic Change in Orange and Greene Counties, Virginia, 1716 to 1860." Ph.D. diss., Johns Hopkins University, 1980.

Shultz, Jane E. "Women at the Front: Gender and Genre in Literature of the American Civil War." Ph.D. diss., University of Michigan, 1988.

Stauffenberg, Anne Lenore. "Albemarle County, Virginia, 1850–1870: An Economic Survey Based on the U.S. Census." Master's thesis, University of Virginia, 1973.

Tripp, Steven Elliott. "Restive Days: Race and Class Relations in Lynchburg, Virginia, 1858–1872." Ph.D. diss., Carnegie Mellon University, 1990.

Index